RADICAL LAMBETH

Simon Hannah

Radical Lambeth 1978-1991

"Let us be judged by our deeds"
Lambeth Council motto

BREVIARY STUFF PUBLICATIONS
2021

Breviary Stuff Publications,
BCM Breviary Stuff, London WC1N 3XX
breviarystuff.org.uk
Copyright © Simon Hannah 2021
The centipede device copyright © Breviary Stuff Publications

All rights reserved. No part of this publication may be reproduced, stored in a retrieval system, or transmitted, in any form or by any means, electronic, mechanical, photocopying, scanning, recording, or otherwise, without the prior permission of Breviary Stuff Publications

A CIP record for this book is available from
The British Library

ISBN: 978-1-9161586-3-4

Contents

About the Author	*vii*
Acknowledgements	*viii*
Introduction	1
1. A Place Called Lambeth	5
2. Lambeth Council	11
3. Housing and Community	21
4. Enter Thatcher	29
5. Resisting Thatcher	35
6. Brixton and Black Resistance	53
7. Setbacks	73
8. Nukes and Nicaragua	79
9. Rate-capping and the Second Front…	85
10. The 1985 Riot and Inner City Blues	111
11. The Left Regroups	119
12. Queer in Lambeth	129
13. Anti-racism and Anti-apartheid	137
14. Reflections on the Housing Battleground	145
15. Lambeth Isolated	153
16. The Vauxhall By-election	171
17. Fighting the Poll Tax and the Gulf War	177
18. Hurtling Towards the Precipice	191
Conclusion: Legacy of Radical Lambeth	199
Bibliography	207
Index	209

"And you shall Reap the whole Earth from
    Pole to Pole, from Sea to Sea,
Beginning at Jerusalem's Inner Court,
    Lambeth, ruin'd and given
To the detestable Gods or Priam, to Apollo,
    and at the Asylum
Given to Hercules; who labour in Tirzah's
    Looms for bread,
Who set Pleasure against Duty, who Create
    Olympic Crowns
To make Learning a burden & the work of
    the Hold Spirit Strife,
The Thor & cruel Odin, who first rear'd the
    Polar Caves.
Lambeth mourns, calling Jerusalem…"

William Blake

About the author

Simon Hannah is a socialist living in South London and working in Lambeth. He is a trade unionist and occasional writer, often found frequenting the pubs south of the Thames. His other books include *A Party with Socialists in it: A History of the Labour Left* (Pluto 2018), *Can't Pay, Won't Pay: The Fight to Stop the Poll Tax* (Pluto 2020).

Acknowledgements

Thanks to...

Many of the veterans of the 1980s were very warm and welcoming during my research, so thanks to everyone who helped by providing materials or giving interviews. In alphabetical order; Sharon Atkin, Linda Bellos, Bill Bowring, Jon Davies, Sean Geoghan, Neil Gordon-Orr, Ed Hall, Noel Hannon, Alison Higgs, Ted Knight, Chris Mullin, Steve Nally, Tim O'Dell, Jan and John O'Malley, Jon Rogers, Helen Shaw, Michael Tichelar, Joan Twelves, Anna Tapsell, John Tuite, Marc Wadsworth, Ansel Wong. Also Abibat and O'Neil and all the Lambeth library staff. David Mezetti and Gay Lee for information on the Nicaragua Solidarity campaign. Eamon Maguire, Jackie Lewis, Reg Morrison, and Andy Tullis at Lambeth UNISON. Sean Creighton for his extensive notes and personal experience. Megan Doolittle for her excellent unpublished MA thesis on squatting on Villa Road. George Gordon for his MA Thesis comparing Wandsworth and Lambeth Councils and Eliot Henderson's on the New Urban Left. John Medhurst for useful critical comments. The staff at Lambeth Archives, Jon, Len and Elisabeth. The staff at Black Cultural Archives for their assistance. Obviously any errors are my own. Anyone I have forgotten over the many years I deeply apologise!

The wonderful support of all my friends who read over manuscripts and helped with corrections and discussed the ideas with me and heard me talk about Lambeth history repeatedly for many years as well as practical help with this book, Ruth, Alex, Steven, and Kieran. Many thanks to Paul Mangan at Breviary Stuff for his patience with the editing and publishing.

Introduction

"During the Eighties, Lambeth council was the acme of municipal madness for the tabloids. Most inner-city Labour authorities were treated as loony, but Lambeth had its own space in the ninth circle of Hell. Although by 1990 the 'Free flying lessons for bereaved lesbians' stories had dried up elsewhere, Lambeth remained a rich source of loonyology."[1]

It is not the literal past that rules us; it is images of the past.
George Stirner

I was partly inspired to write this account when Margaret Thatcher died on 8 April 2013. There had been rumours that there would be a huge party in Trafalgar Square the day that she died, social media pages had been set up to encourage people to go, possibly as a conscious historical call back to the Poll Tax riot that had occurred there in 1990. But on that Monday evening just a short bus journey away in South London, there was a small but notable gathering in Brixton. It was a mixture of local people; anarchists, some older community activists, local trade unionists and socialists all started knocking back bottles of fizz (cava, not champagne of course) in Windrush Square opposite the Town Hall. It was good natured, with drinking and chatting. An impromptu performance by a make shift band replete with guitar and double bass. A few chanted "Maggie, Maggie, Maggie, dead, dead, dead!" and everyone laughed. At some point someone climbed onto the roof of the Ritzy Cinema to rearrange the lettering on the front board "MARGARET THATCHER DEAD YUPPIES OUT!!" An older woman with an old T-shirt emblazoned with a pink triangle and "Stop Section 28" held aloft a sign: *Ding dong the witch is dead*. The look on her face one of ecstatic energy, ghosts of the past finally being exorcised.

Whatever Thatcher was, she elicited extreme passions either way. Eventually the police arrived, as is the way with such things, and sought to disperse the crowd. Gatherings without the proper permits are forbidden.

---

[1] 'Loonies need not apply' *The Independent*, Peter Kinston, Wednesday 27 January 1993.

The revelries continued but in a tenser atmosphere until after midnight when riot police cleared the square. There was some pushing and shoving, some throwing of objects — maybe a symbolic reminder of earlier protests that had dominated the headlines in the 1980s — before people went home.

The impromptu party in Windrush Square, in the middle of Brixton, was a cathartic moment for Lambeth. After all, there was history between Lambeth and Thatcher's government, a deeply unhappy one. For some people the 1980s seemed more like a battle between the peasants against the government on the other side of the river, a river which wound like a moat around the gothic palace of Westminster, where monsters lurked, set upon confrontation and ruin. From the poorest family on a slum estate, to a queer anarchist in her squat on Railton Road, to local politicians and mayors — all of them confronting the nightmarish vision of the British establishment across the Thames.

Lambeth had a strong Labour left who succeeded in winning control of the council. Their brand of left politics, willingness to confront Westminster and strident rhetoric branded Lambeth one of the archetypal 'loony left' boroughs. The attitude of local administrators and councillors, coupled with often wild claims of local corruption and mismanagement earned the borough the moniker "Dodge City" in *The Guardian*.[2] But what really happened behind the headlines?

Whilst the trade unions were often cited as the key enemy of the 1980s Conservative regime, the other institutional force that Thatcher most detested was Local Government, and it was partly in that struggle that Lambeth came to dominate the headlines in the 1980s. During those years Lambeth loomed large in a mainstream demonology that took root in the public imagination. Thatcher scornfully viewed inner-city Labour boroughs as 'resentful colonies'.[3] Not only the marginalised residents of Lambeth — the poor, the blacks, the lesbians and gays — but the very institutions of the borough, here lived the feckless and dangerous radicals of Thatcher's nightmares. It was they who stalked the land, the enemy within, the forces of destabilisation and of wasteful bureaucracy, those that sought to attack the sovereignty of Parliament, upend the racial power relations, those that dared to defy the evangelical crusade of Milton Friedman and the poisonous remedies of Friedrich von Hayek.[4]

This account of Lambeth will focus on the council, campaigns and community struggles during the long 1980s. The story starts with the

---

2 'Tame Dodge City' *The Guardian* 10 December 1994
3 Simon Jenkins, *Accountable to None: The Tory Nationalisation of Britain*, p. 156.
4 Friedrich von Hayek was the author of *The Road to Serfdom*, a defence of classical liberal economics against centralised planning, arguing that personal freedom only came with economic freedom and that meant keeping government out of the free market.
Milton Friedman led the war against Keynesianism and was very influential over Ronald Regan and Margaret Thatcher. He was the intellectual guru behind the 'Chicago School' of economists who helped restructure Chile's economy towards Neo-liberalism capitalism after the Pinochet coup in 1973.

election of Ted Knight as leader of the Labour Council and ends, roughly, with the suspensions of Joan Twelves as council leader, marking the end a long period of left wing politics in the Town Hall. The early 1990s also marked a shift in British politics more generally, as the old fights gave way to new battles over culture, rave music and environmentalism.

It cannot cover everything, and no doubt some will identify gaps by way of what I haven't included. I also can guarantee that everyone will be unhappy in some way with the tale told here. There is no room for halos when you get down and fight dirty in the environs of local politics. But this is a story worth telling, one that gives us an insight into a certain place at a certain time and how it came to be that way. It is a social and political story of Lambeth during a decade of great change and great resistance, of people and place, of hope and fear, of oppression and resistance.

I

A Place Called Lambeth

Lambeth has seen many famous residents in its history. The utopian socialist William Blake lived around modern day Waterloo – the streets near where his home stood (since demolished) are filled with mosaics created by artists to commemorate his life. It was during this time that he wrote some of his most famous works – *Songs of Innocence and Experience, Marriages of Heaven and Hell* and *Daughters of Albion*. His poem *The French Revolution* is a paean to the storming of the Bastille in the name of freedom, of a people rising up against tyranny. W. Somerset Maugham wrote *Liza of Lambeth* whilst working at St Thomas' Hospital, a novel that revelled in depicting the complexities and problems facing working class life in the borough. Charlie Chaplin grew up on Brixton Road, his father was a local entertainer. As a child he was both enamoured and horrified at the vaudeville music hall theatre scene in the borough, the razzmatazz alongside the alcoholism that was slowly killing his father. At the age of seven his mother had a breakdown and took the family into a workhouse to survive. Thankfully the workhouse where they took his indebted mother and broke her body and spirit is a distant memory of another time, today it is converted into the Cinema Museum.

Lambeth is the second largest borough in inner London and by the end of the 1970s was the fourth most deprived area of the country. With high levels of poverty and debt, the borough struggled with social deprivation and the inevitable consequences for an inner city neighbourhood: crime and alienation. The area had struggled with underinvestment for years; once gaudy shopping areas had succumbed to deterioration and atrophy. Half the borough lived in council accommodation though both public and private sector housing were often in a shocking state. One newspaper described Brixton as "handsome but teetering on the brink of decay".[1] Others were less fortunate, large cardboard cities had built up over the years around Waterloo Station and the Bull Ring as the homeless crowded together for support. The area was a run down inner city, vibrant in parts but dominated

---

1 *The Guardian*, 2 February 1981.

by the concrete blocks of modern living with all the opportunities and oppression that entails.

Of course parts of Lambeth, in particular Brixton, are often associated with its large black community. *Time* magazine described it as "a grimy, racially mixed neighbourhood south of the Thames";[2] a decade later the *South London Press* described Brixton as "a rundown inner city slum [in] 1981".[3] Lambeth in the 1970s was 30% black, though 50% of the youth in the borough were black. The second generation, sons and daughters of Windrush, knew that their position in Britain was precarious, that their very existence on the island was a difficult balancing act between vast swathes of middle England with their inherent nationalist conservatism and the authorities, who had initially welcomed them to Britain but who now policed them with a zealous fury. The racial aspect of Lambeth has been far more obvious and deep rooted than much of the rest of south London. The cheap housing (or free if you squatted it) and the vibrancy of the local community, night life and urban buzz all made Lambeth a popular place. The 1970s soul and black power aesthetic was popular in Brixton, Desmond's Hip City record store at 55 Atlantic Road was emblematic of the mood, the latest LPs alongside posters of Muhammad Ali, Che Guevara and Angela Davis.[4] Music was politics and politics was music. It was an area where black owned businesses could operate and do trade (replete with signs above the cashier saying; 'In God We Trust: Others Pay In Cash'), where a community of working class and middle class could mix.

This particular demographic of central Lambeth made it a natural home for anti-racist campaigns. It was never a ghetto, even if the housing was poor quality, it was a genuine multicultural community, both in terms of ethnicity as well as class background. But just down the road leading south westerly, Streatham represented a kind of mirror opposite to Brixton. Streatham was less diverse, the residents often more racist, made up of a large number of better off white flight residents desperate to get away from the blacks making a home in Brixton. The area remained a hot bed of Toryism as a result.

But there are other important things to note. The number of single parent families in the borough was 20%, twice the national average at the time. One in five houses held pensioners. This wide divergence between rich and poor, young and old was not uncommon in inner London but Lambeth was certainly one of the most noteworthy.

The infamous 'Streatham Rate Payer' – a journalistic short hand for home owning, right wing Tories – always complained "Brixton gets this and Brixton gets that", the rumour was that Brixton got all the money because

---

2   *Time*, 'Britain: Bloody Saturday', 20 April 1981.
3   *South London Press*, 9 April 1991,
4   Tanisha Ford, *Liberated Threads: Black Women, Style, and the Global Politics of Soul* (California University Press 2015), pp. 134-5.

immigrants lived there. This boiled over into outright hostility at times; occasional shouts of "get back to Brixton" would be hurled at Black people on Streatham High Road. Perhaps this was a small improvement on being told to return to a country that your parents had come from. Black librarians at the Tate Library in Streatham used to get regular doses of racist abuse at work. Labour was an embattled minority in that part of the borough. To add to the tension and the threat of violence the fascist organisation National Front had an office in Streatham. Streatham was considered "posh", it was the bedrock of the local Tory Party.

As with many inner city areas it was socially mixed, black and white living side by side. There were some middle class streets, but you only had to turn a corner and you found yourself in a dilapidated end of an estate. Vauxhall was described as "Calypso with Chopin overtones" by the *Daily Mail*.[5] This particular mix of the borough, its geographical location and the time we are studying provides for a very political, combustible mix. It was a place where anti-fascist teachers lived alongside social workers, political activists, artists and militant trade unionists.[6] There was a healthy mix of local well organised working class and middle class socialist intellectuals. Lambeth was a radical place. It still retains some of that energy and there are still surviving representations of the various struggles and resistance that occurred in that borough during the Thatcher years, but clearly there was an alignment of social, economic and political interests that ran through the borough in such a way as to make it a particularly radical area.

Clapham Common at the time was home to a lot of low paid workers – the Northern Line was nicknamed the 'Misery Line' by the proletarians that it sucked into London on for their labour value to be extracted on a daily basis. Clapham was rapidly emerging as a popular place for gays and lesbians to go out at the weekend, leading to Clapham Common becoming a regular site for cottaging, a discreet attraction for the gay community who still paddled serious prejudice in the home and their communities. Many a night out would start or end at the Vauxhall Tavern to the north before winding down to several gay clubs and pubs around Clapham North; with lesbian and gay activists getting drunk in the streets, chanting:

> two four six eight
> > gay is just as good as straight
> three five seven nine
> > lesbians are mighty fine

By the late '70s construction was slowly beginning on the Lambeth that will be familiar to people today. Next to the Tate Library in Brixton stood the Little Bit Ritzy Cinema, recently taken over by a consortium of people

---

5 *Daily Mail*, 8 June, 1989.
6 In the words of local historian John Salaway, "a kind of local organic intelligentsia"; *Reading the Riots Acts* (Lambeth Archives 2005) p. 36.

who wanted to show more art house and independent films. Nearby the site of the Brixton Recreation Centre remained a hole in the ground due to a bitter argument between the Council and the Greater London Council over who would fund construction. But there was still the remnants of the failure of post war housing. Estates were run down, some infested with cockroaches, others waterlogged. Many people did not have indoor toilets. Housing was in a bad state across the city. It was the bitter fruits of the ailing modernist post-war dream.

Lambeth has always been full of political and religious sects; from the famous Clapham Sect[7] that opposed slavery through to modern-day street preachers and paper sellers outside Brixton tube. By the 1980s there were also left-wing bookshops scattered throughout the borough. The area was also no stranger to the seedier side of life. At 32 Ambleside Avenue the notoriously flamboyant brothel keeper Cynthia Payne gave luncheon vouchers to her clients to spend on the girls working there – a unique way of trying to get around prostitution laws. The arrangement lasted until the police raided in 1978, catching some notable politicians and other pillars of the community *in flagrante*. At her first trial in the media circus that was the Madame Cyn case, the legal establishment was blind-sided by problems of prosecution, given how many lawyers and even judges had been regular patrons, gripping their luncheon vouchers in their sweaty palms waiting for one of Payne's girls to take them upstairs. Meanwhile at 140 Acre Lane the Workers' Institute of Marxist-Leninist-Mao Tse Tung Thought were busy plotting Maoist revolution in the form of a strange cult whose leader imprisoned young women – only being finally exposed in 2013.[8] For years afterwards his wife still attended demonstrations with leaflets calling for his release.

Its proximity to Parliament also filled the north of Lambeth with politicians of all stripes living alongside Westminster machine men, pin striped lobbyists and journalists. Little happened in Lambeth without being reported, discussed, debated and itemised by the political establishment and the media. The local Labour Parties were largely on the left. Norwood and Vauxhall produced the most left-leaning members of the council and local party leadership. Streatham was more mixed, reflecting the more conservative mood in that part of the borough. Their repeated failures to get Labour councillors elected throughout the 1980s and the presence of the only Tory politician in the borough hardened up a right wing tendency in the Constituency Labour Party who blamed the left for their electoral defeats. But we are skipping ahead. That is all yet to come.

---

7 The Clapham Sect were an Anglican social reform group, active from the late eighteenth to the early nineteenth centuries, who campaigned against the slave trade.

8 For more details read *The Conversation*, 'Inside the paranoid Maoist cults of 1970s Britain' 28 November 2018, accessed at theconversation.com/inside-the-paranoid-maoist-cults-of-1970s-britain-20739.

After all, this wasn't a time for apathy. As the post-war consensus began to unravel and the New Right moved into gear many in the local community knew it was do or die, fight or fall. Those that wanted to just go with the flow, accept the apparently inevitable, were considered part of the problem. They were fifth columnists behind the lines. The yuppies moving in only a short walk from the squatters building alternative communities. Others were putting their bodies and hearts against the wheels, either as a last gasp for a dying old order or as the first salvo in the fight for a new world. It was hard to tell which. As with a lot of historical battles, you usually don't know who's won until sometime later.

2

Lambeth Council

Writing in 1991, the then current chief executive of the Council Herman Ouseley described what he called "The Lambeth Factor". Lambeth was a "rotten Labour borough" in the early to mid-1970s – dominated by "a few powerful politicians (the old guard – 'mafia') and a handful of very powerful bureaucrats who effectively ran the council."[1] He described one director who "took so much power to himself that nothing happened in Lambeth unless he personally approved it and he would block anything not to his liking".[2] The effect of this mafia-bureaucrat control was "the erosion of local democracy, the non-involvement of local people in local government, a total lack of accountability, and rampant institutionalised racism with black people being denied jobs, good quality housing, relevant social services and access to resources".[3] Local government was corrupt – some might argue that all government under capitalism is organised corruption – but local government is perhaps more immediate: you scratch my back and I'll scratch yours; more direct in the form of cash in envelopes under the table. Cynthia Cockburn had described how "even socialist councillors are quickly curbed by the decision-making power of senior permanent officials."[4]

Some suspected it was more than just conservative bureaucracies. There were also the constant rumours that the borough was run by Freemasons. The idea of a clandestine group of gentlemen collaborating together to control things behind the scenes was one that many local residents firmly believed. As with most conspiracy theories it was probably more of a case of entrenched clique in power in a local bureaucracy but the rumour of Masonic control lingered well into the 1990s. When John Mann was a Labour Councillor he would take his fellow local politicians around the

---

1 Herman Ouseley, 'A personal reflection on the "Lambeth Factor" in the affairs of the local municipal machinery' September 1991 p. 2, his correspondence with Labour's NEC during the disciplinary hearing into then Council Leader Joan Twelves.
2 Ibid.
3 Ibid.
4 Cynthia Cockburn, *The Local State: Management of Cities and People*, (Pluto Press 1977), p. 50.

Town Hall pointing to the Masonic symbolism he believed had been incorporated into the building.[5] The shape of the Town Hall itself, similar to the Masonic compass, aroused suspicions.

A new generation of left wingers were coming into the council, idealistic and determined to enact change. Ted Knight was expelled from Labour in 1954 whilst a member of the Labour Party Young Socialists (LPYS). At the time he had been a supporter of the Trotskyist Gerry Healy's secretive association 'The Club' which in 1959 became the Socialist Labour League (SLL). After Knight left the SLL he still retained some close friendships with members in the SLL and its successor organisation, the Workers Revolutionary Party (WRP). During his time outside of Labour, Knight had been active in the Vietnam Solidarity Campaign and served on its Political Committee. In 1970 he reapplied to join Labour. At his NEC meeting to discuss his readmission he was unabashed about his politics, telling them he was very firmly a Marxist, that Marxism was a legitimate tendency within the working class movement, and that Marxists have the right to be inside the broad party of the working class. The mood was clearly far more tolerant by this point in Labour as he was readmitted. In 1974 he became a Councillor in Norwood.

Knight always had an air of seriousness about him. Often well dressed, he appeared formal, even conservative. Cautious with people at first, once he took you into his confidence he became warmer. From the beginning he was ambitious, a socialist who wanted to go places, who wanted to be in the thick of it. He had two qualities that even his opponents admired: he was an excellent public speaker and he was a leader able to marshal people. Most conversations were carefully measured, sounding out someone to see if they were an ally or an enemy. Allies were kept close, enemies, ("those creatures" he would call them), were to be defeated.

Councillor Ken Livingstone was also an ambitious Young Turk, keen to eventually make his name as an MP, maybe even Prime Minister. He knew it was an uphill battle; if you lacked proper connections then you had to go the hard way to prove your ability, spending time at the coal face of local government before the call to glory in Parliament was granted to you. Livingstone was a campaigning housing activist. He worked with the chair of the housing committee, a young John Major, they both uncovered the racist housing practices of the council at the time. In short: white families got the good housing, black families were left on the waiting list or placed in, effectively, slum conditions. They uncovered and stopped a practice by housing officers of marking black applicants' cards with the letter N in the corner to differentiate them from the 'normal' residents.[6]

---

5   Interview with Joan Twelves, June 2016.
6   Ken Livingstone, *If Voting Changed Anything, They'd Abolish It* (Collins 1987), p. 118.

Livingstone was sceptical about the abilities of London Labour Councillors. He described Lambeth's post-war municipal history in scathing terms:

> Like many other inner-city Labour councils, a strong authoritarian, quite conservative Labour administration had been in power since the war, led by a handful of competent working-class men with strong roots in the local area. These men ruled over a group of mediocre councillors who were treated as lobby fodder.[7]

The left during this period fought hard to make the local Labour Party more outward looking. By all accounts Norwood had a healthier approach to getting its activists onto Tenants Residents Associations and into local campaigns, but the other CLPs either actively struggled or resisted it. One person described how "he found his local branch in the Vauxhall CLP to be, as he put it sardonically, closed to new members in the mid-1970s. After joining with some difficulty, he found that members were so few that they nominated each other for the party posts. The politics of the branch changed from right to left when he recruited new members."[8] This was repeated in other areas of the Labour Party, a recalcitrant right wing who controlled the levers of power was actively opposed to new members for fear of them being, at best, disruptive, at worst, left wing. A Norwood councillor complained that "they are Rightists in Streatham, they are all friends. The grossest incompetence in their ranks is tolerated in order to avoid not splitting them."[9]

The council at the time was run by David Stimpson, a traditional Labour rightist who Ted Knight claimed liked to refer to himself as the Prime Minister of Lambeth. The issue that dogged his time in charge was housing, inevitably, given Lambeth's situation. The council was buying up houses at an accelerated rate but didn't have resources to refurbish a number of them. Livingstone and others had secured a deal to give empty council properties temporarily to squatters until they could be refurbished – the famous short life tenancy scheme. This deal was torn up by the Labour Group leadership. Instead the Chair of the Housing Committee and the Director of Housing announced that short life properties would be made 'uninhabitable' – contractors for the council were sent to smash the toilets and sinks in empty properties to deter squatters. This miserable work, (known as 'wrecking'), had to be done by non-union people because the builders' union UCATT had issued explicit instructions not to carry out these operations. The squatting movement fought back, lobbying council meetings and holding

---

7   Ibid., p. 15.
8   James Curran, Ivor Gaber and Julian Petley, *Culture Wars: The Media and the British Left*, (Edinburgh University Press 2005), p. 33.
9   Cynthia Cockburn, *The Local State*, p. 89.

their own regular meetings, issuing pamphlets and other materials about their rights as squatters and the hypocrisy of the council evicting them when so many homes in Lambeth were left empty.

One clash gripped the national headlines: the fight over St Agnes Place. St Agnes Place was a long line of houses running next to Kennington Park. First squatted in 1969, a large number of Rastafarians began to gravitate there, eventually earning it the nickname Bob Marley Street. In fact Bob Marley himself visited in 1977 and lived in a house converted into a Rastafari Temple at the north end of the street where he recorded part of his critically acclaimed album *Exodus*. However in 1974 the council had tried to evict the tenants, prevented from doing so only by incredibly brave acts of resistance: people jumping onto wrecking balls and forming human chains in front of bulldozers. Faced with mounting pressure over images of police roughing up black people and knocking down their homes, the council relented and the squats stayed. St Agnes was a bustling community, home to musicians and even pirate radio stations. It was a living example of the kind of place that had to be obliterated by developers and council officers; its mere existence challenged concepts of property, what community meant, and whether you had to live as part of the machine. Attempts to evict the community in the mid-1970s saw squatters from across the borough descend on the council for a week long vigil that culminated in disrupting a housing committee meeting.

The mood of defiance and rebellion among some squatters was clear. One pamphlet about the movement carried the poem *Doing the Lambeth Squat*, which included,

> Fix a Yale-lock, mend the lights
> Get to know your squatter's rights
> And join us all
> Doing the Lambeth Squat.
> Sunny Brixton welcomes you
> And the Lambeth Council too
> Can't stop us all
> Doing the Lambeth Squat.[10]

Amidst the constant battle over property and community, the rebel alliance of squatters, the poor and community activists were often at loggerheads with the establishment. At a public meeting to discuss the Inner London partnership, Stimpson was booed off the platform by angry local residents. The left saw their chance as the 1978 elections drew closer. The chair of the powerful Local Government Committee was taken by left winger Matthew Warburton in 1977, soon to become a key member of the Knight administration. He was tasked with drafting the 1978 election manifesto based on feedback and consultation with the local Labour Parties.

---

10 Nick Wates and Christian Wolmar (eds), *Squatting: The Real Story*, (Bay Leaf Books 1980) p. 77.

Warburton had lived in central Brixton since 1971 and saw empty homes throughout the borough, (there were 5221 empty properties in the borough according to the 1971 census).[11] Alongside this waste of accommodation there were many homeless families housed in expensive, cramped bed and breakfasts and hotels, often outside the borough. Many people lived in totally unsuitable accommodation, Warburton himself knew a man who had lived for 20 years in a garden shed, a stand pipe outside was his only access to clean water for washing and drinking. The inefficiency over empty council properties being allocated compounded the social injustice of the suffering of so many people and formed a core pledge of the 1978 manifesto: to reduce the B&B bill, bring those empty houses back into use, and renovate the dilapidated private sector housing. The left pushed in several wards to get Labour activists with more radical credentials selected as council candidates.

Knight rallied support a week before polling day, sending every council candidate a notice of a meeting to discuss "what can be achieved by a strong coherent left-wing voice." The letter made it clear that "only councillors prepared to break with the past leadership and work with the Left wing caucus" could attend. The meeting of the incoming left councillors prior to the election agreed a general line of march and divided up the committee positions they believed they would win. Seeing which way the wind was blowing, Stimpson told the *South London Press* that Knight would be a "Marxist dictator" in the borough.[12]

KNIGHT MOVES – THE LEFT TAKES CONTROL

Labour swept the board in the 1978 local elections, winning nearly 50% of the vote across the borough, one of their best performances for years. The election also saw a large turnover of Labour councillors as many of the old guard either didn't stand or were deselected in their wards by the left. A number of the key activists who became left stalwarts of the Council were first elected in 1978, several from radical left wing backgrounds. Bill Bowring worked in the Brixton Law Centre and was initially rejected as a candidate due to having been a member of the WRP from 1970-4. He appealed the decision at Labour HQ on Old Kent Road and was eventually allowed onto the long list. Matthew Warburton had been expelled from the International Socialists in the mid-1970s before joining Labour.

As more left Labour councillors were returned than those of a right wing persuasion, Stimpson declined to stand for leader again, having been advised that he might lose. Instead Peter Lane stood against Knight but was beaten 19 votes to 23. Livingstone, for his part, had by this time left to focus on winning the leadership of the GLC. The fears of the establishment about the trajectories of the two Norwood CLP luminaries found their way into

---

11 Ced Jackson, *Lambeth Interface: Housing Planning and Community Action in an Inner London Borough* (Suburban Press 1975), p. 80.
12 'Battle hots up for control of town hall', *South London Press* 28 April 1978, p. 4.

the House of Commons. One Tory MP was quick to alert the house that "we are faced with a different London Labour Party. We are talking not about the London Labour Party of Herbert Morrison or Reg Goodwin of only a few years ago, but about the party of Ted Knight and Ken Livingstone."[13] After he was dethroned, Stimpson remarked about his successor: "I detest his politics though I don't dislike him as a person."[14] A few years later Stimpson joined the right wing Social Democratic Party (SDP) breakaway, many of whom cited the 'gesture politics' of places like Lambeth as a reason to split.

There were other councillors who were unhappy with the new direction. Peter Mandelson had been elected in Stockwell ward where he found the culture of the local party to be utterly against his own methods: "I remember being warned by a local Labour activist as we canvassed in a local estate one Sunday morning that the party must at all costs avoid 'compromising with the electorate'. My local comrades had absolutely clear views. Criminals were victims of the capitalist system. The police were agents of repression. Riots were popular uprisings against capitalist injustice."[15] Alongside a handful of other moderates like Peter Ormerod, they fought against the left leadership, though Mandelson admitted, "I was not a terribly effective brake on the Labour group's march to the drumbeat of revolution…"[16]

The day after winning the council, Knight entered the Town Hall determined to seize control with both hands. The ornate Town Hall, designed by the Scottish Architect Septimus Warwick, shaped like a wedge and subsequently modified according to a baroque style, remains one of the most impressive local government buildings in London. The clock tower stands at an imposing 134 feet, guarded at four corners by statutes representing Justice, Science, Literature and Art. Previously the Chief Executive had enjoyed large office space whilst the leader of the council had to work in a small room alongside their chief whip and a secretary. Prior to 1978, the head of the council would usually pop into the Town Hall after work, have a chat with the CEO and perhaps imbibe a drink whilst the officer briefed him on their days work.[17] Knight made it clear that he would be working at the council full time and quit his job as a contracts manager of a cleaning firm to work on a £60 a week allowance for attending committee meetings on the basis that "when you are in control of a £150 million budget it is nonsense to suggest that you can do it in your spare time."[18] A journalist at the time commented "there was nothing ostentatious about his

---

13 Cyril Townsend (Tory MP for Bexleyheath 1974-1997), *Hansard* 28 April 1981.
14 'New Lambeth Council steps firmly to the Left', *South London Press*, 9 May 1978, front page.
15 Peter Mandelson, *The Third Man*, (Harper Collins 2010), p. 64.
16 Ibid.
17 Interview with Ted Knight, April 2016.
18 'What's left of Lambeth?', Peter Strick, *South London Press*, 4 May 1979, pp. 16-17.

life style. He drives a 12 year old Rover, smokes thin Dutch cigars and wears sober business suits.[19]

Arriving to work in his most sober suit, Knight immediately moved the CEO into the smaller office and ensconced himself in the larger room. His office had an imposing desk with chairs for visitors and a conference table for meetings. This was no part-time leadership and they were intent on the balance of power shifting from the officer caste to the elected politicians.

With Labour still in government and the radical left moving into position in local councils, Knight and his allies were confident that they were well placed to leverage their position for the cause of socialism: high spending, lots of jobs, an expanded industrial base in the borough. The manoeuvres to get to power in the Lambeth Labour group had been drawn out but the result had been an unqualified success for the left. For the time being, the Knight had become the king.

MUNICIPAL SOCIALISM

Knight and his comrades stood in a tradition of municipal socialism, politics that were in line with the project of the Labour left in local government at the time. Municipal Socialism was the general term to describe a political movement dating back to the Victorian era whereby progressive councillors would use the local state infrastructure to alleviate suffering, provide access to services, and ensure decent wages. Many of those elected in 1978 and again in the early 1980s hoped to use local government as a weapon in the battle for redistribution of wealth and power from the rich to working people and their families (to borrow a phrase from the 1974 Labour Manifesto).

Once the wheels began to come off the post-war mixed economy in the 1970s, socialists in Labour began to formulate alternatives. This produced the Alternative Economic Strategy (AES), the Labour Party's economic programme after 1972 that had been theorised by Stuart Holland (who became the MP for Vauxhall in 1979). The AES looked beyond standard Keynesian thinking to argue for elements of workers' control and more vigorous state intervention in the form of social ownership not just of bankrupt enterprises (as Labour had traditionally done) but of profitable concerns, in an attempt to restructure the economy away from capitalism and towards socialism. The strategy had informed the 1974 manifestos and been the dominant thinking at the Trade Union Congress, but Labour MPs, led by Harold Wilson and then James Callaghan, were far more sceptical and refused to implement its more radical demands. This led to the formation of the Bennite movement and the push to democratise Labour and make MPs more accountable to party members.[20]

---

19 Ibid.
20 The Bennite movement was followers of Labour MP Tony Benn (1925-2014) a leading figure of the left in the 1970s and 80s.

Importantly the intention of the local government left during this period was to fight not just defensive struggles but to forge a credible alternative, a signpost to the socialist future that, in however small a way, could prove to people that the ideas of collectivism and social solidarity were useful. Not just useful but possible. Theirs was a practical politics, not an abstraction; the use of Town Halls to spread messages of solidarity and try to provide economics rooted in social justice was supposed to be a pointer to what a more radical Labour government could do as well. This concentrated minds and energies on the local elections and inspired a new generation, (some of whom used to be revolutionaries), to stand in an arena that was historically the preserve of the 'geriatric Labour right'.[21] The focus was on job creation, using the council workforce to soak up the unemployed. It meant working closely with the trade unions to draw up and implement plans overspending, community enterprises, social planning and work. This had particular resonance in Lambeth: around 12,000 people were registered as unemployed at the Brixton dole office in early 1981 and the left was acutely aware of structural discrimination in both housing and employment against black people.

The pinnacle of the AES in local government was the GLC after 1982. It not only attempted a bold job programme, led by the Greater London Employment Board, it also put into practice new forms of democratic decision making, opening up council meetings to women's groups, LGBT rights campaigners, housing activists and trade unionists. Whilst the dream of the left for an alternative economic strategy was undermined in practice by Labour's more moderate leadership, it was finally killed off by Thatcher after her victory in 1979. After that defeat the left couldn't hope to get progressive economic strategies through parliament any more, which put even more of an onus on the Labour councils to offset the Thatcherite attacks on jobs and working class communities.

The municipal socialist ethos was inevitably going to clash with the New Right in Parliament. Labour councillors emphasised the public sector and more economic planning, the Tories prioritised the private sector and wanted more capital accumulation. The left focused on the methods of production and how to improve them, for the right the market was sacrosanct. The constitutional crisis that was brewing was the insurmountable gulf between the political commitments of local councillors elected on a growth budget and the slash and burn policies of a Tory party in central government elected to end 'profligate' councils. Faced with such an obstacle the left councillors knew they had to fight.

The Labour left was organised in several tendencies and also made up of several high profile individuals not in any grouping, like Benn himself. Of course there was the Militant Tendency, a rapidly growing formation in the Labour Party that claimed to be 'just a newspaper' yet was suspiciously well

---

21   Patrick Seyd, *The Rise and Fall of the Labour Left*, (Macmillan Education 1987), p. 138.

organised and coordinated.²² Militant had control of the Labour Party Young Socialists (LPYS) by the early 1980s and was very influential on Liverpool Council after 1982. It also had two Labour MPs, Dave Nellist and Terry Fields. Despite a significant following nationally, Militant had little impact on Lambeth Labour politics with a couple of notable exceptions. Another smaller tendency was the Socialist Campaign for a Labour Victory (SCLV), made up of Trotskyists and radicals of various backgrounds. A split in their ranks formed London Labour Briefing and later the Labour Representation Committee, whereas SCLV went on to become Socialist Organiser.

A strategic debate on the left was whether you could offset cuts by increasing local rates. Rates were the primary form of raising money locally, the revenue came from both domestic and business rates. Rates were based on the nominal rental value of the property but valuations were only done sporadically – the last one in England had been carried out in 1973. Some on the left believed that increases in rates was a tactic that was justified in the overall fight against cuts, others, (for instance, Socialist Organiser), criticised rate increases as being a regressive tax on working class people as it wasn't based on an ability to pay. But proponents argued that rates levied against big business could reap dividends. Lambeth Council had the advantage of the massive Shell Headquarters and the GLC offices in the north of the borough to extract money for local services. The left organised around the magazine *Labour Briefing* believed it was permissible to raise rates (but not rents) as a tactic to offset cuts whilst also mobilising for a mass campaign. As we shall see, this debate was set to dog the municipal left in the early 1980s.

The strategy of municipal socialism was challenged from the left by various Trotskyists who deemed it an 'illusion of power'²³ and mocked the pretence that you could build socialism in one borough. Cynthia Cockburn, a Marxist academic, wrote an analysis of local government, using Lambeth in the 1970s as a case study, deriding it as effectively just an arm of the capitalist state.²⁴ Local government in a capitalist society was concerned primarily with the social reproduction of the local population keeping them housed, ensuring they had parks to use, that there were social workers for people with various issues, and so on. The management structure of local government was entirely functional along the lines of the private sector techniques of social control and engineering, behind a democratic façade of local elections. In short, socialist aspirations in local government would always hit the rocks of capitalism and roll back.

The left Labour councillors at the time read Cockburn's book and discussed it. They were aware of the dangers of integration into merely managing the capitalist state locally, but they had to offset it against the possibilities that a radical Labour council could act as a beacon of local

---

22 Report of the 1982 Annual Conference Labour Party, p. 41.
23 For instance, Socialist Organiser pamphlet, *Illusions of Power*, 1985.
24 Cynthia Cockburn, *The Local State*.

redistribution and resistance to central government if it was needed. Surely better to be in power, no matter if there was the danger of compromise, rather than refuse the opportunities it provided? This debate was had throughout the 1980s.

It wasn't just in the Labour left that significant changes were happening, the trade unions were also moving left. The working class of Lambeth was well served in the 1980s. The Town Hall was covered by NALGO a white collar union, NUPE which covered lower grade NHS and council staff and the NUT. The builders union UCATT had a headquarters in the borough, a beautiful brick work piece along Abbeville Road, near what was known locally as the 'French Quarter' in Clapham for its Gallic residents and restaurants. In the job centres the Civil and Public Services Association (CPSA) was very active.

The largest was Lambeth NALGO, led by Mike Waller, its branch secretary throughout most of the 1980s. Waller was a member of the Socialist Workers Party and a tough union negotiator. He was part of a team of militants in the late 1970s who had worked to take over the union and move it away from its stuffy post war existence. NALGO had traditionally been a very conservative organisation, its officers were usually upstanding gentlemen of the community, senior officers who wore gold chains around their suits like the mayor. Old photos of NALGO meetings showed very austere white men in chains of office, almost as if they were the Lord Mayor himself. By the 1970s, however, this old way of working was rapidly coming undone, women were involved, revolutionary socialists had become active in local government, black workers were demanding a place and a voice. The old branch chair, Bill Pitt, was a prominent Liberal, having stood for Parliament on a number of occasions, much to the derision of some of the more socialist minded members of his branch. He reflected the old guard, the way that NALGO used to be – essentially a gentlemen's club, an 'association' and not a union. At the AGM in 1981 when the left consolidated their grip on the branch, they passed a symbolic motion that the chair shouldn't sit on a raised platform overlooking the members and shouldn't wear their customary gold chain. When the motion was passed, Pitt shook his head with anger, ripped the chain off, threw it on the floor and left the room. Avowed liberals like himself were no longer welcome in a class struggle union.

3

Housing and Community

> In thirteen hundred and eighty one
> They made a famous lore
> T'was all for English Squatters
> Of whom you've heard before
> This lore has stayed the same my friends,
> Five hundred years or more
> Tis one of old England's liberties
> THE ENGLISH SQUATTERS LORE.
>
> Musical Barricades, performed at the
first Villa Road Carnival, 1976

One of the blights of local government at this time was corruption, with councils regularly undergoing reports and internal inquires uncovering financial irregularities, nepotism, or outright theft. There was the old vice of using public office for private gain.

Graft and theft has been a feature of local government for a very long time, and not just in Britain. Whether it was Tammany Hall system between 1854 to the 1930s as a way of binding different ethnic groups to the machine politics of New York city or *La bustarella* (the bribe) culture in Italy in the 1970s, local government has often been synonymous with the back-hander, the inflated price, and the 'you scratch my back' mentality of municipal politicians. Local government lends itself to these kinds of practices because, unlike central government, it is far more rooted in defined communities, with a direct impact on the distribution of resources.

These factors led to the rise of figures like T. Dan Smith in Newcastle or Dame Shirley Porter in Westminster. Smith served time in prison after it was revealed that his public relations firm had received significant sums of money from John Poulson, a local architect, which had also been used as a bribe for local councillors to back Poulson's regeneration schemes for Newcastle city centre. Porter was famously ousted from Westminster Council and fled the country after her 'homes for votes' gerrymandering to get more Tory voters into the borough was exposed by the District Auditor. Wandsworth engineered its own social cleansing with an aggressive right-to-buy scheme, driving poorer working class residents out of the borough through underinvestment in estates, and the hiking up of rents to encourage the 'wrong sort of people' to leave. The one mistake that Porter made was being too flagrant about it.

A lot of the issues focused on housing and building more generally. Local Government in London had employed its own builders in Direct Labour Organisations (DLOs) since 1892, as a way of competing with the private sector builders and driving down costs. Lambeth's own DLO had been established in 1972 and by 1981 it employed around 1,200 people. It was a huge organisation responsible for everything from building to repairs and maintenance on housing, roads, council amenities and so on. Lambeth's DLO was based on Acre Lane, in a depot that later became a large supermarket. On the corner of Acre Lane there used to be an old pool hall where all the plumbers and builders would socialise after work. The *South London Press* pointed out that the DLO's turnover was £20 million and made nearly £1.5 million in surplus for the council. The cost of running such a large DLO meant that housing maintenance in Lambeth worked out at about £195 per house, the most expensive in inner London.[1]

The concept of Councils employing direct labour to building and capital maintenance remained popular in Labour. Ann Taylor, the MP for Bolton West made the point in the Commons when she defended the DLOs from new policies that would effectively lead to their abolition in order to create more space for the private sector building firms: "I should make it clear at once that Labour Members positively believe in Direct Labour Organisations. We recognise that, by and large, direct works departments have a good record of service to local authorities and to tenants and provide value for money to ratepayers. They have also set an example for the rest of the building industry in terms of security of employment, pensions rights, employment of the disabled, health and safety at work and apprenticeships."[2]

However, DLOs were often accused of being involved hot beds of corruption, everything from minor overcharging for repairs to missing building materials to outright gangsterism. The Lambeth DLO had a history of such issues. During the building of Myatt's Field estate in the 1970s around one million bricks were 'lost' as trucks were driven onto the site and then the bricks siphoned off by unscrupulous individuals. As one ex-DLO man put it, "a few people were on the thieve, nicking copper and wood". Many local residents laughed about the 'Lambeth Price', when contractors or council workmen would charge extortionate amounts for simple repairs to the Council, skimming money off the top. A number of staff would dryly

---

1 'Aims' Broadside at direct labour', *South London Press*, 11 August 1978, p. 3.
2 *Hansard*, 30 March 1982.

point out how flashy the contract managers' expensive cars were, as they zipped around the borough, meeting contractors and arranging payment for building and repairs.

As a result police operations against the DLO were fairly common. In May 1978, 31 workman at the Council depot at Carew Street were detained in a dawn raid by police for allegedly doctoring the requisition forms for materials.[3] Knight emphasised at the time that it was the council's own internal procedures that had uncovered the corruption. The construction union's stewards committee called a walk out at work for the entire morning until assurances were given by management that workers detained and then released would be paid their wages if there were no charges.

Whilst the media and Tory politicians would focus on the corruption of the DLO as part of their war against the public sector, it was often the case that the private sector wasn't exactly shy when it came to over-charging and massaging contracts with hidden extras. An inquiry by the Council headed by Ousley in the early 1990s found that there had been around £10 million lost in corruption and malpractice during the 80s, largely as a result of huge ever-expanding contracts gobbled up by the private sector.[4] The expansion of the private sector into local government building works didn't discipline the prices or act to drive down costs, in fact in some cases they rocketed. Private sector contractors had several schemes to inflate their costs, including having different copies of tender documents – the ones they would send to the council had fewer pages, then when the bill was presented for payment the Council would discover pages with additional quotes and charges which had allegedly been part of the original tender. Another example of private sector behaviour was one that many people who have hired cowboy builders encountered: the original contract looks cheap (for instance offering 10% 'sweetener', discounts to initially get the job) but significant delays force the council to shell out more money to finish the project. One plasterer firm that was hired managed to secure an additional 15% funding out of the council when he explained delays caused by 'the inadequate labour strength of plasterers'.[5]

But there were also failures of procedure within the Council itself. A lot of money also seeped away in smaller contracts: the Directorate of Construction Services was supposed to secure reliable tenders for works under £10,000 that should have been signed off by the Councils solicitor but this was rarely done so. The systems were not robust enough, with not enough checks and balances across departments. In some ways the main difference between the Labour Councillors in Lambeth or the Tory Councillors running Wandsworth was whether you were more concerned by

---

3   '£50,000 council theft probe', *South London Press*, 19 May 1978, front page.
4   Lambeth corruption suspicions 'were reported nine years ago', Stephen Ward, *The Independent*, Sunday 24 January.
5   Cited in the 1987 report into DCS p. 106.

some of your own workforce over-charging or the private sector greasing their palms. Construction has rarely been a well regulated industry whether nationalised or not.

THE POLITICS OF THE CROWBAR

Despite only just being elected as a councillor, Warburton was placed in charge of the all-important Housing Committee. Like Knight he also pledged to work full time for the Council to get a handle on the various problems in the borough. Warburton moved to try and introduce a fairer system for dealing with squatters. Squatting was a huge movement in Lambeth, campaigners reckoned that in 1975 there were over 3,000 squats in the borough.[6] The Family Squatting Advice Service (established 1970) led the charge in helping to house homeless families. The establishment figures who believed that squatting was merely drop-out hippies and drug addicts tended to avoid dealing with families who needed housing, preferring to leave them in hostels until a council house became available some years down the line..

However it wouldn't be right to imagine that this was simply a question of housing vulnerable and desperate families. By the mid-1970s the idea of communes, alternative lifestyles and attempts to live your lives independently of the politicians, the state and the *status quo* were also common – the politics of the crowbar. This could be because of political idealism or a more base desire to simply avoid paying rent – which meant some squats had revolutionaries alongside petty criminals. It was a diverse movement of people – living between the gaps in society as the post war social democratic model began to crack.

By the 1970s the squatting movement was organised with lawyers acting on their behalf. Squatters' rights activist Ron Bailey had already devised the by then ubiquitous notice that was stuck on the front doors of squats alerting the authorities that squatting was a civil matter and not a criminal one. Notices on doors citing the 'Forcible Entry Act 1381' and the rights of the commons to unoccupied land would leave many landlords and police constables nervous and confused. Activists would 'crack' an abandoned house using various methods, screw a bolt on the door and then stick the sign on the front. Bailey argued that the best approach was not a militant one, but "ultra-reasonableness", merely of highlighting the contradictions of an affluent society that left so many in poverty and destitute, and collaborating with council officials to turn squats into short life property.[7] This approach had worked very well in Lewisham and was the approach adopted in Lambeth.

Many of the Lambeth squats were buildings scheduled for slum clearances or road widening. If there was no money in the budget that year

---

6   Nick Wates and Christian Wolmar (eds.), *Squatting: The Real Story*, (Bay Leaf Books 1980), p. 41.
7   Ron Bailey *The Squatters*, (Penguin 1973), pp. 132-3.

for those redevelopment schemes then they weren't going to happen, which allowed for more squats to be temporarily made legitimate in a deal with the council. Initially, 80 squatters were offered council flats that were in disrepair and rejected by housing associations. They would pay rates but no rent but in return they were responsible for their own repairs. The tenancies would last at least two years or until the council got around to bringing them back in house.[8] Defending the policy from its critics, Warburton was adamant: "Better a licensee than a squatter."[9]

But in many ways it was more than a question of a debate over the legal question of ownership or occupation. It was that a space was created in the decline of post war social democracy, a pivotal moment where the old slums and near-derelict houses offered a chance – before their gentrification – for experiments in living. It gave a generation of mostly young people a historic opportunity to imagine what a different way of living could be outside of the stifling conformity of the nuclear family unit and the mortgage. They were experiments that were inevitably going to end under the relenting pressure of housing demands, Thatcherite social engineering and the *yuppification* of inner city areas, but for a time they were the grassroots growing among the grey concrete of inner city life. It had its own local heroes like Olive Morris, who had intervened as a teenager in 1969 when police began to harass a Nigerian diplomat driving his Mercedes Benz through Brixton, was arrested and beaten for her troubles.[10] She went on to join the British Black Panthers and helped found the Brixton Black Women's Group, as well as becoming an expert squatter.

Some squats were cultural centres. Anarchists and other radicals flocked to Railton Road to establish cafés, meetings rooms and bookshops – various revolutionary collectives published countless *samizdat*, everything from a celebration of Maoism to guerrilla gardening tips. Railton Road became known locally as the Frontline, an indication of how people saw the symbolic nature of the area, a battleground against the police and a refuge from racism. Its nature as a 'reclaimed space' from the state meant it was a beehive of left radicalism too.

In 1981 the 121 Centre was established, a base for anarchists which became the headquarters of several punky, iconoclastic magazines. The building had originally been squatted by Olive Morris herself alongside her ex-Black Panther comrade Liz Obi back in 1972. One resident-activist, Paul Petard, described the assembled folk at 121 Railton over the years: "There would be real agitated ANARCHIST meetings in the back room with young punks, ageing Spanish veterans, anarcho-nerd bookworms, romantic insurrectionaries, hardcore squatters, urban saboteurs..."[11] The building was

---

8 'Lambeth gives squatters a new deal', 27 June 1978, p. 2.
9 Interview with Matthew Warburton, November 2017.
10 She died tragically young, aged only 27.
11 Urban 75, urban75.org/brixton/features/121_1.html.

a base of operations for many networks who were keen to defy the state in whatever way possible, even single issue campaigns like the Fare Dodgers Association. Despite the plurality of people who would visit, the aesthetic of the 121 Centre was definitely anarcho-punk, the basement held host to some outstanding punk gigs before electronic dance music took over as the new *zeitgeist* counter culture towards the end of the decade. Railton Road had also been host to a gay squat at number 78 (which hosted the Gay Liberation Front for a time who were very active in the area) and the Women's Centre at number 207. These places were political organising spaces as well as necessary accommodation for people who had either fallen between the cracks or made a conscious choice to live a precarious lifestyle for the revolution. They scavenged anything that was usable, found supermarket food in skips ('skipping') and tended "to live on the left-overs of capitalist society" – as one anarchist pamphlet put it.[12]

Many squats started off as residential. Sometimes whole streets were squatted on both sides, over the years being connected by knocking down walls and digging rabbit warrens of tunnels between basements. One such squat was Villa Road, a street of Victorian housing first squatted in 1974. One previous occupant, Megan Doolittle, wrote an account of life on the street which captures a flavour of the times: "Marxism, the Trotskyist vanguard, libertarian socialism, women's liberation, gay liberation, ecology, anti-racism, anti-fascism and the peace movement, all vied for attention on the street. Villa Road also contained many of the experiments in forging new social relationships at that time, through communal living, collective working, alternative therapy, sexual liberation and lesbian separatism."[13] These kinds of people were liable to be labelled as 'bad' squatters, as opposed to the 'good' squatters who were just desperate people trying to deal with homelessness. This led to divisive rhetoric around squatting as a life style versus squatting as a necessity, allowing some squats to be seen as 'fair game'.

Such a heterogeneous community had much to disagree about, but they were forged as a community under siege for a considerable time. Despite political or social differences, resisting eviction through direct action, attending court summonses, lobbying local councillors and MPs, and battles with the police and bailiffs were not an uncommon event. A distrustful approach to the state alongside a hostile local press deepened the sense of *me against the world*. But it also encouraged a sense of autonomy and of self-reliance – indeed in a strange way the very values that Thatcher claimed to admire. The difference of course was that this was not about the hyper-

---

12 Eyewitness account from the 'We Want to Riot, Not To Work Collective', 1982 urban75.org/brixton/history/riot.html
13 Megan Doolittle, 'Living in Villa Road: A Brixton Squat 1974-1981', MA thesis, University of Sussex, October 1989.

individualist selfishness of Monetarism, this was an autonomy born out of a radical vision of a new world, a new way of living.

The spirit of taking over disused property and reconverting it for public use was quite common even beyond the political activists. In the mid-1980s an abandoned shop on Brailsford Road in Tulse Hill was taken over by a group calling themselves Brixton Parents Self Help Group. They opened the shop as a crèche, appealing to the council to let them 'go legal'. The shop had been empty for eight years – an example of the economic decline of inner London at the time.

Everyone was in agreement that work needed to be done to regenerate the borough and improve housing. The slums had to be cleared, other houses renovated and decent estates built. The nature of the redevelopment was controversial however and disagreements emerged between the new administration and the Architectural Department of the council headed up by the renowned Edward Hollamby. Hollamby had been hired in 1962 to revolutionise the council's ambitious design of new estates and buildings. His work included unique estates like Cressingham Gardens. Hollamby liked large open space and pleasing geometric curves of housing, where space permitted he had patio gardens built and houses would overlook open, green spaces. Livingstone praised Hollamby because he "passionately believed that council housing should be as good if not better than private housing".[14] His innovative architectural vision and commitment to excellent working class homes were largely driven by his Communist Party background – not the large blocks of Soviet era homes (he was opposed to monumentalism as well as any unnecessarily stylish aesthetic) but the modernist ideal of the post war period. But Knight and the left were intent on undermining the autonomy and power of the council officers, even ones from left backgrounds such as Hollamby. During one tense housing meeting where one of Hollamby's developments was being criticised, Hollamby confronted Knight afterwards: "What are you doing this for?" "Well, you're too powerful" was the reply.[15]

The Councillors sought to divide Hollamby's role into two parts, effectively handing part of the architectural work over to another officer. This infuriated Hollamby. But what he also rejected was the new 'confrontational' style of the leadership. In his mind the council had always worked well with central government and secured money for their projects. Why couldn't Knight have the same attitude? Despite this, Hollamby's garden estates were a prized possession of the borough, an attempt to create idyllic, serene green spaces in an urban landscape more often than not marked by rotting timbers and smashed windows in run down streets. Hollamby went on to work on the controversial London Docklands Development Corporation, a Thatcherite project that transformed East London in the interests of the private sector.

---

14 Rowan Moore, *Slow Burn City: London in the Twenty-First Century*, (Picador 2016), p. 228.
15 *The National Life Story*, Collection Ref. No.: C467/22.

The battle to regenerate communities and provide council housing — determined by an aesthetic linked to the health and well-being of residents, rather than just 'pack 'em in' high density or a developer driven dream of luxury flats for overseas investors — was a living tendency which fought and lost. The desire to regenerate was obviously right. Ending slum housing and providing homes for everyone was a vision shared by every progressive. But it directly conflicted with one of the key features that provided the material basis for radical communities in Lambeth: the squats and short life properties that acted as a base of operations for activists, organic intellectuals and community campaigners.

It is also worth considering how many iconic estates and buildings in Lambeth were designed by female architects. Rosemary Stjernstedt designed Central Hill; Kate Macintosh, (described in *The Guardian* as one of Britain's great unsung architects of social housing), designed a social housing complex on Leigham Court Road, and Magda Borowiecka had been placed in charge of the Southwyck House redevelopment. They were all left wing, motivated by various egalitarian principles or inspired by cutting edge Swedish architectural innovations of the '60s and '70s. The living space in Lambeth has always been a battleground of radical ideas of how people could live their lives. But these are contested spaces, and occasionally even high ideals can result in clashes with residents and campaigners.

4

Enter Thatcher

Now we have set the scene, let's go back to 1979, the year that changed everything. The Conservative victory over Labour was heralded as a brave new dawn of opportunity, a new direction for Britain, though few at the time knew how far Thatcher and her acolytes were willing to go. This is why Thatcher looms so powerfully as a leader. In her was the living philosophy of the New Right. Thatcher's politics were defined by her opposition to collectivism, driven by a Methodist concept of self-reliance, underpinned by neo-liberal economic theories. In her first speech as leader she praised self-reliance, thrift and individualism. It was bureaucracy that was the enemy, holding back progress and entrepreneurship. And there were few places more closely associated with wasteful red tape than the town halls. This necessitated a fundamental attack on the 'paternalistic' nature of the state.

This marked a decisive shift in Conservative attitudes to local government. There was nothing inherent in Toryism that predisposed it to a violent dislike of municipalism, indeed there was a strain of Toryism dating back to the 19th century which saw local government as far preferable to central. But these were new, dangerous times. The social democratic settlement of the post-war period was coming undone, the economy was sclerotic and the scissor crisis of inflation and workers striking for higher wages convinced a wing of the Conservatives that the mixed economy was bankrupt as an idea and the free market had to let rip to restore both profitability and workplace discipline.

In particular, the Conservatives knew that the remains of the Bennite left had taken a turn to local government to try to pursue their Alternative Economic Strategy from there. The shift in Conservative approaches to local government has to be seen then in the context of the Cold War and the fierce and historically embedded anti-communism of the Conservative Party. Influenced by Sir Keith Joseph and the ideas of von Hayek, they asserted the primacy of the market against bureaucracies and the free exchange of a multitude of individuals versus the elite decisions of a few in the state.[1] But

---

[1] Ken Young and Nirmala Rao, *Local Government since 1945* (Blackwell 1997) p. 265.

this new paradigm was also the product of cracks in the social democracy itself. Thatcherism was the monstrous child of the post-IMF crisis. The IMF in 1976 had demanded huge cuts from the Labour government to expenditure in order to secure a loan. Denis Healey's proto-Monetarist letter to the IMF in 1976 and the statement by Anthony Crosland to local authorities that "the party was over" provided the basis for the wider New Right ideology of the Thatcherite administration.[2]

Thatcherism, bloody in tooth and claw, was a renewed Conservative party with old scores to settle. The bitter experiences of their last government under Ted Heath (1970-74) still weighed heavily on them. Heath had faced mass working-class opposition to their trade union laws and had been eventually brought down by a miners' strike. They had also encountered opposition from Clay Cross Council over rent increases – the first serious open defiance by councillors against central government since the Poplar rebellion in the early 1920s.[3] This partly explains why there appears to also have been a personal motivation for Thatcher's crusade. One biographer referred to her "irrational, almost visceral dislike" of local government when she was Prime Minister.[4] This may partly have been a result of councillors' opposition to Thatcher's policies when she was head of the Department of Education under Heath, the mocking refrain of "Thatcher, Thatcher Milk Snatcher".[5] Quickly it became clear there was now a vendetta being waged from Westminster against the Town Halls.

The rising period of municipal militancy in the 1970s was seen by Conservative figures as part of the growing anarchy in the country and Thatcherism was chiefly concerned with restoring the supremacy of parliament as the sole sovereign power in the country. Other forms of local or institutional power that challenged parliament from a collectivist viewpoint were the 'enemies within'. This vitriol was primarily aimed at trade unions and local government, both of which were seen as defiant to the democratic and proper form of government from Westminster. Thatcher's theoretical hatred of both unions and councils came not just from her Hayek-influenced worshipping of the free market but from a famous book about the unwritten constitution, *Relation between Law and Public Opinion in England during the Nineteenth Century*, by Albert Venn Dicey.[6] Dicey had identified the two main enemies of parliamentary democracy as trade unions and local government back in the early 1900s.

---

2 John Medhurst, *That Option No Longer Exists: Britain 1974-76* (Zero Books 2014).
3 J Chandler, *Explaining Local Government: Local Government in Britain Since 1800* (Manchester University Press 2013) p. 211
4 John Campbell, *Margaret Thatcher Volume Two: The Iron Lady*, p. 375.
5 Referring to the withdrawal of milk for primary school children when she was Education Minister under Ted Heath's 1970-74 government.
6 Albert Venn Dicey, *Lectures on the Relation Between Law & Public Opinion in England During the Nineteenth Century* (AMS Press, University of Michigan 1978).

Based on the above political principles, the Thatcherite reforms of local government can be understood. The fundamental reform of local government by breaking the old model apart could be summarised in three policies: control of the money, sale of council homes, and privatisation of local services. With strategic thinking, they could kill two birds with one stone. So-called reforms to local government gave them a chance to undermine the strength of public sector unions as part of a wider battle against trade unionism generally. The municipal unions had played a key role in the Winter of Discontent strikes in 1978, (though in Lambeth the worst of the strikes were avoided through fostering of good industrial relations by the left administration), and the Conservatives viewed them as unrepresentative interest groups dominated by ideological concerns over collectivism which ran *contra* to the new spirit of individualism. The vehicle used to break the unions would be "introducing market discipline into service delivery through competitive tendering and de-regulation."[7] Councils would be 'freed' to focus on setting targets and standards for service delivery while the tendering process would determine the nature of the service delivery. It would allow the private sector in through the front door, undermine the public sector ethos of local government and transform it into a model based on managing private sector contracts. The war fought by the Conservatives in the 1980s against local government would later be characterised as "cumulatively the most serious threat" to councils "health and vitality which has been posed during its entire history."[8]

In addition, as Prime Minister, her statecraft prioritised a ruthless particularism, the Conservative government were determined to preserve the social order through enriching certain sections of the electorate.[9] The political project of the Conservative government from 1979 focused on rolling back the provisions of the state as part of Thatcher's concern that collectivism was sapping the energy of working people. The goal was to "decontaminate the middle classes of collectivism and socialism, while persuading aspirational workers that restoring small government and free markets would create the conditions in which they, and their families could 'get on'."[10] This meant a political, social, cultural and moral war. Thatcher summed up both means and ends in an interview with *The Sunday Times* in 1981: "Economics are the method: the object is to change the soul."[11] Thatcher had declared that Callaghan would be the last ever Labour Prime Minister, so confident was she on establishing Conservative rule for all time. Towards the end of the 1980s people began to wonder if she was true to her word.

---

7 Stoker, *The Politics of Local Government*, p. 191.
8 Hugh Butcher, Ian G. Law, Robert Leach and Maurice Mullard, *Local Government and Thatcherism*, (Routledge 1990), p. 28.
9 Ben Jackson and Robert Saunders (eds), *Making Thatchers Britain*, pp. 82-3.
10 Ibid., p. 140.
11 Ronald Butt, 'Mrs Thatcher: The first two years', *The Sunday Times*, 3 May 1981.

THE BATTLE FOR THE STREETS

But Lambeth wasn't just a target for its left wing socialistic local council. The Tories had an inveterate class hatred of the urban sprawl and everything that it represented. The working class, immigrants, unions, republicanism and non-conformism. They were class conscious fighters, determined to prevent Labour from ever establishing a political hegemony again as they had after World War Two. They had to turn the local people against their councillors, inculcate in people a love of property, a suspicion of profligacy. "Property enters like a fury into the human heart,"[12] as Paul Lafargue once wrote, and it was the sincere conviction of the Hayek-reading, Friedman-worshipping Tory right that that fury would transform Britain into a property owning democracy, inoculated from ideals of collectivism or flirtations with socialism. Convincing working class people to vote with their pockets, not with their social conscience or their class interests was key. Break down solidarity. Exalt the individual. Make you so concerned about not paying your mortgage that you don't go on strike. This was the whole narrative to denigrate the collective, that *there was no such thing as society, only individuals and their families.*[13]

But the government knew there would be opposition to their plans to roll back the state, to defund communities, local councils and to smash workers' unions. Whilst the state was being lambasted as a provider of social provision in favour of the market, the police were retrained, re-equipped and deployed to put down urban riots and break up picket lines. Given the kind of politics that dominated Lambeth, it was of particular concern to trade unionists and the urban black population that the police were being armed with protective helmet gear and thick polycarbonate shields. The equipping of police for urban combat against large crowds started on the UK mainland after the Lewisham protests in 1977 and then escalated into the miners' strike. The kind of tactics and violence used against the Catholic community in Northern Ireland was now coming to Britain. They were authorised to use plastic bullets after 1981, though never did. Police used CS spray in Toxteth during the riots for the first time. Many began to talk of a police state emerging, lawless and unchecked power being wielded by the elites against the poor.

If people were paranoid, perhaps they had a reason to be. Many decades later some of the extent of police infiltration of left wing organisations and trade unions would become clearer. Joe Gormley the head of the NUM before Arthur Scargill was an asset for the intelligence community. In 2002 a TV documentary series titled *True Spies* revealed that around 20 senior trade union leaders were in regular communication with MI5 or Special Branch.

---

12 Paul Lafargue, *Social and Philosophical Studies*, (C.H. Kerr & Co 1906), p. 110.
13 Interview with Margaret Thatcher in *Women's Own*, 23 September 1987.: "...they are casting their problems on society and who is society? There is no such thing! There are individual men and women and there are families..."

Harold Wilson still maintained that he had been subjected to a conspiracy against him to undermine or even overthrow his government. The Queen's relative Lord Mountbatten was regularly named as someone who would head up a new government, installed and protected by right wing private militias in the event of a left Labour government takeover. His assassination by the IRA in 1979 sent shockwaves through the British establishment, making many powerful people feel incredibly vulnerable. In 1982 Labour activist Chris Mullins wrote *A Very British Coup*, a 'what if' novel about what would happen in the event of a reforming Labour government, its slow strangulation by the civil services and the dubious and nefarious powers of the establishment to thwart popular democracy.[14] The CIA backed *coup* in Chile in 1973 that overthrew a democratically elected leftist government was still fresh in people's minds.

The Republican movement hated Thatcher's government and her bullish support for the Ulster Unionists. Inevitably the 'Troubles' began to dominate politics more and more. The IRA's bombing of the Conservative party conference and the subsequent crack down on Irish people living in the UK increased the atmosphere of distrust. By 1988 three unarmed IRA men were shot dead by the SAS in Gibraltar in what looked like a state sanctioned extra judicial killing. Given the experience of the left and the black community in Lambeth, the fears ran deep about the police and their increasing authoritarianism. The way the election played out, it looked to many people like white Middle England giving Thatcher *carte blanche* to impose a more authoritarian regime. It looked to some that the blacks, the Irish and the trade unionists were all part of a dangerous force, intent on overthrowing the government or destabilising society.

The TV screens of the 1980s were regularly filled with images of violence, buildings on fire, police cars overturned, strikers with bloodied heads. You cannot impose neo-liberalism without being prepared to crack skulls – that had certainly been one of the lessons from the Chilean coup in 1973. People were expendable. They knew there would be casualties. Later it was revealed that they had planned to depopulate Liverpool. In Lambeth rumours of Masonic control continued to linger in pub conversations and hushed whispers even in the council itself.

The 1979 election saw long-standing Vauxhall MP George Strauss finally stand down. Strauss was the longest serving Member of Parliament, having been elected in 1929 – before the Wall Street Crash. He had been a prominent left winger in his youth, was temporarily expelled from Labour for backing the Republicans in Spain during the civil war, and had been involved in funding an assassination plot against Hitler in a beer hall in 1943. He had also ended theatre censorship in the 1960s, outraged that the official censor had tried to ban Gilbert and Sullivan's *Mikado* during a visit by the

---

14 Chris Mullin, *A Very British Coup*, (Hodder & Stoughton 1982).

Prime Minister of Japan, in case it offended him.[15] Strauss was replaced as the Labour candidate in the ultra-safe seat of Vauxhall by the left intellectual Stuart Holland, the principle architect of the Alternative Economic Strategy. Strauss standing down had caused something of a crisis for Vauxhall Labour as his flat was the party headquarters and had been so for decades. There was a desperate scramble to find a suitable venue, one that could also fit a social club for local members. In Streatham Bill Shelton beat Labour's candidate T P C Daniel, 19,630 to 14,130. Shelton's vote had increased considerably since 1974, driven up even further by a rightward mood among the residents in the south west of the borough.

Things were febrile. Within a week of the election, councillors came to blows in the Council Chamber. There had already been a walk out of Tories that evening over the spending on the *Rock Against Racism* festival in Brockwell Park that year, so tensions were running high. When order was restored there was further uproar over an inappropriate speech by Tory Group leader Robin Pitt for the outgoing mayor Frank Quenhalt when he appeared to accuse Quenhalt of biased chairing. Labour representatives took exception to his language – the Mayor's wife Jean burst into tears and the local press reported she called Pitt "a few strong names".[16] A scuffle broke out and one Tory Councillor, Malcom Hollis, accused his Labour counterpart, Johnny Johnson, of kneeing him in the groin. Johnson for his part was relatively unfazed: "I went to comfort the mayoress, but Cllr Hollis tried to hold me back. I told him three times to take his hands off me. In the end I had to use force to get out of the chamber."[17] It was probably a sign of the times that, despite being a Tory, Pitt was a housing worker in nearby Lewisham and held a prominent elected committee role on behalf of NALGO in pay negotiations.[18]

---

15 *South London Press*, 6 April 1979.
16 'Members go wild in council clash', *South London Press*, 11 May 1979.
17 Ibid.
18 *South London Press*, 27 May 1979, p. 24.

5

Resisting Thatcher

Municipal Socialism may have been the theory but in practice it was much harder to implement. The primary obstacle was, of course, the Tory government after 1979. The Tories were, ideologically and morally, totally opposed to redistributionism and – in particular – to local government. Within months of the election the Secretary of State for the Environment, Michael Heseltine, said the government would recoup grant money from 'over-spending' local councils. Heseltine asked all local councils to reduce their expenditure by 1.5% as the Rate Support Grant (RSG) was being arbitrarily reduced by £300 million. The RSG was money given to local councils from Westminster, an annual sum of money that helped pay for local services because in most places the local rates alone would not cover the costs. Heseltine punished Lambeth for their refusal to make budget cuts. The Council lost £2.1 million from the RSG in penalties, resulting in them incurring more charges in interest rates.

In its 1980-81 annual report, Lambeth Council laid out the arguments against cuts: "The reality is ... that for the majority of its services, Lambeth's costs are within the general range for inner London boroughs. Only social services, housing and environmental health costs show significant variations. There are very clear reasons for the high levels of expenditure on these services, briefly, these are related to the problems of inner cities; housing shortages, poor standards of housing, and the socio-economic factors, including the high instance of one-parent families, unemployment, and low incomes."[1] This was the key argument for Lambeth all through the 1980s, despite repeated insistence from central government that the key issue was inefficiency and mismanagement.

The Lambeth Councillors earnestly believed that the cuts were politically motivated and aimed at some of the most vulnerable residents. Accepting the cuts meant accepting the implications on social welfare, housing and other services.

---

1   *Lambeth Annual Report 1980-81*, p. 16.

In reply, the standard Conservative view was that councils like Lambeth spent money frivolously. Shelton spoke in parliament about how "if one examines the wilder flights of fancy by Lambeth council, one finds that a poet and an artist are in residence and paid out of the rates. In addition, a gentleman is paid to sculpture with a chain-saw dead trees wherever he finds them in the borough."[2] These seemed an outrageous expense but Municipal Socialists would have seen it as perfectly acceptable to employ people working in culture and the arts for the benefit of the local community — why not? Should a council only collect bins and look after vulnerable people? If a man was paid to do tree sculpting on estates around the borough and it made the place look nice then who could possibly complain?[3]

One poet who also worked for Lambeth was Leo Aylen. In 1979 he won the Cecil Day Lewis Fellowship by the Greater London Arts Association. Part of the prize money for the fellowship had come from Lambeth and it stipulated that he was required to act as a 'writer in residence' to the people of the borough, including performing at the Country Show, in old people's homes, youth clubs and schools. Writing in *The Guardian* after his time there he concluded: "Lambeth as a governable district appears to be breaking apart, just as New York is breaking apart. And yet... and yet... celebration. I wonder if any of the citizens of Lambeth saw that I was trying to celebrate them. I don't know what I did for Lambeth. One basic thing perhaps. Time and again, I have been to places where the organiser has said to me, "You see, they think all poets are dead." I hope that I have showed some of them that it is possible to be a poet and still alive."[4]

In defiance of the new direction of government, Lambeth Council and the local unions called an anti-cuts march on Parliament. On 7 November 1979 around 20,000 people marched from Brixton to Westminster, the first ever protest against the new Tory government. Despite the lack of official endorsement from the major unions and the Labour Party, the demonstration was well attended with union and Labour Party banners scattered among the protesters. Knight used the platform to demand the TUC and Labour's NEC issue a call to action from the many millions of trade unionists and Labour members. The first salvo of the decade-long battle against Thatcher had begun, fired from the steps of the town hall in Brixton.

CRISIS IN LOCAL GOVERNMENT CONFERENCE: 1980

Feeling that they had momentum, the Labour Group threw their weight into a bolder anti-cuts initiative. Ted Knight himself proposed a motion to the

---

2 *Hansard*, 12 January 1981.
3 The artist in residence was Gordon Wilkinson and poet Ms Michell Roberts. Wilkinson cost local rate payers £750 and Roberts £850, the rest of their wages were paid from central government from a scheme to help inner city areas. The tree surgeon in question was David Brodie who became quite renowned and exhibited at the Saatchi Gallery.
4 *The Guardian*, 9 August 1980.

1980 Labour conference at Blackpool, delivering what was described as a 'blockbusting speech' in support of a motion calling for "massive industrial action on cuts to force the government to retreat and if it will not retreat, to force it out."[5] The widely held belief was that Thatcher's government was an aberration, a historical abortion, one that would not last more than a term. By March 1981 the approval rating of the Tories was at minus 58 points, Thatcher's personal rating languished around minus 37 points. The left knew that Thatcher was still a threat, not least due to her clear ideological determination. She was no 'wet' Ted Heath. And they felt they had the public on their side. Thatcher*ism* as a distinct hegemonic ideology was yet to properly emerge and the forces of resistance seemed to be growing.

In September 1980 Lambeth Councillors met with the Lambeth Trade's Council to organise a national 'no cuts' conference, scheduled for 1 November 1980. The call for the conference was warmly received by the British left, many of whom looked to it as the start of the real campaign against Thatcher where all the new struggles from her first year in power – primarily austerity and the sale of council homes – could be debated and a movement built against them. There was clearly a little antagonism at this stage between the politicians and the unions. Vanessa Wiseman, the secretary of Lambeth Trade's Council and a member of the International Marxist Group, made clear what the unions perspective was in the run-up to the conference: "we are not just asking trade unionists to take action against Heseltine's Bill, but asking to see Ted Knight and Labour councillors throughout the country calling on the trade unions to take action and committing themselves to also be on the line with those trade unionists, to commit themselves now to not make more cuts, not to wait and see how November's conference goes but to undertake not to make any further cuts, not to sell any council houses and not to make any further rate increases."[6]

The official party leadership were more sceptical about attending or endorsing the event. The organisers of the conference even received a letter from Labour Party General Secretary Ron Howard asking why Lambeth Council had called the conference in the first place, surely Labour was doing enough already?

In terms of turnout, the meeting, held at Camden Town Hall, was a huge success, with delegates from nearly 600 labour movement organisations attending, including 72 Labour controlled councils. Lambeth NALGO Branch Secretary Mike Waller played a key role in organising the event and spoke on behalf of his union branch. "The conference reflected the deep concern among the labour movement about the effects on services and employment. It did for the first time bring together all the local authority

---

5 Geoff Bell, *Socialist Challenge*, 9 October, number 167, p. 4.
6 *Socialist Challenge*, 11 September 1980, p. 7.

trade unions, NALGO, NUPE, UCATT, TGWU GMWU etc., Labour councillors together to discuss a plan of action."⁷

Knight moved the main resolution opposing the Tory cuts and lambasted the TUC and Labour's NEC for not having called a similar event. He also criticised the Labour right's position that the only response was to hunker down and focus on winning the next election.⁸ This point of view was represented by John Lebor, head of Brent Council, who argued "we have to accept reality", which meant a waiting game until the electorate came back to Labour nationally.⁹ His position was one of paralysis and retreat and it received only lukewarm applause from the assembled delegates.

The only representative of a national trade union in attendance, Ron Keating from NUPE, also got a rough ride. Keating moved a motion on behalf of NUPE which proposed to raise the rates as much as possible then for all councillors to resign and stand on no cuts platforms. He argued "there is too much fear in the land" to expect any mass resistance against the Tories, only anti-cuts propaganda was possible at this stage. Mike Waller protested: "it isn't enough to pass the buck from councils to unions and then from unions to councils. Ron Keating's amendment falls short of the necessity that the Tories cannot be defeated by Labour councils alone, without us being prepared to take action too."¹⁰ What really torpedoed Keating's position was the rank and file NUPE members in the room, who rose to their feet to add their voices to calls for a more militant opposition. Conference rejected the motion in favour of a united fight back by unions and the council.

As an alternative, Waller proposed a motion from Lambeth NALGO which he said had been passed at a "long and heated" meeting of 1,700 local members. It called for a national campaign against cuts, for strikes against redundancies, non-cooperation with new technology to replace jobs and "measures to build a broad based campaign prepared for an all-out strike if the Tories try and replace Labour councillors with commissioners."¹¹

Vanessa Wiseman amended the motion (proposed by the Lambeth Trade Council and supported by Vauxhall Labour Party) to include: "a policy of no cover for vacancies and a campaign against voluntary redundancies and natural wastage. Create and defend jobs by stopping overtime and fight for a shorter working week."¹² Wiseman also proposed an amendment calling on miners and engineers to join the local government unions in solidarity strike action and for Labour Councils to organise rate and rent strikes in the event of any councillors being surcharged. These amendment were also passed by a large majority.

---

7   Lambeth NALGO Cuts bulletin, 5 November 1980.
8   *Socialist Press*, 5 November 1980, p. 12.
9   Ibid.
10 *Socialist Organiser*, 27 September 1980.
11 Ibid.
12 *Socialist Challenge*, 27 November 1980, p. 5.

Lambeth NALGO didn't hold back on giving their local Labour councillors grief. As chair of housing, Matthew Warburton received a cool reception when he explained that Lambeth had decided not to openly fight the sale of council houses, as the Labour Group felt that the general issue of cuts and not council house sales was the one to campaign on. Lambeth NALGO used the conference to express public anger at the Councillors for not taking a firmer stand. The amendment that Wiseman proposed contained a veiled barb against Lambeth Council, where some on the left felt that the lack of a national campaign was being used as an excuse to hold back action: "Labour Councils [should not use] the inactivity of others to justify implementing or accepting cuts themselves."[13] *Socialist Organiser* was more direct: "[Knight's] statement hinges the whole cuts fight on a general strike by council workers in January 1981. The unvoiced let-out clause is that if the unions do not meet this arbitrary deadline, then the Labour councils will go ahead, include cuts and rate rises in next spring's budget – and claim they have no alternative!"[14] A motion urging the General Secretary of the TUC Len Murray to call a general strike was also passed, although the Lambeth NALGO leadership opposed it. They were sceptical that the TUC would do anything, Waller ridiculed it, saying "Len Murray's action ... was to go on holiday!"[15]

Feeling a lot of momentum and energy in the room, the 50 strong steering committee called a follow-up conference for January, two months later. Plans were also put in place to organise for a week of strike action in February against Tory cuts. Whilst the Lambeth unions urged for strikes, others felt that public demonstrations might be easier to organise and garner more support. The Transport and General Workers Union (TGWU) and the NUT branches called strike action, (in fact the local NUT executive was suspended for taking part by the national union), NALGO and NUPE didn't strike though members attended a large demonstration.

Though 430 delegates showed up for the next conference, the mood was more sombre, many feeling undermined by the actions of Lambeth Council. Despite moving a motion against rate and rent rises and in opposition to council house sales, Lambeth had ultimately implemented both. The Labour group proposed a considerable supplementary rate increase at the start of 1981, mere weeks after passing a motion agreeing not to do so. This had the effect of angering the left, who accused Knight of selling out, and the right who accused him of taxing local people just to prevent cuts. The *South London Press* editorial described Knight "waving his baton in predictable style... orchestrated his Labour group in the latest chords of his Marxist melody against the Thatcher government."[16] The supplementary rate increase meant households paying £50 more, small shops £140 and larger

---

13 *Socialist Press*, 29 October 1980.
14 Ibid.
15 Lambeth NALGO Cuts bulletin, 5 November 1980.
16 'Why deeper in the red, Ted', *South London Press*, 9 January 1981, p. 14.

department stores like Morley's £11,600. The massive rate increases to stop the cuts to local services caused outrage across the borough. In a series of council by-elections the newly formed SDP and Liberals won seats in Labour heartlands. Labour canvassers were confronted by local residents furious about the rate increase. Similar problems were encountered in other municipalities, Lothian council announced huge job cuts in education and Coventry Council agreed to hold a referendum on the question of 'cuts or rate rises'.

The chair of the Streatham Residents and Ratepayers association, Geoffrey Southon, wrote to the local press complaining that; "ratepayers of Lambeth are being sacrificed on the altar of Cllr Knight and his friends' ideology."[17] But reactions from those accessing council services, like the elderly in a Lambeth run day centre were far more positive. Pensioners in Lambeth Tower's Day Centre were glowing about the local services: "Our rates are high, but we are getting the best services ... we get a lovely meal, bingo, old time dancing and tonight there is a party – all free of charge."[18] Another pensioner was clear whose side she was on: "If Ted Knight walked in here now I would shake him firmly by the hand."[19]

Councillor Graham Norwood wrote a scathing attack in *Socialist Challenge* over the rate increases, describing the bitter exchange in Lambeth Labour. Knight's argument for raising the rates was that there was no sign yet that there was any serious fight against Thatcher and Heseltine because "it had no backing whatsoever from the national Labour and TUC leadership."[20] Councillors Steve Stannard and Neil Turner rejected the rate increase, arguing it would fall disproportionately on poorer working class communities as it would not be covered by rate rebates. Knight argued against. He publicly criticised his comrades on the Labour benches "you are not socialists in my opinion... your policies are disruptive and will play into the hands of the Tories."[21]

The opposition in the Labour group took a different view, Neil Turner argued that as the rate rises were part of Heseltine's plan to punish 'overspending' councils, by setting the local residents against Labour, it was Knight who was playing along to the government's tune. Any Labour council that passed on the cost to the local rate payer was falling decisively into the government's trap – drawing the battles lines to turn the electorate against the councillors.

Town Hall workers were more inclined to back the rate increases as they saw it as a way to protect jobs whereas local residents resented the rate increases. The radical left argued that Lambeth shouldn't fall into the trap of squeezing its own residents. Instead it was time for political action, either a

---

17 *South London Press*, 16 January 1981, p. 6.
18 'So where does all the money go?', *South London Press*, 16 January 1981, pp. 14-15.
19 Ibid.
20 *Socialist Challenge*, 22 January 1981, p. 10.
21 'Labour split as rates go soaring up', *South London Press*, 16 January 1981, p. 9.

mass resignation, forcing bankruptcy, or refusing to step down and making the Tories send in commissioners. These proposals had been rejected in the Labour group. Certainly for some, there was a sense of retreat and demoralisation setting in after the high point of the November anti-cuts conference.

Despite these setbacks, the left hoped to re-launch the anti-cuts movement with a week of action called for February. Peter Coles from the TGWU branch in Lambeth called for solidarity: "The Tories frighten people, but they're not going to frighten us. Some people have said we're jumping the gun on calling strike action in February, but if we don't fight we don't have a job left anyway."[22] The conference affirmed a position of no cuts, no rate rises and no council house sales. Wiseman spoke in a fringe meeting at the event, criticising the Lambeth Council leadership, especially the sense that some had that the left councillors were being reticent about joining the struggle: "We don't want anyone to go to prison or be surcharged, but if you are a councillor and you are against the Tories there is that danger. Trade unionists run the risk of arrest every day they are on picket lines. Councillors should be prepared to make sacrifices too."[23] A steel worker from South Wales also stuck the boot into the beleaguered Lambeth Councillors, "Lambeth should have done a charge of the light brigade and made a stand."[24] He compared the council unfavourably to the Clay Cross fight in 1972.[25]

Knight was furious at these criticisms, seeing them as deeply unfair to the efforts that the left councillors were making to raise opposition to the government. From his perspective the bastions of the left like Lambeth were in a difficult situation and had to act tactically, to rush into a confrontation with Thatcher so soon risked events escaping from them, and despite the success of the anti-cuts conference so far, there was little practical working agreement between the councils on how to fight back. For Knight's left critics however, it looked like backtracking and ducking the fight, and it completely went against the spirit of the motions passed at the November conference.[26] *Socialist Newsletter* was scathing in their conclusion: instead of a fight the council was "soaking council tenants with huge rate rises to temporarily maintain jobs and services."[27] It was untenable and something had to give.

The February week of action in defence of local government was more muted than expected. Finding themselves in the vanguard, the Lambeth

---

22 *Socialist Challenge*, 22 January 1981, p. 10.
23 Ibid.
24 Ibid.
25 *Socialist Challenge*, 22 January 1981, p. 10. Under the 1970-74 Heath Government there was a law passed to force councils to put up rents. Despite most Labour councils voting to oppose the policy only only three really opposed it. Clay Cross Council in Derbyshire saw its councillors surcharged for their stand
26 Marie Jones, *Socialist Newsletter*, number 11, p. 2.
27 *Socialist Newsletter*, February 1981, number 13, p. 4.

unions organised some strike action but precious little of that materialised elsewhere. The lack of militant response led to a search for scapegoats. Couldn't people see the need for action against Thatcher? Some on the left blamed Knight for demobilising the movement, arguing Lambeth should have led by example. Knight was still reticent, preferring to leverage the bigger forces of the TUC and Labour Party into action – when confronted with accusations of timidity Knight replied, "we aren't going to throw ourselves at the government like Kamikaze pilots".[28] Ken Livingstone was forthright in his defence of his old comrades: "I have nothing but contempt for those left tendencies who have sought really to go after Ted Knight and attack Lambeth, while bypassing the appallingly right-wing councillors that have passed on every cut in order to keep the rates down right the way across London."[29]

After the week of action, six NUT members in Lambeth were suspended by their union for taking part in the action without national approval. After teaching activists from Lambeth, led by Dick North, an NEC member of the union, attended the 4th February rally, Fred Jarvis the secretary of the NUT wrote to them informing them that they were all suspended. In order to have the suspension lifted they were told to write a letter expressing complete loyalty to the union and to Jarvis' leadership.[30] There were serious manoeuvres happening in the trade union movement to keep a lid on wildcat action that wasn't officially sanctioned.

LAMBETH MAKES CUTS

After Heseltine announced cuts to the Revenue Support Grant (RSG), once again the issue of cuts versus rate and rent increases was posed, but this time for the left it wasn't an abstract debate, they were in charge of the budget and now they had to make the tough choices. The dividing lines were clear – those on the left that argued the rate and rent increases were an excuse to avoid the fight over cuts and those that thought they bought valuable time. For some it was a matter of principle, others a matter of tactics.

The Labour Group was advised by council officers that the scale of the cuts to the RSG meant they needed a 45% increase in the rates to sustain current spending levels. Knight feared that was too high and local residents would revolt, instead proposing a 39% increase. This would have led to £1.5 million of cuts – mainly falling on under-fives provision and housing maintenance. The initial decision by the Labour Group and councillors was to make the cuts "in the least damaging way" whilst preparing the ground for a future major fight with the government on the issue. The key thing was to

---

28 'Leading London leftwards?', *Socialist Review*, June 1986.
29 Pete Goodwin & Chris Harman, *Leading London Leftwards?* [Interview with Ken Livingstone], *Socialist Review*, June 1981.
30 *Socialist Challenge*, number 14.

see if there was movement from the other left run councils to mount concerted resistance.

At the Council meeting 9 March 1980 the proposal was made to keep the rates increase down to 37.5%, cut £11 million and raise council rents by £4 per week. Knight backed a cuts package that would "reduce current revenue expenditure yet protect essential services and existing job holders".[31] Knight said the council had received legal advice to increase their rents (a further £2 a week in April and again in October). Few of the proposals were very detailed because NALGO had instructed its members not to cooperate with any cost cutting measures so many officers blanket refused to suggest budget cuts. If no cuts were made or rents increased then the rates would increase 57.9%.

The Labour Group met on 9 July and agreed to 4.5% of cuts, including £1 million from social services and £800,000 from housing. There was a fierce debate at the meeting, where observers from the local parties were also present. However Mike Bright's view was that the budget was "full of fat" and that cuts could be made that would not impact on jobs.[32]

Inevitably, the response from the trade unions was not a happy one. Waller wrote bitterly in the NALGO anti cuts bulletin that: "The 'wall of resistance' to the cuts that Ted Knight once promised to build around Lambeth was breached on Wednesday night when the Policy and Review Committee voted to cut next year's budget by £10.3 million. The Council pledged no redundancies but did say some staff would be redeployed." NALGO's message to the council workers was unwavering: "Members are reminded that the present Branch policy is one of total opposition to cuts in JOBS AND SERVICES".[33] Lambeth Trade's Council launched an anti-cuts organisation called the Lambeth Fightback Campaign.

Norwood CLP called an anti-cuts meeting for 27 July, followed by a meeting of delegates from each party two days later. The local party activists roundly criticised the cuts proposals. They felt betrayed that the left had just made a great show of winning on a radical programme and seemed to have buckled so soon. At the GLC Livingstone blamed Knight's approach for the failure to foresee the scale of party opposition to the cuts package. The cuts budget in Lambeth also caused consternation across the wider left. Ron Heisler, a councillor from Hackney slammed the decision at an SCLV discussion: "It's a disaster. Ted Knight has got himself national publicity as "The Marxist" in local government and now he is supporting cuts. The Lambeth cuts will sanction every right-wing Labour council that's making cuts."[34] His point was echoed by Ken Livingstone, at that time a GLC councillor "for all the posturing as Marxist Lambeth, already the right wing councillors here say, 'we'll do no more than Lambeth'. The real tragedy is

---
31 NALGO Cuts bulletin, no 7.
32 'Illusions of Power', *Socialist Organiser*, p xx.
33 Lambeth NALGO cuts bulletin number 8, 16 March 1981.
34 Cited in 'Illusions of Power', *Socialist Organiser*, p. 27.

that Ted has given a cover for every right-winger to put through cuts."[35] From his perspective the structure that Knight had implemented meant that he couldn't canvass wider opinion on the question of cuts.[36]

Facing the stern rebuke of the local party and wider left Knight and the Labour Group agreed to ditch the cuts. For the councillors this was a steep learning curve: left opposition out of power was easier than the reality of managing a local government under capitalism. They claimed they felt forced into their position by the officers and financial advisers and their inexperience meant that didn't feel confident to take a stand.[37] Nevertheless they seized upon the opportunity to be accountable and carry out the wishes of the party that they were members of and represented in the council chambers. Instead recruitment was slowed down, leaving some vacancies to try and offset the lost money from central government.

More financial woe was coming down the road. One of the first pieces of legislation from the Tory government was the Local Government Planning and Land Act 1980, which allowed Westminster to set guidelines for what local authorities should be spending. There were inbuilt penalties in the RSG in the form of "holdback" if councils overspent on the targets. The targets themselves were determined by the Grant-related Expenditure Assessments (GREs) but the formulas were not made available to councils.

Local authorities, including Lambeth, publicly attacked the GREs on the basis that the 'educated assessments' were based on an unclear methodology, seemingly known only to the Civil Servants in the Departments of the Environment. Like arcane magicians or medieval priests they would guard the secrets of their financial incantations, hiding their formulas and ledgers from the local authorities, magically deciding on an amount to cut and, after declaring it, demanded that it be made so. Alongside these financially binding spells, the rules governing the targets were subject to constant change, as were the penalties which made budgetary planning involve even more guesswork than usual based on the capricious mood of the mandarins in White Hall. It all looked thoroughly arbitrary and biased against local government.

The penalties became more savage year on year until eventually councils were receiving less money in absolute terms than they had been prior to 1979, despite rising costs. Talk of a legal challenge against the penalties was scotched when the 1982 Local Government Finance Act retrospectively legalised all of them.[38] John Fraser, MP for Norwood, complained in parliament that the Tories were putting Lambeth in an impossible situation: a

---

35 Ibid.
36 As Livingstone explained, "With a more open and wider consultative process he would have detected much sooner the scale of party opposition to his proposals", Livingstone, *If Voting Changed Anything, They'd Abolish It*, p. 125.
37 Interview with Ted Knight, March 2016.
38 Brian Jacobs, *Fractured Cities: Capitalism, Community and Empowerment in Britain and America* (Routledge 1992) pp. 132-3.

triple crisis of finance, housing and unemployment. He damned the government for malice towards inner city boroughs, but towards Lambeth in particular.[39]

Inevitably, these financial problems had a seriously detrimental impact on the councillors' attempts to fix the housing problem. Substantial savings were made by slashing the B&B expenditure, but it wasn't enough to meet the 10% cuts required across the board. A voluntary redundancy package to reduce staff costs saw many experienced long-term housing officers take early retirement. Half the staff in the Brixton housing office left, leaving a strained service and more inexperienced officers to deal with the hugely complex housing and often social needs in the area. The vacancy recruitment freeze in place resulted in a series of strikes by the unions which closed the housing offices, disrupting the rent collection and service delivery. Other staff had to be drafted in from other parts of the borough but this only caused more problems in other area offices. Warburton and the housing director struggled to get to grips during that difficult year, their directorate lurching from one crisis to another to try and achieve their ambitious goal of getting the housing situation under control.

NO RIGHT TO BUY

The Conservative's Right to Buy policy was a centrepiece of their 1979 election efforts. Indeed, the subsequent Housing Act 1980 could be regarded as one of the most socially far reaching and politically ingenious pieces of legislation of the 20th century. It was the cornerstone of the drive for a 'property owning democracy', where working class people would have a stake in the economy through home-ownership and their communities would become whittled away as council homes became commodities to be bought and sold for a profit. It was hoped it make workers less amenable to egalitarian or redistributive policies from the left. Heseltine's summary of the role of home ownership was that it "stimulates the attitudes of independence and self-reliance that are the bedrock of a free society."[40] The Tories saw this as a necessary palliative to the post war council house building programme of the London Labour Party which they suspected was gerrymandering to get more working class voters in the capital. Well anything that Labour could do, the Tories would do better.

Lambeth had already clashed with the Tories in 1978 when the Tory run GLC (before Labour won the election in 1981) tried to sell off its housing stock to residents. By late 1978 around 70 homes a week were being sold in what was called the 'sale of the century' as council tenants got onto the property ladder. Wandsworth Council, under Tory control since 1978, was enthusiastically selling council homes before Thatcher was even Prime

---

39 'Lambeth has triple crisis', *South London Press*, 9 January 1981.
40 Cited in Richard Ronald, *The Ideology of Home Ownership: Homeowner Societies and the Role of Housing*, (Palgrave MacMillan 2008) p. 128.

Minister. In 1979 Thatcher visited a couple in Balham who had bought the 2000th council homes sold, promoting the new deal for 'hard-working' residents who just 'wanted to get on the properly ladder'. To ease the transfer of property, residents were given a sizeable discount, starting at 32% and rising to as high as 60% or £35,000.

Clearly selling off council homes was anathema to the politics of the New Urban Left. Back in Brixton, Warburton initially went on the offensive, the council newsletter *Lambeth Local* carried a front page article urging "Let the buyer beware" and followed it up with a leaflet to every GLC tenant outlining reasons why they should not to apply to buy their house.[41] Lambeth refused to assist the GLC in selling a single property in the borough. But this was only the first skirmish in a huge battle that would change the social and economic face of the country.

The resistance to Right to Buy in Lambeth wasn't just ideological, it was also practical – the borough had the highest levels of homelessness, overcrowding and the longest waiting list in the capital. It was costing the council around £20,000 a year to house a family in a bed and breakfast; rehousing them in council property would have cost only £9000.[42] Half the houses in the borough were pre-1919 and as such the quality of the housing stock was poor. By 1981 14% of homes were unfit for habitation and a further 13% needed major renovation. Large slums still existed in the borough, for instance along Mayall Road in Herne Hill, and an aggressive compulsory purchasing scheme was in place in Lambeth to buy up derelict houses to renovate them into council homes. In that context, selling off valuable council homes in a way that brought very little money back to the council (receipts from council house sales couldn't be used to build more housing) was simply going to make a bad situation much worse.

However, Lambeth was faced with a difficult choice. Having committed themselves to the fight against budget cuts, Warburton counselled against the council opening up a fight on two fronts. Better to focus energies on the anti-cuts campaign which could potentially generate huge public support than breaking the law so directly by refusing to sell council housing – at least openly. He pointed to the reticence of the local CLPs to mount a campaign against the sales – what hope was there in the councillors going it alone in such conditions?

At the Council meeting to discuss the legislation, Knight and Warburton decided against outright defiance. Instead, Lambeth would just delay individual sales as long as possible. Knight explicitly argued against opening up a front against Right to Buy: "We're in a war, and in a war every possible battle is not necessarily won. The objective is to defeat the enemy and we felt this could be a diversion…"[43]

---

41 'A tale of two councils', *South London Press*, 5 September 1978, front page.
42 'Whitehall farce', *South London Press*, 29 March 1985, p. 12.
43 *South London Press*, 10 October 1980, p. 2.

Lambeth NALGO rejected this approach. They pointed to Rochdale and Waltham Forest Councils who had publicly taken a more defiant stand against the council house sales. Mike Waller and the housing convener Simon Berlin led the charge in the branch to agree to refuse to cover anything associated with Right to Buy – "blacking" the work to frustrate the sale of council houses. There were 18,600 people on the housing waiting list, another 6,000 tenants who needed a transfer, and 480 families in homeless accommodation ranging from short term properties to hostels. In the face of such issues, the union made it clear to the Councillors that they would fight them on this issue if necessary.[44] It wasn't just Lambeth doing this, NALGO branches in Southwark, Glasgow, Hackney, Newcastle and Sheffield also refused to process the initial forms.

Nationally, NALGO made clear that taking industrial action over a political issue would not be appropriate but a democratic vote for industrial action should be respected if it was done regarding workplace issues. Waller had to pitch the dispute as something that could pass national scrutiny. The NALGO conferences in 1979 and 1980 had passed motions supporting industrial action against Right to Buy so long as it was due to workload – essentially did the council provide enough additional resources to carry out the work? That was Waller's way in. Since Lambeth was providing no additional funding for housing officers to Right to Buy this was the technical excuse NALGO needed to boycott the work.

At a well-attended branch meeting a motion was passed instructing NALGO members not to process any council house sales "as a consequence of Lambeth Council refusing to provide *additional* resources to carry out such sales without detriment to existing services". This was a narrow terms and conditions argument, the unions were still squeamish about being seen to organise political strike action. Lambeth NALGO received the support from their NEC. Waller was clearly only fudging the issue to get official backing, from his point of view, "even if Lambeth Council employ 300 people tomorrow to sell the houses we would not budge".[45]

At this time NALGO had a very high density rate among the officers at the council which effectively meant that, if the boycott was enforced, the council couldn't enact the Housing Act. Waller was infuriated when it was discovered that the Housing director, Bill Murray, was processing applications. Murray argued he was bound by the law to carry out his duties. Even after two NALGO branch officers visited him at home and threatened to suspend him from the union he refused to follow the union's instructions.[46] Union members took matters into their own hands and expropriated around 300 Right to Buy application letters from the Town Hall post room. The scandal in the national press led to some letters being

---

44 Kate Ascher, 'The politics of administrative opposition – council house sales and the right to buy', *Local Government Studies*, vol. 9, no. 2. 1983, pp. 16-18
45 Quoted in *Women's Voice*, November 1980, issue 47, p. 11.
46 'Housing Chief in trouble with union', *South London Press*, 27 January 1981, p. 3.

returned, though the union said they would only direct all post to the Chief Executive, Frank Dixon Ward, as none of their members would handle the post, as per union instructions. The union's recalcitrance was raised in the Commons, by Streatham MP Bill Shelton, addressing Thatcher he asked, "During her busy day, will my right hon. Friend turn her thoughts to Lambeth? Is she aware that NALGO – with, I fear, the tacit support of Lambeth council – is still totally blocking any action on council house sales? Does she agree that this is a denial of the rights of the tenants and citizens of Lambeth and indeed the tenants of all socialist councils which are behaving in the same way, and a denial of the will of the electorate as expressed at the last general election?" In response, Housing Minister John Stanley promised to investigate. Tony Durant MP asked whether it wouldn't be necessary for commissioners to go in and take over operations in the council to defend the rights of citizens being blocked by union officials.[47]

A group of housing managers wrote a letter to the *South London Press* defending Murray and accusing NALGO of "leaving no stone unturned to achieve their own ends".[48] Simon Berlin, the NALGO Housing convener, summoned them to a meeting to explain their actions which they refused to attend. Hugh Williams, the NALGO press officer pointedly asked if they even cared about their union and its campaigns. The senior managers joined the rival union NUPE, which earned them a suspension in the NALGO rule book against dual carding. Waller was unrepentant however, addressing a letter to NALGO members in March 1981 where he proudly declared that "during the last five months, this branch has played a significant role in developing a campaign in this country against the Right to Buy Provisions of the Housing Act 1980. Members have successfully prevented any Council dwelling being sold…"[49]

In early 1981, the irrepressible local Tory activist, Mary Leigh acted as solicitor for a mini-cab driver who felt that the Council had taken too long to process his form, the mandatory limit being four weeks. Lambeth had already admitted they were outside the statutory guidelines but Leigh wanted her day in court anyway. This was the first legal decision on the 1980 Act – once again Lambeth proved to be a legal test case for Tory legislation. However Judge McDonnell refused to set a deadline for the Council to process the application because the reason for the delay (the boycott by NALGO) was outside the Council's control. Immediately the Tories used the court ruling to call on the council to discipline staff taking part in the boycott.[50]

---

47 *Hansard*, 10 March 1981, Volume 1000.
48 *South London Press*, 12 March 1981.
49 Letter to Lambeth NALGO members, 15th March 1981, Lambeth UNISON archives.
50 'Town hall at fault for taking too long to accept tenant's Right to Buy home', *South London Press*, 13 January 1981.

The *South London Press* was unequivocal in its condemnation: 'Hypocrisy and Democracy' was the headline of the editorial on 10 March 1981, slamming NALGO for taking political action to stop residents exercising their legal right to purchase their council homes. The union had become a "law unto itself" warned the newspaper.[51] Waller declined to comment. However, the high point of union opposition to the Housing Act was by then already passed, the forms were eventually being processed. The union branch annual report contained only a short paragraph on the Right to Buy: "difficulties occurred as a result of an industrial dispute which hampered the implementation but these have been overcome during 1981/82"[52] And with that brief summary, the social housing in the borough began to be sold off, the majority of properties ending up in the hands of landlords.

STRAINS BETWEEN THE COUNCILLORS AND WORKFORCE

Despite being socialists, the left Councillors accepted that in relation to their workforce, they were employers. They could aim to ameliorate the worst effects of the capital-labour wage relation but they knew they could not abolish them – there was no possibility of socialism in one borough. Whilst the existence of a left Labour Council mitigated against some of the conditions that led to the Winter of Discontent in 1978/79, as the years went by there were increasing disputes with the Council trade unions that couldn't be ignored.

By 1981 the no cuts policy was under impossible strain due to the cuts from Heseltine and the constant penalties being imposed. Lambeth ended up making 10% cuts to their budgets whilst still having to bring in a 37% rate increase. This ended up angering both residents and the workforce, seemingly an impossible position. The consequences of this will be returned to later.

NALGO for their part stood solidly with the councillors when they opposed cuts to services but were not reticent about calling strikes or demonstrations against the council when they needed to. One campaign in 1984 to get decent wages for the Home Care Workers saw Knight's office occupied by over 50 women, many of them with small children. Knight was accosted by the workers who initially described their negotiations with him as "unproductive". They did manage to secure an extra 15p an hour however.[53]

The most explosive fall out was the residential workers strike in 1983/84. The dispute was over reduced working hours and unsocial hours payments. The national employer refused their demands which led to a national work-to-rule in September, then an escalation of action in October and December. The workers were certainly militant, 200 of them invaded the NALGO HQ

---

51 *South London Press*, 10 March 1981, p. 8.
52 *Lambeth Council Annual Report 1980-81*, p. 29.
53 *Lambeth Summer 1984*.

in December in protest at the slow progress by the union officials in winning their demands.

Within a week of the work-to-rule starting, four Lambeth care homes for children had closed. Senior and middle managers refused to cover the additional work. Knight sent a statement to the strikers offering support and saying he would pressure the national employer to come to the negotiating table. But relations began to sour in late September when a delegation of workers and children from the care homes attended the Council meeting. Councillor Steven Bubb harangued the union members, accusing them of kidnapping the children. During the argument the union accused him of threatening violence against a member. Bubb was clearly furious in that he felt the union was using children in their dispute. A delegation of strikers went to Knight's house in protest but in response he firmly placed the blame on NALGO for the breakdown in negotiations. The union accused the council of leaving children in care homes over the weekend with no staff supervising them.[54]

NALGO were highly critical of Councillor Bubb, who was a member of the National Union of Teachers, and Councillor Jock Quinn, who they alleged called the police to eject them from a Town Hall meeting.[55] This was followed by an angry *communiqué* from the NALGO Black Workers' Group which accused the Councillors of ignoring their own equal opportunities policies to rush recruit new residential workers during the strike.

Relations deteriorated further when shop stewards in the Housing directorate were banned from meeting during work hours and managers in NALGO were excluded from management meetings due to their trade union activity. The most serious blow was when the Labour councillors demanded that the residential workers lift the ban on working unsocial hours in the middle of the ballots on that issue. The union saw this as a direct attack on their industrial base by the council. In the 1983 Lambeth NALGO Christmas bulletin NALGO Chair Anna Tapsell warned that "when this Labour group came to power in 1978 it was welcomed by the vast majority of our membership; we wanted to be loyal partners. Despite frequent periods of disillusionments that loyalty remained until the outset of the residential workers' dispute. The Labour group with its intransigent, divisive manoeuvres has done what may prove to be irreparable damage to its relationship with NALGO and other council unions."[56] The dispute ended with a whimper, the strikers returning to work with the promise of an inquiry into their pay which reported back eight months later and promised nothing.[57]

---

54 *Lambeth Action News*, no. 7, 29 September 1983.
55 Ibid.
56 Lambeth NALGO Christmas bulletin, 1983, p 2..
57 Roger Seifert, Mike Ironside, *Facing Up to Thatcherism: The History of NALGO, 1979-1993*, (Oxford University Press 2000) pp. 177-8.

This was the most extreme example of the often tempestuous contradiction within the labour movement between the unions and the left councillors in Lambeth. NALGO declared that the damage done to industrial relations in the handling of the residential workers' dispute was possibly beyond repair. Nevertheless, the public sector unions rallied to the Councillors over the coming years as the fight against Thatcherism heated up. Knight himself was phlegmatic about the situation. They may have been socialists who wanted to overthrow the system but as councillors difficult choices sometimes had to be made. The key for them was to try and work collaboratively with the unions where possible to apply political pressure to the Tories, not simply to acquiesce and implement cuts or privatisation. This was a precarious balancing act however and one that became increasingly difficult to manage.

6

Brixton and Black Resistance

> Lawd of mercy child, is why you luk so?
> Look what me cme a England fe set eye pon,
> Is what around wid yuh, what no you live in a
> Council flat and de pon welfare?
> good lawd that you died in my womb
>
> Poem published by Black Women's Group, 1980[1]

Black people had lived in Lambeth for hundreds of years before the *Empire Windrush* landed in 1948, when 240 Jamaican men were sent to stay in the old air raid shelter at Clapham Common underground. The government pressed Lambeth Council to make efforts to house the new arrivals, so the Mayor organised a welcoming meeting for forty representatives with tea and cake at the Astoria Cinema (today the Brixton Academy) and showed a movie. The men returned to the underground shelter and conveyed the good news: "Brixton is a place that we can call home".[2] It was a sign of how much things were changing, the first movie shown when the Astoria opened only 20 years previously was *The Singing Fool*, featuring Al Jolson in black face.

The welcome turned out not quite so warm as they had wanted. Many were attracted to Brixton and Stockwell largely because of the number of black landlords that owned property there. In the racist climate of Britain few whites would rent a room or a house to a black family. Therefore it was a safer space, a place to build communities in an otherwise hostile environment, although the conditions were often cramped, with few amenities and poor sanitation. Local schools were badly equipped and many of the teachers displayed varying degrees of conscious and unconscious discrimination, particularly against black boys.[3] The imperial myth of lazy or dangerous black people that had been fostered in the British Empire was prevalent across society.

---

1 *Speak Out!*, Issue 1, Black Women's Group, 1980.
2 Jerry White, *London in the Twentieth Century: A City and Its People* (Bodley Head 2001) p. 135.
3 Chris Mullard, 'Multiracial education in Britain: From Assimilation to Cultural Pluralism' in J Tierney (ed.), *Race, Migration and Schooling* (Holt, Rinehart and Winston 1982).

Although they had been invited by the government to work in the rapidly expanding public sector, the immigrants found themselves discriminated against in housing, jobs and education. It was made clear early on that the police were not their friends. This was at a time when the Met Police still marked young black people being stopped and searched as "Negroid" in their internal documents.[4] They faced a resurgence of Mosleyite fascism; graffiti was seen daubed in large letters in Notting Hill and Brixton saying 'K.B.W.' (Keep Britain White) – a call to arms for local whites and a warning to the newly arrived immigrants. In 1968 Enoch Powell had given his 'Rivers of Blood' speech, leading to the formation of the National Front, which made inroads into parts of the white working-class, calling for forced repatriation of all Blacks and Asians. By this time "Powell for Prime Minister" graffiti was a regular sight around the Brixton area. When David Pitt, a black socialist, stood for Labour in Clapham in the 1970 General Election, thousands of copies of the notorious 'If you desire a coloured for a neighbour vote Labour' leaflets were distributed throughout the constituency on the eve of the election. Several were even posted to white people with black neighbours. The Tories denied any involvement and denounced the leaflet but they were certainly the primary beneficiaries. Pitt lost the safe Labour seat with a 10% swing to the Tories. He tried to put a brave face on it, blaming various factors, but he and his comrades knew that his skin colour had been a decisive factor in his rejection by the local voters.

But the organised racist movement did not limit itself to only graffiti and leaflets. The black community faced regular violence that targeted their homes, shops and organising centres. Black people in Streatham would put a bowl of water behind the door in case racists put fireworks or rags soaked in kerosene through the door. Desmond's Hip City had a regular book stall outside which was trashed by far right activists. In March 1973 a series of black-owned businesses on Mitcham High Road and Streatham High Street had been fire bombed. The same night, the Black Panther affiliated Unity Centre was burnt down. The loss was devastating; "from an empty shell at 74 Railton Road we created with our own hands the first and only cultural and political centre serving the black and working community in Brixton."[5] The Black Power movement knew who the culprits were, "It is well known in South London that the Conservative party is the political mouthpiece for the fascist fire bombers of the National Front." But the movement remained defiant; "We have survived four hundred years of terror, torture, fire, sword and guns and we are still resisting."[6] There were thirty-one murders between 1976 and 1981 of black people across the country by racists.[7]

---

4   *The Guardian*, 19 January 1979.
5   *Black Life Brixton*, 16 March 1973.
6   Ibid.
7   Peter Fryer, *Staying Power: The History of Black People in Britain* (Pluto Press 1984).

The community also felt that there was a concerted effort by police to target them. The arrest of four black men, Sterling Christie, George Griffiths, Constantine "Omar" Boucher and Winston Trew, in 1972 at Oval station serves as an example of the kind of treatment that black people received: An undercover Met Police squad operating on the Northern Line would accuse black people of 'nicking handbags' and then arrest them for 'resisting'. The four men were arrested under this operation and were subjected to a five week trial, being sentenced to two years, reduced to eight months on appeal. The charges were totally fabricated; a corrupt police officer, Derek Ridgewell, who himself was sent to prison in 1978, was part of this undercover Met Police squad.[8]

These turbulent times led to a range of militant responses from the black community, determined to fight for their right to stay. The short lived British Black Panthers Party had their headquarters at 38 Shakespeare Road, paid for by the left-wing art critic, John Berger, after he won the Booker Prize. (Their newspaper headline declared that "NEW INFORMATION IS THE AMMUNITION FOR UNITY".) Berger had given half of his £5,000 prize money to them in recognition of the damage that the Booker McConnell Corporation had inflicted through exploiting indentured sugar workers in British Guyana. The occasional provocative presence of the National Front outside Brixton tube station were never left unchallenged by the left, anti-racist campaigners or local residents. In September 1978 the Anti-Nazi League (ANL) held a *Rock against Racism* festival in Brockwell Park, with thousands of marchers from Hyde Park joining a feeder march from Wandsworth. Over 20,000 people attended to listen to music and hear anti-racist (anti-racialist, to use the language of the time) speeches. But relations with the police were poor – a widespread view of the residents of Lambeth was that the police were racist and unfairly targeted young black men in particular. The 1980s would see two explosions of anger over this issue.

By the turn of the decade, it was clear to that there was a social malaise in the borough was reaching crisis proportions. Patterns of decline were obvious, too many communities were in a spiral of deprivation and the borough was sitting on a powder keg waiting to explode. Brixton centre was pretty run down, though with some gaudy splashes of community efforts to brighten the place up. Considering Brixton had the first electrified street and the first department store in the country, it had become very run down. There were very few restaurants, an Indian Curry house on Atlantic Road, the Jacaranda restaurant, a trendy vegan lefty place. One person remembered the "ghastly shops selling ghastly furniture" all burned down by fires in 1981 and '85.[9] The arson of the riots forced the area to be rebuilt, clearing the area for regeneration, though of course that was little comfort for the local

---

8   "Oval Four' men jailed in 1972 cleared by court of appeal in London', *The Guardian*, 5 December 2019.
9   Interview with Abibat Olulode, July 2018.

businesses. The area had a BHS but it only sold seconds, just piles of cheap tat. There was a small Marks and Spencer. The market was better, with loads of stalls selling cheap, quality food. All in all the dramatic decline of the post-war social democratic consensus was obvious to any visitor and painfully real for people who lived there.

Housing was the major problem, there was a shortage of 20,000 dwellings and 12,000 homes were over crowded. About 25% of the housing stock was substandard and many homes lacked one or even two basic amenities. Access to good jobs was also tough for the black community. The social and economic neglect of a whole group of people was no accident in a country where race was weaponised by politicians and racist views were commonplace.

Inevitably a community began to grow. Some semi-derelict buildings are put to other uses; "Empty houses are also used by local blacks as drinking and gambling clubs, dope centres and venues for all-night blues parties or bashment with sound systems pumping out non-stop reggae."[10] As Railton Road evolved into the Frontline, it became the centre of black resistance both culturally and politically. On the Frontline the local Black community made itself heard in patois – the use of which was designed to facilitate cultural dissemination and exclude outsiders – one writer described it as an "assertion of racial and class identities".[11] It was also the Frontline for its proximity to the looming fortress of Brixton police station – a building where black men were taken, beaten and charged, then for many to be disappeared into the maze of the British prison system.

Only a minute's walk from Railton Road, on Shakespeare Road, was the Headquarters of the *Race Today* collective, headed by Darcus Howe, Linton Kwesi Johnson and CLR James, among others. Howe was considered a rabble rouser, a prominent campaigner for black rights who had been involved in the Lewisham protest. Johnson, the founder of dub poetry, a well-known figure in Brixton's Little Jamaica community. His poem *Di Great Insohreckshan* was a righteous and unapologetic retelling of the Brixton riot. CLR James was an older Trinidadian revolutionary socialist, an ex-Trotskyist, cricket correspondent and powerful writer. His view that you had to build a black-led revolutionary movement for liberation was popular among black intellectuals at the time – these kinds of ideas were common currency among Black Panther types as well as the Black Liberation Front. The *Race Today* collective monitored comings and goings from their offices on Shakespeare Road, speaking to local black residents, with one eye on the police officers who would skulk around nearby.

Political activists produced a lot of local magazines and publications aimed at various groupings within the local community. A lot of the

---

10 'We Want to Riot, Not To Work Collective', 1982.
11 Dick Hebdige, *Reggae, Rastas and Rudies, Resistance Through Rituals: Youth Subcultures in Post-War Britain* (Routledge 2002), p. 136.

publications and community magazines were produced on a Gestetner, a clunky printing machine designed for short runs. Words would be typed on a typewriter into columns like a newspaper, stuck on a page alongside photos which had been cut out from a newspaper or magazine, and then run through the Gestetner. It was a cumbersome process before the desktop publishing revolution in the 1990s but it provided opportunities for large circulation of printed materials. The idea of finding a distinctly black voice, of creating cultural as well as physical space was a central aspect of the struggle. Black Ink (based at 258 Coldharbour Lane) was an example of a black owned business that was concerned with carving out an intellectual and cultural space for the local ethnic minority community. They secured a grant from Manpower Services Commission to create jobs for several local black people who were employed in every stage of the process from editing to printing. O'Neil Williams, who was involved in the publishing house, remembered that, "Unemployment in Lambeth was a scandal, we had to do something for younger black people." Black Ink sought out first-time writers, primarily younger people, to give them a chance to be published. They went to the local schools, (some still around, others long since demolished), Vauxhall Manor, Stockwell, Michael Ramsey, Tulse Hill School. They contacted the English Departments and asked to speak to sixth formers, reading their short stories and essays which made up the bulk of the first book the collective produced.[12] The second book they published was called 'School Leaver', a play written by a 16-year-old black youth Michael McMillan, who went onto become a respected playwright and curator.

Many of the squats had mainly white residents, whereas St Agnes Place was predominantly Rastafari. Starting in the 1960s the Rastafari movement was gaining popularity in Brixton. Its mix of pan-Africanism and religion, of Christianity and cosmology, provided a political and a spiritual foundation for many. Although reggae was not exclusively Rasta, there was a symbiotic relationship between the various Jamaican style sound systems that toured south London and the Rasta movement. Bob Marley was obviously a crucial cultural figure for making reggae and Rastafarianism so mainstream. In the racial tensions at the time, young Rastafari men occupied a special place in the fears of the racist imagination. Dark skinned, with long dreadlocks and apparent allegiances to an African god-figure, when the media talked about black muggers this was the stereotype that middle-England, the far right, and the Police fixated on. Photos of 'Dreadlocks' (as young Rastafari men were known) being harassed by police made for good newspaper sales; but for their part, Dreadlocks were also heralded as street-fighting heroes by the local community if there was any trouble with the police.[13] Britain was part of the Rastafarian concept of Babylon, a part of the oppressive white

---

12 Interview with Oniel Williams, August 2018.
13 See Eddie Chambers, *Roots & Culture: Cultural Politics in the Making of Black Britain* (I B Taurus 2017)

structures that brutalised and enslaved black people globally. Babylon was spiritually crippling, it was a lived oppression and permanent policing, a form of mental slavery designed to make black people forget their past, their cultures and traditions and make them hate themselves. As such, black empowerment focussed on consciousness raising, both about the nature of racist oppression and the heritage of African people. Given how difficult life was in Lambeth, it is no surprise that Rastafarianism, bold, strident and unapologetically black, was popular.

It was clear from the start that Thatcher's government was not going to be a liberal one when it came to progressive values. From the late 1970s onwards there was public hysteria around 'muggers'. The phrase was a new one, only coined in the 1960s, but it had quickly become synonymous with young black men.[14] The notion of mugging was radicalised and used to target the black community in highly discriminatory ways. Newspapers ran repetitive, salacious articles which all seemed to feature the same story, usually gangs of black muggers attacking an old white woman. There was a sense of dread about the image of the mugger fostered by newspapers and politicians – it was short hand for urban society, for a fear of lawlessness, that there was an uncontrollable menace. Within two years of her election Thatcher's government moved to a legislative programme specifically aimed at undermining any sense of collective belonging or citizenship for black and Asian people in Britain. Thatcher made the notorious comment in 1978 that "people are really rather afraid that this country might be rather swamped by people with a different culture" – an explicit dog whistle to the kind of extremist arguments that the National Front (NF) were making.

Given this context the British Nationality bill that was winding its way through parliament was of particular concern as it changed the rules for who would have automatic right of abode in the UK, from allowing anyone born in the UK to claim a right of abode to only people with at least one parent who was British or a 'settled resident'. Many feared it would become *carte blanche* to deport so a demonstration was called, attracting tens of thousands on 6 April 1981. Some participants were chanting slogans calling for Thatcher herself to be deported. It is clear that race, racism and the idea of who was welcome or not in Britain was certainly a topic of some intense discussion for many people.

Anti-racist activity in Lambeth had picked up significantly in the 1970s. There had been a marked increase in violent fascist activity in south London and the fielding of a National Front candidate in the 1978 Lambeth Central by-election was a flash point for protests and counter demonstrations. A mass NF leaflet and paper sale in Brixton on Easter Saturday 1978 saw 100 fascists gather across the road from the tube station, protected by several hundred police and shouted at by a sizeable Anti-Nazi League presence. The presence of the fascists was criticised by Lambeth Council for Community

---

14 Stuart Hall, *Policing the Crisis: Mugging, the State, and Law and Order*, (Macmillan 1978)

Relations. Brian Hodges from Lambeth Trade's Council said that the NF "appeared able to break the law with impunity."[15] People were not surprised, there were irrepressible rumours that there was not one but two NF branches organised in Brixton police station. The National Front even set up a print shop on 221 Streatham High Road for their leaflets and newspaper, until the Council found a planning regulation issue they could use as an excuse to shut them down.

In the run-up to the 1979 election there was what the local press described as a "mini Lewisham" at Loughborough School when the NF held a public meeting there to build support for their election campaign. Only the back two rows were put aside for the public and NF leader Martin Webster personally vetted entrants, turning away many known left-wing 'trouble makers'. Nevertheless, when the meeting started anti-fascists in the audience started to disrupt proceedings, leading to Webster and others engaging in a scuffle that led to thirty-four arrests.[16] Twenty ended up in court, including four teachers and three students.[17] Webster himself was fined £60 and £80 costs for his role in the fracas.[18] As a result the All Lambeth Anti-Racist Movement (ALARM) and the NUT appealed to the Inner London Education Authority (ILEA) to stop NF meetings in schools. Subsequently, full page advertisements were taken out in the *South London Press* to oppose *racialism* and anti-Semitism in Lambeth and Southwark with a long list of signatories.

The Lambeth central by-election set a new record for the number of candidates contesting, a total of eleven.[19] Labour's John Tilley won, though his majority was halved to 3,141 votes (a total of 10,311) whilst nine of the eleven candidates lost their deposits. Tilley described the victory as "a double victory for the working people of Lambeth" because it showed significant support for Labour and a total rejection of the far right. The NF candidate, Helena Stevens, won 1,291 votes, loud jeers at the count when her result was read out forced the Mayor to halt proceedings several times.[20]

The defeat of the NF at the election didn't stop the problems around racism. The black community had not only violent fascists to deal with but also the predatory institutional racism of the Metropolitan Police, and daily discrimination when it came to housing, education and employment. Indeed, black organisations in the late '70s were weary of the white left's preoccupation with anti-fascism. Colin Prescod, writing in *Black Liberator*, argued that the left tended to conflate anti-racism and anti-fascism, "The clearest representation of this tendency is the ANL. If the white masses are

---

15 Row over 'protection for the NF', *South London Press*, 21 April 1978, p. 2.
16 Martin Webster, 'NF clash leads to a new demand for school ban', *South London Press*, April 18 1978.
17 'NF school clash', *South London Press*, 3 May 1978, p. 2.
18 'National Front organiser fined', *South London Press*, 30 June 1978.
19 *South London Press*, Friday 14 April 1978, p. 16.
20 'Lambeth swings to the right', *South London Press*, 25 April 1978, p. 2.

led to believe that it is only if and when fascists like the National Front (NF) have public platforms, or come to power, that Black people will really experience heavy racism – if this is to be believed, then with regard to the gross physical, economic, political, cultural and psychological attacks that are already being made against us, what's that?" Or, as the Black Women's Group put it, "it is not enough to like reggae and jump around the street wearing badges."[21] Prescod reported on a meeting of eight black organisations held at Brixton's Abeng Centre (today called the Karibu Education Centre) opposite the Police Station in 1978 to establish Black people Against State Harassment (BASH) in the wake of the call by Metropolitan Police Commissioner David McNee for a significant increase in police powers. At the meeting Martha Osamor spoke from the campaign against the 'sus' laws, whereby mainly young black men were harassed by the police merely for "acting suspiciously". Cecil Gutzmore spoke from the Black People's Information Centre on the racism in the courts and the violence of the special police groups that had been formed under the Callaghan Labour government; "Those hard shock troops, at the front of those police lines, were always SPG [Special Patrol Group] men. They are now being used against the working class as the shock troops of the state in industrial actions. The white working class did not mind the development of the SPG, because they thought it was meant for blacks. They were deluded: it is meant for them as well."[22]

The SPG were an elite unit of the Met Police which specialised in meticulous and thorough violence against protesters and people they considered 'undesirables'. In 1974 Kevin Gately had been beaten to death by the police during an anti-fascist protest in central London. He suffered a brain haemorrhage from blunt force trauma – a policeman's baton. In 1979 SWP member Blair Peach was killed by SPG police, after a counter-protest against the NF in Southall. He was killed in a side street, from blunt force trauma blow to the head. The coroner's report found that it wasn't a normal truncheon, but some kind of special weighted baton that was used. An internal police investigation raided SPG lockers and found an array of such weapons, including crowbars, a lead-weighted leather stick, a whip and knives. The internal confidential report was released 30 years later, stating that a member of a team of SPG officers had killed Peach, but since they had all lied, covered up the facts and disposed of evidence, it was impossible to say which officer committed the murder. These were dangerous times.

Tensions were high in south London since a suspect arson attack in New Cross led to a fire in January 1981 which killed 13 black youths. The police had dismissed the view that it was arson, but many people suspected it was deliberately started by violent racists. More upsetting was the muted and

---

21 *Speak Out*, issue 2.
22 Colin Prescod, 'Black People Against State Harassment (BASH) campaign – a report', *Race & Class*, (2016), 58(1), p. 98.

meek response from the media, who barely covered the fire, let alone investigated it. There was no condolences or public displays of sorrow from the Queen or the Prime Minister. It was almost as if black lives didn't matter. Leaflets with "THIRTEEN DEAD AND NOTHING SAID" appeared across the capital.[23] In response, a large protest in early march saw tens of thousands of black people and their supporters march on Parliament, the biggest black political action Britain had ever seen. Many young people from Lambeth had attended the protests and were clearly fed up with the attitude of the police. They not only didn't investigate racist violence properly, they even carried it out themselves. The New Cross Massacre Action Committee was launched in 1981, based at 74 Shakespeare Road, the same office as *Race Today*.

The Labour left in Lambeth knew that they were governing a community which faced serious threats against its very existence. As such they were keen to tackle the social and political problems facing the black people in their borough as well as the wider community. Top of the list was the issue of police-community relations. To investigate any grievances Lambeth Council commissioned an independent working party to look into community and police relations in March 1979, proposed by Mike Bright. The working party was aided by some of the councillors, notably Bill Bowring with his background in law, but worked separately from the council. In six months they amassed 275 submissions from individuals, and organised 41 public meetings/hearings, publishing their final report in January 1981. The report was a clear indictment of the way that police treated black people, notably young black men. The Tories greeted the establishment of the working party with both derision and outright hostility, one Councillor wrote to the *South London Press* that Mike Bright was – unconsciously – acting as "the mouth piece of every crook, twisted mugger, vandal and cowardly brute in the Lambeth area."[24] Her conflation with monitoring the police and the mugging threat was a telling example of how deep the racism ran.

The report recommended "no increase in police powers" because "at the moment police in Lambeth are over stepping their powers",[25] to repeal the Vagrancy Act 1824 which was being used to target black youth and to discontinue the controversial Special Patrol Group deployments.[26] However, the report stopped short of recommending police monitoring units, as the working party considered that a political question outside of their remit. At the public launch of the report Knight forewarned, "if the Home Secretary

---

23 See Robin Bunce and Paul Field, *Darcus Howe: A Political Biography* (Bloomsbury Academic 2014), Chapter 14.
24 *South London Press*, 6 April 1979, p. 50.
25 Final Report of the working party into community/police relations in Lambeth (1981), p. 87.
26 Ibid., p. 88.

takes no notice of this report, he will be acquiescing in an explosion in areas like Lambeth."[27] That was published in January 1981.

And an explosion there was.

UPRISING 81

> it woz in april nineteen eighty wan
> doun inna di ghetto af Brixtan
> dat di babylan dem cause such a frickshan
> dat it bring about a great insohrekshan
> an it spread all owevah di naeshan
> it woz truly an histarical occayshan
>
> Linton Kwesi Johnson, *Di Great Insohreckshan*.

The last flashpoint on the road to Brixton's uprising was the events in the St Paul's district in Bristol during April 1980. Police had violently raided a café, sparking a backlash. The largely black community fought back, driving the police from the area for several hours. The clashes in St Paul's were heralded by some as a harbinger of things to come, a sign of the times for how the police would treat black people. Within days of those events, graffiti went up across Lambeth: "Bristol yesterday, Brixton today".

That day came a year later in April 1981. The Metropolitan police launched Operation Swamp in Brixton. The code name was not lost on the local community – only a few years earlier, when she was Shadow Education Minister, Thatcher had warned of Britain being "swamped by an alien culture".[28] Police targeting Brixton using such a code word was more than dog whistle politics. Darcus Howe firmly believed that the police operating out of Stockwell, Clapham and Brixton were racist. By this stage residents regularly claimed they saw plain clothes police wearing National Front badges as they harassed young black men on the street.

The operation saw the usual heavy-handed policing as Brixton was flooded with plain clothes police carrying out stop and search under the notorious Sus laws. The ability to harass and arrest people considered to be acting suspiciously (hence 'Sus laws') came from the 1824 Vagrancy Act, a reactionary law that gave police sweeping powers to target 'rogues and vagabonds'. Suspicious behaviour seemed to cover anything that a black person did, as the number of arrests for minor offences or even for complaining about the police operation was huge. The police regarded black people as the enemy, as an uncivilised and uncivilisable element – all that could be done was repression and control. The pathological fear generated by racist bigots and the media around "black muggers" and the, by then, commonplace rhetoric around immigration concerns meant that hanging around in public was considered an act of wilful subversion by young blacks.

---

27 'Police silent on 'crisis' report', *South London Press*, 3 February 1981.
28 Mary F. Brewer, *Staging Whiteness* (Wesleyan University Press 2005) pp. 172-3.

Around 1,000 people were searched by teams of police in six days, leading to confrontations and anger from local residents.

Outraged by the attacks on the local community, Ted Knight lambasted the Met Police operation amounting "to an army of occupation". His detractors immediately seized upon these apparently inflammatory words, accusing him of criticising a police force that was overstretched and dealing with difficult situations. But one ex-police constable admitted in 2011 that young black men were "routinely fitted up, beaten up, tortured and worse" by police. He claimed police would rip dreadlocks out and pin them on the station noticeboard like trophies. Commander Adams proudly refused to inform the local police liaison committee of the activities of his boys: "no good general ever declares his forces in a prelude to any attack".[29] Such a comment provides a useful insight into the mentality of the serving officers. Ted Knight was right – the police did see themselves as an army of occupation, fighting the blacks, fighting anarchists and battling people that they considered scum.

The exact events are inevitably hazy, with many competing versions of what happened. What is known is that on Friday 10 April a young black man, Michael Bailey, was stopped for "acting suspiciously". It turned out he was badly hurt with a four-inch stab wound and had been running from a gang that was pursuing him. But police initially didn't get medical help, instead they searched him, treating him like a suspect. Some local onlookers said they saw the police punch him in the stomach. A crowd gathered around the distressed youth and started to hector the police, urging them to take Bailey to the hospital. He was put into a police car; afterwards the police said it was to take him more quickly to the hospital, but it looked like he was being arrested. As more people gathered, police backup arrived, creating an inevitably escalation. Rumours spread that the police had let a black man die rather than help him. Members of the enraged crowd began to throw bottles through the windows of police cars. Mayall Road and surrounding areas cleared out as evening drew on, but it was clear that more was coming. That night in Brixton there was a febrile calm, a *quiet before the storm* mood was palpable.

On Saturday morning the Labour councillors met with black community groups and discussed how to improve conditions in the borough. They had a final meeting with the police to warn them that if they didn't radically alter their approach then there would be serious consequences. The council organised a 24-hour watch at the Town Hall in case any trouble started, an officer standing anxiously by the window and hovering near the phone. Knight, Lesley Hammond and Len Hammond were playing cards at the Hammond's home in Herne Hill when the phone rang around 6pm. It was the officer at Brixton Town Hall on watch. "You better get down here." The councillors jumped in Knight's car and drove to Brixton, already they could

---

29 Robin Bunce, Paul Field, *Darcus Howe: A Political Biography*, p. 209.

see smoke and the crowds as they got closer. Flashing their council ID badges they made their way through the protest. Knight was approached by a member of the Workers Revolutionary Party who had been monitoring the police all afternoon and explained what was happening.

During the day, Home Secretary Willie Whitelaw walked through Brixton, flanked by police and advisors and accompanied by a media circus. He took a moment to praise the police and call on "all law abiding citizens to support them."[30] More protests started in the late afternoon. It was one stop and search too many, one arrest too many, and one arrogant police officer too many. At about 5pm on Saturday, 11 April, a young Black man was arrested by police and bundled into a van. People started throwing bottles and bricks at police and within an hour the centre of Brixton was engulfed in violent protests. It was a scream of rage against the racist police who were clearly targeting and persecuting black people. People were charging the police lines shouting "remember Bristol!" in the faces of the cops.[31] But it was also born out of the frustration over people's quality of life, the lack of housing, the rocketing unemployment, the sense of social deprivation and alienation.

As with many violent protests, it saw people take out their frustrations on shops, cars and even passers-by. Over 400 police were injured during the weekend. People said it was the most serious urban disturbances of the 20th century. People said that Leeson Road saw a petrol bomb thrown at police on the UK mainland for the very first time. Railton Road, Atlantic Road and Coldharbour Lane were filled with police, vans and police cars were on every corner. At one point local youth commandeered a bus and drove it towards the police lines; the driver's window was shattered by a brick thrown by police, causing the young driver to jump out of the vehicle before it hurtled into police lines. immortalised in the lines of Kwesi Johnson:

> wen wi run riot all ovah Brixton
> wen wi mash-up plenty police van
> wen wi mash-up di wicked wan plan
> wen wi mash-up di Swamp Eighty-wan[32]

This wasn't only a black uprising however, a number of white people were also involved. There was a generalised sense that the racially mixed community of Brixton was being targeted, that it was the people versus the police. Clearly social anxiety and rage also went beyond race issues – a general frustration with inner city life, with the government, with the callous disregard shown by those in power. The mass looting that happened saw some memorable scenes; one participant remembered seeing "one old lady

---

30 ITN News report, April 11 1981.
31 'St Paul's riot DID spark 1981 race riots across Britain, as researchers find 'direct connection'', *Bristol Post* 14 September 2017.
32 Linton Kwesi Johnson, *Di Great Insohreckshan* from the album *Making History* (Island Records 1984).

on a Zimmer frame [asking] for something to be brought from a window, which an agile youth courteously handed her."[33]

All the police could do was contain the revolt, setting up a cordon and directing traffic elsewhere. Some forays by police with riot shields into the protest turned out to be forlorn hopes, they were met with bottles, petrol bombs and stones, and were forced to retreat. Some police decided to deal with the situation in their own way. One freelance photographer near Brixton Police station saw a group of police in jeans and jackets, civilian clothes, arm themselves with "a pick-axe handle, rubber tubes ... and a piece of chain about 18 inches long" before heading out to find some local youths to beat up.[34]

The clashes lasted all weekend before the energy was finally spent. By the end over twenty buildings had been destroyed or badly damaged through vandalism or fire. A number of pubs were burnt down where landlords were known to be racist – such as the George Pub on Railton Road (the landlord had also been accused of barring gays from drinking there). A local reporter described it as "an act of revenge for years of racial discrimination".[35] By comparison, the Atlantic (now the Dog Star) was left untouched – a black pub run by Irish landlords in the heart of Brixton. The collapse of several structures had damaged water pipes, which caused some areas to become flooded. Residents living in central Brixton were advised to boil water and store food safely away from rats and cockroaches. The area looked like a war zone right in the heart of London.

On the Monday morning Ted Knight called an emergency meeting with senior councillors and officers. They felt that their warnings from January 1981 had been ignored and the uprising was an inevitable consequence of the crisis that was brewing in the borough and elsewhere. By midday Knight wrote to Heseltine asking for a delegation to Parliament to discuss financial assistance to deal with both the aftermath of the fighting and the chronic social problems. Heseltine's office phoned Brixton town hall and agreed to a meeting the next day.

On Tuesday 14 April Knight, Warburton and a delegation of officers crossed the river to the House of Commons. They hoped that more money would become available. But Heseltine flat out refused, claiming he'd be certified insane by his cabinet colleagues if he gave money to a left controlled council like Lambeth. Instead he proposed Lambeth sell off some land and assets to raise the cash needed to rebuild the centre of Brixton. Knight and his colleagues were incredulous, Lambeth had few assets and the land they owned was earmarked for urgently needed housing. The only financial relief was a grant of £800,000 towards Brixton Rec, based on the

---

33 Albert Meltzer, 'I couldn't paint golden angels', spunk.org/texts/writers/meltzer/sp001591/angels21.html
34 *Sunday Times*, 19 April 1981.
35 *South London Press*, 14 April 1981.

assumption that if young people filled their time with sport then they wouldn't riot. The dejected councillors trooped back to Brixton, picking their way through the clean-up operation.

After Knight labelled the police an 'army of occupation', one local Labour Councillor declared he had had enough. Councillor Peter Mandelson told a journalist in no uncertain terms that "given the choice between having the Labour Party and Ted Knight in the borough, or the police, 99 per cent of the population would vote for the police."[36] After this, however, Mandelson subsequently struck a more conciliatory tone, saying that he "supported much of what Ted stands for… He has devoted great energy to get the right response to the Brixton problems but on the other hand he speaks to fringe left groups and goes over the top."[37]

The narrative following the events in April 1981 became typical of how the local police and press covered the events of the rest of the decade. As it was Brixton, some started to label it a race riot, which bought into the whole media narrative of wild, black lawless youths running amok. Obviously, Brixton had a much higher concentration of black people than the rest of the borough but it still only made up around 36% of the local demographic, and there were large numbers of white people involved as well. In media appearances, Knight said that he didn't feel it was a race riot as he and the other councillors had walked unheeded through the streets, the violence was mostly directed against the police, not white people. This was a community response to hostile and aggressive policing. It was Brixton against the cops. Desperate to distance themselves from accusations of racism, the police also denied it was about any prejudice to the local black community, pointing to the large number of white people they had also arrested. Thatcher's Press Secretary, Bernard Ingram, had a different take. He saw the riots as a product of the loss of respect for elders, for the family and for law and order.

Not wanting the events to be seen as a racist attack on the black community, the security forces blamed the violence on the fact the area was home to "number of squatters" and was a "hotbed of extreme left wing political activity." A local community worker was quoted in the press warning of the danger that "political extremists could move in and try and take over the situation."[38] Police Commander Brian Fairbairn was quoted saying that he was "keeping an open mind" about the claim that the violence was largely caused by outside agitators. Still there was a search for easy scapegoats. A subsequent report submitted to the Prime Minister specifically highlighted the concentration of far left organisations in the area at the time of the riot:

> 'Militant Tendency' were operating 'from an address in Railton Road'

---

36 Peter Mandelson, *The Third Man* (Harper Collins 2010), p. 65.
37 Cited in Andy McSmith, *Faces of Labour: The Inside Story* (Verso 1997), p. 255.
38 'The blitz of Brixton and the politics of fear', *South London Press*, 14 April 1981.

'the Workers Revolutionary Party has a book shop in Atlantic Road and a Youth Training Centre in Stockwell'

'the Revolutionary Communist Group has its headquarters in Railton Road';

'the Revolutionary Communist Party set up a Lambeth Unemployed Workers Group shortly before the Riots, and has since formed a South London Workers Against Racism group, similar to the East London Workers Against Racism which attracted some notoriety for organising vigilante patrols'

'the Race Today Collective has offices in Brixton. The edition [sic] of its magazine is Darcus Howe, who has been associated with campaigning in support of the H-block hunger strikes, the New Cross Massacre Action Committee'

After the riot the Socialist Workers Party circulated a leaflet in Brixton in which it said 'it was a magnificent way for Brixton to fight back'."[39]

Whilst it was certainly true that the area had a large number of socialist and revolutionary organisations assembled there, the events in Brixton were not of their making. Authorities prefer to blame 'agitators' for disturbances because it gives them a handy scapegoat to ignore the social problems that festered in troubled inner-city areas like Lambeth. Certainly it doesn't explain that similar riots happened across England in 1981 in different cities.

To ascertain what happened, the Government called on the services of Lord Leslie Scarman to chair an inquiry into the causes of the events. This led to serious disputes and disagreements locally over whether to engage with the process or denounce it. The general feeling from the black community and the left was that Scarman would produce a report which defended the conduct of the police and would be a whitewash. *Race Today* organised the Brixton Defence Committee (BDC) and had one-time local Councillor Rudy Narayan, a local lawyer from Streatham lead it, alongside Cecil Gutzmore. The BDC called for the boycott of the Scarman Inquiry on the grounds that it would likely just provide a legalistic whitewash to the government's view that this was a breakdown of law and order by a minority of black criminals. There was also the pressing matter that it would be dangerous for people to give evidence to the inquiry about the 'immediate causes' of the uprising that might prejudice a fair trial for anyone accused. The BDC started from the point of view, (widely held by people from the local area), that it was the police that were out of control, not due to a few bad apples, but the entire institution was part and parcel of a racist society.

---

39 Report on the 1981 riots in South London, cited at libcom.org/history/1981-riots-south-london

When the issue of outside agitators was put to Narayan he responded bluntly: "The only outsiders were [David] McNee's storm-troopers, the Special Patrol Group, some armed with guns, who came to attack and terrorise our community". Sivanandan confirmed the view of many from the local area: "In April Brixton exploded in rebellion... for blacks, Afro-Caribbean and Asian alike, all distinction between police and fascist had faded."[40]

Rather than condemning the violence, the socialist left sought to build a political movement out of the issues. Militant organised a mass meeting at the Town Hall a few days after the riots, handing out 30,000 leaflets to build support. Around 600 people filled the hall on short notice and passed a motion which declared that "the responsibility for the riots in Brixton rests with the police... Also responsible are the Tories and the class they represent, whose system – being run purely for the rich – has pushed unemployment up to three million and bred poverty and slum housing".[41] Off the back of that Militant supporters in Lambeth set up the Labour Committee for the Defence of Brixton. The Liaison Committee for the Defence of Brixton (LCDB) organised meetings to discuss the police violence and circulated leaflets calling for the disbanding of the Special Patrol Group and more spending on social welfare. They also raised funds for the defence of those arrested during the rioting. The LCDB was run by Militant people like Clare Doyle and Lynn Walsh, both Editorial Board members who lived in Lambeth, and Tony Saounis from Labour's NEC. Shortly after the riots Lambeth NUT (alongside their comrades in Hackney) passed motions of non-cooperation with police refusing to invite police into schools.

The LCDB also denounced the Scarman inquiry for its links to the police and called for an independent workers' inquiry into the disturbances. Their position of calling for democratic control of the police force clashed with more radical voices on the left who wanted the disbanding of the police as an institution and an end to the entire notion of what 'policing' meant. At the other end of the movement the TUC General Secretary Jack Dromey visited the local Trade's Council and argued that the unions should collect evidence to give to the Scarman inquiry, despite deeply entrenched opposition to what local people saw as an inadequate inquiry by a Tory judge. That conflict between taking part in the organs of state management or challenging and boycotting them was a regular feature of community politics – a distinction more generally between revolutionary conceptions of social change and gradualist notions of working through the system.

Only two weeks after the riots the People's March for jobs started off from Liverpool, winding its way through the cities and towns of England to

---

40 A. Sivanandan, 'From resistance to rebellion: Asian and Afro-Caribbean struggles in Britain', *Britain, Race and Class Journal*, October 1, 1981.
41 '1981: Brixton erupts', *Socialism Today*, Issue 147, April 2011.

arrive in Brockwell Park, where the marchers were greeted with a concert headed by Pete Townshend and Aswad, compered by alternative comedian and ex-Communist party member Alexei Sayle. Whilst the march was going on news came through on 5 May that Bobby Sands had died whilst on hunger strike. Sands had been elected as an MP to the British Parliament whilst he served time in prison for his IRA activities. Sands had been in prison since 1977 and had become known internationally for his resistance in the H-Block cells and demanding political prisoner rights for IRA people behind bars. The hunger strike was a protest – similar to the suffragettes before World War One – to demand more rights for Republican prisoners. He slowly starved himself to death, his emaciated body a testament to the determination he had for the cause. He was the first of ten. But as each man died, Thatcher remained implacable, determined not to give in to the Republicans. "Sands was a convicted criminal. He chose to take his own life" she said scornfully in the Commons.[42] The riots that followed Sands' death and each other man that died in the hunger strikes were an inevitable result of the cruel, purposeful indifference of the British establishment.

Within months there were ten more Republican men dead. A milkman, an upholster, a drapers' assistant, all ardent Republicans who had died for their cause. It struck a chord that these were the kinds of jobs that anyone could be doing – working-class jobs. They didn't seem like elite terrorist gangsters when their bodies were displayed. As the summer wore on urban uprisings happened in Toxteth, Moss side and Handsworth, all following a pattern laid down by Bristol and Brixton. It was a year of riots and starvation, a desperate fight against the tide, and at the heart of it all lay a British establishment determined to crush all resistance and opposition.

When the Scarman Report was published in November 1981, it rejected outright labelling of the police as institutionally racist, though Scarman did criticise the "the ill-considered, immature and racially prejudiced actions of some officers". That verdict would not be delivered until 1997 when Lord MacPherson looked into police failings over the murder of Stephen Lawrence. The portrait of the violence in the Scarman report was one of insurrection, that if it hadn't have been for the 'thin blue line' then the rebellious masses might have marched on parliament itself. Local youths had no such intentions of course, for them it was about their homes (or lack of them), their neighbourhood, and their rights in the face of police repression. Lord Scarman's report did, however, conclude that, "the disorders in Brixton cannot fully be understood unless they are seen in the context of the complex political, social and economic factors to which I have referred. In analysing the communal disturbances such as those in Brixton and elsewhere, to ignore the existence of these facts is to put the nation in peril."[43] He also

---

42 *Hansard*, 5 May 1981.
43 Leslie George Scarman, *The Scarman Report: The Brixton Disorders, 10-12 April 1981* (Penguin Books 1982), p. 203.

concluded that "the raw material of the explosion was the spirit of angry young men."[44]

Scarman partly blamed the lack of stable families for the problems. He attempted to exonerate the Rastafarians in the most patronising ways, dismissing them as "essentially humble and sad" people, dreaming of a return to Africa, who had been whipped up by outside trouble makers. The fact is that the real cause of the crisis was outside of Scarman's remit. Housing, education and employment were all in crisis for the black community in Lambeth and elsewhere, but they were only at the most acute end of inner city urban decay that was wracking central London at that time. Scarman did acknowledge that young black men felt "hunted" by the police. But Howe and others felt that Scarman had soft-pedalled the police violence and the systemic problems, it wasn't "just a few bad apples" – the whole barrel was rotten.

Nevertheless, the further riots in Birmingham, Liverpool and Leeds over the summer persuaded the Thatcher government to act. They decided to loosen the purse strings temporarily and increased the Revenue Support Grant in 1982/83, in addition to another £3.6 million for the housing budget. There was a sense that more cash was needed for some poverty stricken areas, but with a refusal to acknowledge any deeper political issues at stake, and Scarman himself also declined to look too much into the issues. Having an economic response – looking at more investment in areas of dense urban poverty – wasn't going to get to the core of what was essentially a political problem, one of systemic racism in British society.

In the middle of the Scarman report, just after the first phase of the inquiry was concluded, 176 police attacked several houses on Railton Road. The actual warrants for the raids on several buildings were concerned with "unlicensed drinking", whilst others were raided under the auspices of Section 6 of the Criminal Justice Act 1977, that of "using or threatening unauthorised violence". They were looking for alcohol and petrol bombs. The report into the haul from the raid reveals a slice of life on the Frontline. Number 47 was found to have "a new record player and a small quantity of drugs", 54 Railton Road was the site of a gathering of 30 people, whilst another building had a pool table. One of the premises was found to have a "quasi-Masonic temple" complete with two swords and various regalia stored in a glass cabinet, no doubt a place of worship for one of the many religious sects that operated in the area.

In the words of John Fraser MP, "a large number of policemen had deliberately set out to wreck the houses, to make them uninhabitable, by taking up floorboards, breaking water pipes, removing gas and electricity meters, handrails and bannisters and smashing almost every window."[45] All

---

44 Ibid, p. 66.
45 Cited in John Salway, 'Reading the Riot Acts: Behind the Headlines and the Frontlines', (Lambeth Archives 2005), p. 30

the police involved were exonerated of any wrong doing. It was clear that the cycle of state violence and community retaliation was not going to end any time soon. Raids on the Frontline increased throughout 1981 and over the following years. What most of the residents had in common on Railton Road was antipathy to the police, whether it was a reggae music shop, counter cultural squat, an anarchist or socialist organising centre or a building connected with the LGBT or Black rights movements – all had their own hostility to the police and the police shared that hostility right back at them, only in their case with the full weight of the law behind them. The police didn't want to take a softly-softly approach, nor to lose ground to the local community; they had to impose their authority. But this time they were more political about it; they knew they had to begin the process of clearing out Railton Road and the surrounding environs.

When Sir Kenneth Newman was appointed Commissioner of the Metropolitan Police it caused a significant backlash. Newman had been head of the Royal Ulster Constabulary in Belfast and was notorious among radicals in Lambeth for his "blood steeped history of torture and violence in Northern Ireland."[46] The fear was that this veteran from the war against the Republicans would seek to apply similar techniques to Britain. He imbued a thoroughly racist sentiment, claiming that, "in the Jamaicans you have a people who are constitutionally disorderly… it's simply in their make-up, they're constitutionally disposes to be anti-authority." His experiences in Northern Ireland meant he understood the politics of policing. In a society that was divided, it was not simply a civil matter, it was a battle for space and control. His methods were closer to conventional guerrilla warfare techniques: target enemy bases, smash their communications, and harass their leaders. His view was that this was a political war against dissidents, whether they be Republicans, socialists or black. This meant he was particularly exercised about places like Railton Road, its very existence as a space beyond the grip of the police pointed to the fragile nature of the state, of the mechanisms of control and domination. He designated such places as 'symbolic locations' – meaning a place with high black youth unemployment and also a politically charged atmosphere which was explicitly counter-cultural. The police viewed such areas as powder kegs that had to be destroyed before they blew up again.

But not everyone supported this new 'political' turn in policing. The Chief Constable of Manchester's police force, Sir James Anderton, a born-again Christian who believed that God was directly communicating with him, was very concerned about the direction: "We are now witnessing the domination of the police service as a necessary prerequisite of the creation in this country of a society based on Marxist Communist principles… it is the first conscious step manifesting itself towards the political control of the

---

46 *Speak Out*, issue 4, p. 11.

police, without which the dream of a totalitarian, one-party state in this country cannot be realised."[47]

Many locals continued to complain about the frequent raids on the Frontline, often shops would be ransacked by the police and windows smashed from the inside by truncheons. There was always a degree of vicious retaliation involved in the raids, frustrated police who wanted to punish the local blacks and 'scum' who lived in the squats. Raids were often provocative and provoked a reaction.

Over the next couple of years, many of the semi-derelict buildings were finally torn down. The council approached it with clinical rationalism, that this was prime real estate in central Brixton, and, after all, converting them into houses was an essential part of sorting out the homeless problem. Many suspected, however, that behind these rationales lurked the political mind of the police, clearing out the rabble and rebellious left, decimating the community, breaking through the centre of the black community on the Frontline. And it wasn't just Railton Road, the nearby Generva Road, which housed many black families, had also just been torn down and replaced by the Moorland's Estate and the infamous Southwyck House. Southwyck was known locally as the 'Barrier Block' because it was designed to block any sounds of motor cars from a motorway that was supposed to tear through Brixton but was never built. Local people felt that there was a lot of 'modernisation' changes going on, and all of them seemed to be disproportionately affecting the black community.

After the evictions some black activists tried to look on the bright side, that the buildings might be gone, but in fact the Frontline was more than a point on a map, it was a state of mind, it was what the black community created, wherever it was. History delivers a different verdict, that the clearing out of the Frontline was the end of an era for black community and self-organisation in Lambeth.

---

47 *The Times*, 18 March 1982. Such political statements from a chief police officer were frowned upon by the establishment, but Anderson was certainly seen as 'one of us' by Thatcher. In 1986 she personally intervened to save his career after he made homophobic comments concerning HIV and AIDs sufferers.

7

Setbacks

The trap that Heseltine had set for left councils was sprung in Lambeth; even though Knight and the others saw it coming they felt unable to escape it. The backlash against the rates increase had been considerable, and there was still no serious national campaign against local government cuts worthy of the name – Labour hadn't got its act together nationally and apart from a few isolated 'days of action' the TUC confined itself to limp rhetoric. The Tory's push to back Labour councils into a corner was certainly working. Across South London it was the same story. In Southwark the Labour council increased the rents. Lewisham put its own rates up by 50% and had protests from its workforce who blockaded the Town Hall entrance. In Wandsworth the unions were lodged in a bitter war against cuts, with 700 blue collar workers due to lose their jobs. NALGO and NUPE proposed blockading the Council committees to prevent them meeting. As a result several stewards were sacked from the workforce. Lambeth had its problems but it was not alone.

In February 1981 Knight addressed an angry mass meeting at the Town Hall called by the Clapham Rates Action Group. With 500 people in the assembly room and another 3000 blocking the streets outside listening to the debate over a PA system, Knight knew he faced serious opposition. He was heckled throughout, being called both a "Marxist" and "Hitler" and told in time honoured 1980s fashion to "Go back to Russia!" Knight gave as good as he got, cited the 1,400 young people without work, the 6,000 elderly that needed looking after, and the 1,800 meals on wheels that were sent out every day. This was being done in the face of £20 million in cuts in the first 20 months of the Tory government. "I won't expect a standing ovation" he joked to a room of faces that stared solemnly back at him. Instead Bob Shelton got the standing ovation when he repeated the standard refrain that Lambeth was profligate and poor value for money.[1]

Local Tories complained bitterly about examples of supposed profligacy. One of the most controversial was the £2,000 given to three artists for their

---

[1] 'Hardly Ted's night', *South London Press*, 13 February 1981, p. 3.

mural, *Nuclear Dawn*, on the side of Carshalton Mansions in central Brixton. No doubt also enraged by the subject matter, which was highly critical of the pro-nuclear weapon policies of the Thatcher government, the mere fact that rate payers' money was being spent on street art was also offensive to the Conservatives. Brian Barnes, the artist who did most of the work on the mural, and fresh from a huge clash with Wandsworth Council who had torn down his last effort on the Doddington Estate in Queenstown, was unrepentant: "Of course people will object to it but what we are saying is that if the Government stopped spending money on nuclear weapons then Lambeth would not have the problems it does because the Government would be able to give it its full grant."[2] A reasonable point – welfare not warfare – but one that fell on deaf ears for many enraged local rate payers.

Under huge pressure, the Labour group and the Local Government Committee agreed cuts in March 1981 totalling £11 million in order to keep the rate increase down to only 37.5% and £4 a week rent increase. The cuts fell on services for the "mentally sick[, t]he old and the handicapped" reported the *South London Press*.[3] The budget meeting that agreed it in late March saw rival protesters; the right wing led rate payers' campaign squaring off against the left and unions furious over the cuts. It seemed that Lambeth Council couldn't please anyone.

The chairs of the committees reported back that services were in danger of serious decline if more cuts went through. After long discussions with the officers Labour decided to raise an additional supplementary rate. They argued this was necessary to offset the £11.2 million in cuts that Heseltine was forcing on them. It would mean Shell paying £625,000 and the GLC paying £1.6 million extra, which led to a haughty reply from the Tory leader Sir Horace Cutler that they would seek to move their building out of the borough as soon as possible.[4]

The supplementary rate, on top of the previous rate rises, triggered significant rate payers protests. It was one of the few times that the Tories managed to organise a mass movement in the borough. They aped the methods of the left, flooding the public gallery with people to shout down the councillors, placards and leaflets appeared as if from nowhere, making the case that Marxist Ted Knight was stealing from the pockets of honest Lambeth residents to pursue his own ideological agenda. At council meetings one particularly vocal Rate Payers Alliance activist called Margaret Wescott would heckle Knight whenever he spoke "What are you going to do with all our money you're stealing, Ted?!"[5] With a flash Knight would retort with a long explanation of his spending priorities for the borough.

---

2 'Political mural upsets Tory Councillor', *South London Press*, 24 February 1981, p. 3.
3 'Cash cuts hit sick and old', *South London Press*, 27 March 1981.
4 'Charge of the Knight Brigade', *South London Press*, 9 January 1981.
5 Ibid.

The local press were also less than sympathetic. The mood of the time was against big spending. There was also a sense that just throwing more money at services wasn't going to improve them. Perhaps some cuts would actually force a degree of efficiency on the sprawling council? Scenting blood, in the run up to the 1982 local election the All Lambeth Rate Payers Organisation launched a series of demonstrations across the borough. In March 1981, they called a protest outside the Clapham Common bandstand. Expecting 10,000, only 600 turned up, leading one organiser to complain about the "high winds and rain" for keeping the enraged local rate payers of Lambeth at home. The wet local residents protesting about the 57% increase in the supplementary rate were regaled in the rain by entertainment from the Pearly King and Queen of Crystal Palace whilst Lambeth's recently reinstated Finance Director Jack Halligan[6] was also spotted under an umbrella.[7]

These protests continued in the Council chamber – before the rate setting meeting in March 1981, the Tory opposition led a robust, though not particularly tuneful rendition of the national anthem. Mary Leigh, who went on to become the Tory group leader on the Council, led a delegation of rate payers protesting at the Labour Party "pouring rate payers' money down the drain". One of the delegation even made a threatening move towards Ted Knight during the questions and answers, leading to a sharp rebuke from the Mayor Pam Verden who "invited" the resident to leave the chamber.[8]

The *South London Press* also editorialised several times against the council's rate increase – publishing articles on their front page about the possibility of a rates strike by residents and local businesses, even though the heads of the Conservative front group Rate Payers Alliance hadn't even suggested such a tactic. The newspaper then published a helpful piece on the launch of a "non-political alliance" to oppose rates with the phone numbers of key organisers and the dates and times of its meetings.[9] The *South London Press* sadly reported shortly afterwards that only the 'far left Socialist Workers Party' had decided to advocate a strike against the supplementary rates.[10]

At the May 1982 election Labour suffered a major upset. Their support collapsed from around 50% to only 33% of the vote. Tory and SDP/Liberal Alliance councillors temporarily took control of the council after Labour lost ten of its councillors (five to the Tories and five to the Alliance). The result was nominally tied, but in a fit of spite against Knight, the out-going Labour Mayor Johnny Johnson voted to elect a Tory Mayor with a casting vote, then

---

6   Halligan was suspended from his post as chief of finance by CEO Frank Dixon in early 1981 over 'corporate management issues' after he clashed with the Labour group on issues like rent increases and moving the Council's bank account from Barclays as part of the South Africa boycott.
7   'Town Hall Union split', *South London Press*, 10 March 1981.
8   'A real song and dance as rates go up', *South London Press*, 31 March 1981.
9   *South London Press*, 23 January 1981, p. 2.
10 'Lambeth needs sense on rates', *South London Press*, 27 January 1981, p. 24.

immediately joined the SDP. This last act as mayor granted the Tories the narrow lead they needed for a coalition. Naturally they were jubilant — they had claimed the scalp of Lambeth Council and beaten the Marxist leadership of Ted Knight.

The victory was partly the result of well-coordinated campaigning by the various Rate Payers Alliance groups that made loud noises about the rates and their alleged misuse by the public sector. The Rate Payers Alliance spokesperson claimed that Lambeth had "the reputation as being the most profligate local authority in Britain".[11] Some Labour councillors also thought that the Falklands war which had been waging for a month by the time of the election impacted on their result, though in Southwark Labour only lost three seats so it is doubtful that it was a major factor.

The coalition, led by Conservative group leader Robin Pitt, immediately went to work on a recruitment freeze and reducing expenditure on staffing. There was already several hundred job vacancies at the council that had not been advertised yet. In January 1982 the vacancies at the council had rocketed to 18%. NALGO had a policy of not covering vacant posts which seized up a lot of the running of the council in some key departments.[12] Pitt proposed a reduction of £8 million from the budget, £4 million of which would come from salaries.

They proposed selling off all vacant lots to private companies for development, thus massively restricting further public sector house building efforts. They also moved to shut down the Lambeth Walk and Streatham Consumer Advice centres. Tories in Lambeth had a history of vitriolic attacks on the Consumer Advice centres, which offered advice on buying and using white goods like fridges and microwaves. Labour traditionally saw them as a cheap means of helping poor people get value for money from their purchases. They also pioneered debt relief and advice programmes, some of the first in the country. Nevertheless, the Tories denounced them as a waste of money, even though the actual cost of the advice centres was only £1.25 per year for each Lambeth resident. Immediately Knight went to the Lambeth Walk advice centre to speak to staff there and offer his support.

A period in opposition was actually beneficial to the disparate left forces in the Labour Group. They were forced together in mutual struggle against the coalition, forging a bond that consolidated them as a force during the rate capping struggle. They adopted a policy of filibustering — keeping the Tory and Alliance councillors up all night in committee meetings to exhaust them. Psychological warfare as class struggle.

Knowing they would find it harder to break the Tories, instead pressure was brought to bear on the SDP. Ex-Labour members in cahoots with the Tories to run the Council were an easy target as traitors to the cause. The coalition only lasted until November when Gordon Ley, an SDP councillor

---

11 *The Times*, 20 May 1980.
12 *The Cutlet* from January 1982.

defected from his party. He declared himself an independent but made a deal with Labour to support them in the council chamber on key votes. Ted Knight wrote a triumphant article in *Labour Briefing* under the headline "We're back!" One of their last acts of the Tory/Alliance administration in October 1982 was to introduce huge rent rises for tenants.[13]

THE IRON LADY REIGNS SUPREME

In early 1982, Thatcher had the lowest approval rating of any Prime Minister since polling began. Only 12% thought that the Tories would win in 1983. However, the Conservatives' poll boost after the Falklands war and the SDP split led to a heavy General Election defeat for Labour. It was this election victory which really allowed Thatcher to launch her full programme for reshaping the country along the policies of the Monetarist Radical Right, it was now that Thatcherism really began to take its fullest form. It was during this term that she established a truly hegemonic power. It is clear that Thatcher's personal approval rating had shot up over the Falklands. The old imperial colonial mindset of the British is a powerful reserve for reactionary politics of all kinds. But it was the electoral rivalry with their ex-comrades in the SDP that hammered the final nail into the coffin of Labour's hopes for government.

In the 1983 General Election the Conservatives gained 100 extra MPs, wiping the floor with Labour. Thatcherites particularly revelled in the polls that suggested more working-class voters had voted Tory than for their traditional party. Lambeth had also featured in a Conservative Party political broadcast for the 1983 election campaign, comparing it unfavourably to neighbouring Wandsworth. The Labour right immediately made the defeat about the left wing manifesto and Michael Foot being an unpopular out of touch, old socialist who couldn't connect with the new Yuppies of the 1980s. They set the narrative, they set the agenda, they set the terms for the left's retreat over the next 30 years.

As Thatcher consolidated her grip on society and progressives geared up for another few years of counter-revolutionary onslaught, the mood of the country changed. The disparity between the new urban types, working in banking and media and abounding in Gordon Gekko's 'greed is good' philosophy was stark compared to the beginnings of de-industrialisation of large parts of the country.[14] The brutality of the government provided the backdrop for a looming sense of catastrophe.

Rumours had spread about the sinking of the obsolete Argentinian cruiser the *Belgrano* by the British nuclear submarine *Conqueror* under direct orders from the British War Cabinet meeting in Chequers. Labour MP Tam

---

13 *Labour Herald*, October 1982.
14 "Greed is good" was the ironic message of Oliver Stone's 1987 movie, *Wall Street*, a film critical of the new spirit of hyper-capitalism and brutal individualism.

Dalyell repeatedly made the claim that the entire Falklands conflict was allowed to happen in order to boost Thatcher's flagging approval rating. He accused her of "calculated murder ... for her own political ends"[15] and challenged her to sue him if she disagreed. The fact she never did was cited by Dalyell and his supporters as proof that the Thatcher government was a malicious and malevolent force, capable of starting a war merely for political ambition.

Despite Thatcher's claim to be rolling back the borders of the state, the signs of growing authoritarianism appeared all around. The banning of trade unions at GCHQ, better to facilitate spying against the malcontent population, sent a warning shot to the unions that they were clearly the enemy within. The intelligence community looked like it was closing ranks – Thatcher personally and obsessively tried to stop the publication of the reveal-all book on MI5, *Spycatcher*, by ex-intelligence officer Peter Wright. A high ranking official of the Ministry of Defence called Clive Ponting was prosecuted under the Official Secrets Act for trying to warn MPs that government minsters had lied to Parliament.[16] Thatcher and ministers were implicated in ordering police raids on the BBC and ITV to prevent transmission of programmes that they considered subversive.

In Lambeth the mood was sombre. This was a government that had been elected to abolish the GLC and limit local government spending, that had sided with the police against the people during the 1981 riots and had a leader that seemed more ruthless than any Tory leader in generations. Labour suffered such a spectacular defeat in the polls that John Fraser in Norwood was the southern most Labour MP in the whole of the country. Everywhere from Gipsy Hill to the south coast was true blue. The GLC building across the Thames from Parliament defiantly hung a banner presenting the number of unemployed in London – a persistent reminder of the economic policies of Thatcherism ripping through the city, the casualties in the war monetarism was waging on the country. It seemed like an enraged tide was circling, Lambeth on the front line fighting for the grand old cause even as it looked like everyone else was giving up or suffering defeats. The Conservative MPs gathered in the Commons and drank in its bars, ominously looking across the river at the enemy.

---

15 Edgar Wilson, *A Very British Miracle: The Failure of Thatcherism*, (Pluto Press 2013), p. 128.
16 Jonathan Aitken, *Margaret Thatcher: Power and Personality*, (Bloomsbury 2013), p. 275.

8

Nukes and Nicaragua

Among Labour circles even 30 years later it is a common refrain for a moderate councillor to remark 'we need to have policies that people can relate to ... not just bang on about things like Nicaragua.' In post-Kinnock Labour politics, 'Nicaragua' is a code, a cypher, a nudge and a wink, a knowing reference to the Labour councils of the 1980s and their overblown internationalist politics. Support by councillors for the embattled revolutionary Sandinistas in their fight against the CIA-backed Contras was seen as a ridiculous waste of time and tax payers' money. It seemed to epitomise the entire problem of the municipal left, that they were hopelessly ideological and out of touch. Others saw it as a natural extension of a kind of socialist, radical municipal agenda, helping the poor and using local government as a platform to raise the political issues of the day, not just relegation to bin collection and cracked pavements (important as those were). It should come as no surprise that one of the councils most associated with the Nicaragua Solidarity Campaign was Lambeth.

The Sandinista National Liberation Front had taken power in 1979 after President Anastasio Somoza Debayle was overthrown, ending 46 years of rule by the Somoza dictatorship. To appeal to their mass peasant and urban poor base, the Sandinistas had a broadly socialist programme and some commitment to resolving the huge inequality in the country over issues like land ownership and wealth. In the midst of the Cold War, the Sandinistas were portrayed as just another Communist menace in the USA's backyard. Right wing opposition militias sprung up, the Contras (from counter-revolutionaries), funded and trained by the CIA and US military. Nicaragua was plunged into a civil war, the global right backed the insurgent Contras and the global left backed the Sandinista government. The country also suffered an international economic boycott led by the USA. Nicaragua was a poor country, blighted by the usual crises of under-development that the west had inflicted on other states in Central America. This led to thousands of young radicals going to Nicaragua to 'help the revolution', just as many young socialists had gone to Yugoslavia in the 1950s because they were inspired by the workers' self-management movement. Given there was a life and death struggle for the revolution in Nicaragua, for left wing councillors it made sense to try and provide practical solidarity in whatever way they could.

Cllr Hazel Smith proposed twinning with the town of Bluefields in Nicaragua as an act of solidarity with the revolution. The original idea had come from representatives of the Latin American Community Project in the borough. Many of them were refugees, and they had asked Lambeth to show some solidarity with the plight of people in central America. The borough was already twinned with Vincennes in Paris and Moskvoretskiy District of Moscow in Russia (since World War II). Lambeth was the first local authority to twin with a Nicaraguan municipality; six others followed in the space of a year.[1] Bluefields was chosen largely because they spoke English, due to the large number of black Caribbean people who lived there. It was felt that there was a potential connection with Lambeth. Despite some local press outrage over what was perceived as a thoroughly political act, in fact twinning with Nicaraguan towns was Labour Party policy; Norwood CLP had proposed it to National Conference in 1983 and it had been adopted. By 1987 there were 20 local authorities twinned.

At the annual Lambeth Country Show in 1984 there was an official ceremony attended by Franciso D'Escote, the Nicaraguan ambassador. Above the councillors and signatories the French, Russian and Nicaraguan flags fluttered above the stage. Lambeth took the twinning seriously, it wasn't just a propaganda exercise. They appointed an officer to work on developing the twinning programme, which led to the sending of £1,500 of medical, educational and sports equipment, a medical student attending Bluefields Hospital to assess its needs, and a carpenter and a bricklayer working there for six months. But it wasn't just the Council, the initiative was also a big rallying point for the local union movement. NALGO agreed to ask the national union for funds to send a council officer (Giles Dolphin) to Bluefields from the planning department to share knowledge and experience; they also donated tools and raised money alongside the Trade's Council for medicines. UCATT also sent a grant of £100 for tools. The broadcast union ACTT sent two members to Nicaragua to assist with improving broadcasting facilities.

Inevitably, the international aspect of the councillors politics was low-hanging fruit for the newspapers. They lampooned their internationalist politics, describing the twinning projects as a waste of rate payers money. The *South London Press*, normally so accepting of the government cuts to local budgets launched a front page attack on Lambeth in August 1985 under

---

1   Oxford with Leon, Leicester with Masaya, Manchester with Puerto Cabezas, Sheffield with Esteli, Liverpool with Corinto and the GLC with Managa. The link was usually made according to an identifiable connection between the two towns, so Leicester and Masaya made shoes, Leon was a university town, just like Oxford and Corinto was a port as was Liverpool.

the headline "Trip of a lifetime: It's all abroad on the rates". They cited the cost (£5,800) of sending the mayor and his wife to Japan to attend a conference – for all civic leaders of nuclear free zones – on the anniversary of the Atomic bomb being dropped on Hiroshima, and the cost of sending Knight, Smith, Bowring and Amelda Inyang to Nicaragua, £11,500.[2] The *South London Press* ran the story alongside comparisons of how much the Lambeth Dial-A-Ride service would benefit from £17,000. Even when the councillors opted not to stay in a hotel but instead in a free government guest house they were still excoriated in the press for it.[3] Knight was jokingly referred to as 'Eduardo Noche' by the editor of the *South London Press*.[4] He met with Interior Minister Tomas Borge and Foreign Minister Nora Astorga who had become a "legend when she lured an enemy general to her bed during the revolution and had him killed by guerrillas."[5]

Smith defended the trip – she had been twice before at her own expense – "we have been working closely with the British Council and Oxfam on particular health projects for Bluefields."[6] Lambeth was prevented from donating any money to Bluefields by law, but they could facilitate British Council and NGO money for healthcare. There was also the matter of the 4,000 Latin Americans living in Lambeth, and the borough having the largest South American refugee population of anywhere in London, nearly 2,000 people. Most of them had fled from military and totalitarian dictatorships in central and South America. It wasn't that the Nicaragua solidarity actions were a diversion from the needs of the local population, they were a specific response to a particular part of the community. The people of Nicaragua had overthrown a dictatorship, so it was a symbol of hope for the region. Moreover there were historic political considerations that socialists had to consider; as Smith wrote in an internal memo to the Council: "Britain is a developed country because it actively 'under developed' Africa, Asia, West Indies and the Atlantic Coast… It's not just Charity that we owe – It's a debt."[7]

It is no wonder that with such hostile coverage the relations between the councillors and journalists was a cool one. On the trip to Nicaragua the Lambeth delegation was pursued by two *Daily Mail* reporters desperate to get the inside scoop on this outrageous internationalist profligacy.[8] Their pursuit of the councillors, whom they lost at the airport, ended badly when they were thrown into the swimming pool of the Intercontinental Hotel, where

---

2 Other local activists went on their own funds. When Greg Tucker, an activists in the Fourth International, flew to Bluefields he was very disconcerted to notice a hole in the side of the plane.
3 'A tale of two cities', *South London Press*, 30 August 1985, p. 6.
4 *South London Press*, 14 February 1986, p. 6.
5 'Knight's Weighty Matters', *South London Press*, 23 August 1985
6 'A tale of two cities', *South London Press*, 30 August 1985, p. 6.
7 'Twinning in solidarity: Lambeth - Bluefields', Lambeth Archives.
8 Interview with Joan Twelves, February 2016.

they were staying, the only Western hotel at that time in Managua following the earthquake of 1972 which destroyed much of the city.[9] The Lambeth delegation were staying elsewhere. Members of the delegation visited Bluefields, which was then under attack by Contras. The Americans wrongly believed that the black, Protestant population of Bluefields, most of whose links were with the Caribbean, would rise up against the Sandinistas. They were wrong. Shooting could be heard at night, and the Contra invaders were slaughtered. After flying by light plane into the jungle, the councillors could not use their usual mode of transport as the Contras had blown up the jetty for the boats. Instead they were taken by canoe on the Rio Escondido to Rama, where the road began, a day's journey through the rain forest, in danger of attack by Contras.

Yolanda Campbell, a Nicaraguan local politician thanked the delegation: "I am sorry there was controversy over the visit but it was an honour to receive you. The Lambeth people tried so hard to put into practice what most others just say, such as 'Love your neighbour'."[10] Stephen Bubb was very moved by the trip: "I have never seen poverty like it. ... When you visit a town such as Bluefields, you suddenly realise how lucky you really are." He was most taken aback at the total lack of any water sanitation system, the water came from wells that were contaminated with sewage. The town had a state of the art hospital but no one trained to use the equipment.[11]

In Lambeth the most vexatious complaints came from the particular issue of the poor quality of services whilst councillors were abroad expressing solidarity with a revolutionary movement in Central America. In real terms the cost of the trip, £11,000, was of course very little and certainly wouldn't have provided much extra for service delivery. Nevertheless, what was really at the heart of the controversy was competing values. The councillors, and Labour left more generally, saw themselves as internationalists who wanted to use their position to highlight important issues abroad and provide practical solidarity with a left wing government resisting a CIA backed coup. Others saw it as a colossal waste of time and energy when broken windows on estates were not being fixed for months on end.

But it wasn't just the councillors organising solidarity work. In the late 1980s enterprising local activists, led by Robert Todd, bought a dilapidated house in Tyres Street, Vauxhall, and started to do it up to sell on as a fundraising opportunity. Todd had been active around cooperative living in Bonnington Square, a group of houses saved from demolition and turned into a communal living space. Bonnington Square succeeded in developing into a radical alternative space with its own gardens, café and newsletter.

---

9   Ibid.
10 'I have never seen poverty like it before', *South London Press*, 20 September 1985, p. 6.
11 Ibid.

The house on Tyres Street was previously an old cobblers' shop and needed considerable work. Todd struck upon the idea of converting the premises into housing and selling it on. He turned up at the Lambeth Nicaragua Solidarity Campaign group with his ambitious idea and proceeded to recruit a small army of between 200 to 300 local people. The volunteers that renovated the house on behalf of the Nicaraguan revolution were largely women, providing training opportunities for female crafts and trades people. The radical journalist John Pilger helped to promote the initiative through the *New Statesman*. After years of work, the house was eventually sold in 1991 for £250,000, which was used to help fund women's organisations in Bluefields, including women's building cooperatives. In addition the campaign also lobbied the Council to buy two old dust carts from the refuse department, fix them up and send them over packed with supplies.

LAMBETH THE NUCLEAR FREE ZONE

The other controversial initiative by the Council related to the threat of nuclear war. In 1983, Lambeth was declared a 'nuclear free zone' by the Council.[12] This was seized on as an example of the kind of 'gesture politics' that the Labour right routinely criticised. For the Lambeth councillors and unions however, it was a point of principle based on their proximity to the potential epicentre of a nuclear blast. The Reagan administration had become more bellicose and was flexing its considerable military might. In late 1983 NATO conducted its infamous Able Archer exercise, simulating a nuclear attack by the Soviet Union. Earlier in the year the USA had assembled an armada of 40 ships to conduct military exercises near Soviet waters to study the response capabilities of the Warsaw Pact. Looking back a few years later USSR president Mikhail Gorbachev commented that: "Never, perhaps, in the post-war decades has the situation in the world been as explosive and more difficult and unfavourable as in the first half of the 1980s."

As an inner London borough, Lambeth had a real existential crisis during the Cold War. The government literature suggested that a nuclear bomb landing in Westminster would only affect 30% of the borough. Local Campaign for Nuclear Disarmament (CND) activists argued that the civil defence initiatives were part of whitewashing the true impact of a nuclear war, which was mutually assured destruction. A Lambeth NALGO Annual report argued that "There can be no realistic protection for the people of Lambeth in any nuclear war, and to suggest they can be, is to make people believe that they can survive any global conflagration, and acclimatise them is the possibility, even the inevitability of an horrific event."[13] A one megaton bomb dropped on St Paul's Cathedral would wipe out Lambeth, a similar

---

12 Peter Dickens, *One Nation?: Social Change and the Politics of Locality*, (Pluto 1988), p. 172.
13 Lambeth NALGO, *Annual Report 1984/85*, p. 34.

sized bomb dropped on Croydon would also exterminate the entire population of Lambeth. In July 1981 the Council passed a comprehensive motion aligning it politically with the aims of CND. From 1983 the government required local councils to make contingency civil defence plans in the event of a nuclear strike, but the councillors and local trade unions were implacably opposed to taking part – NALGO formally decided to instruct members not to take part in any drills or emergency planning.

By the middle of the decade the government had planned to spend only £9 million on civil defence, which a GLC pamphlet on the Greater London Area War Studies Risk concluded was "worthless against any likely nuclear attack."

But it wasn't just the waste of money on training and preparing evacuation plans and resource distribution in the event of the city being blasted by a volley of nuclear weapons from Russia that caused consternation. It was also the pervading sense of control and policing from the Thatcher government. Writing in the local trade union paper, activist Andrew Simpson argued against participation in the civil defence exercises, because the government's directives were simply "documents which determine how you and I will be shot, controlled, governed and otherwise assigned to the crematorium during pre and post-nuclear attack planning."[14] There was little faith that a Thatcher government would really protect the average citizen and many people refused to accept the official line that most people would be safe in the event of a nuclear attack as long as they put sandbags against their windows. After all, the types of nuclear warheads being deployed across Europe in the early 1980s were hundreds of times more powerful than the ones dropped on Hiroshima and Nagasaki.

Cllr Joan Whalley was the one most associated with the concept of publicly making the borough a Nuclear Free Zone. It was her idea to place the blue road signs dotted around the borough declaring "Welcome to Lambeth – a nuclear free zone". In fact, the nuclear free zone had practical implications. During the 1980s spent nuclear fuel from the Chatham Naval docks was transported through the borough via the railroad that ran directly through Tulse Hill and Brixton. Concerns were raised over a number of derailments of nuclear waste trains and the potential impact of an irradiated flask landing in the middle of Brixton. If shoppers buying vegetables at the Atlantic Road market place had cared to look up as one of the trains trundled overhead they would have seen nuclear waste from Germany making its way through the centre of the capital. By the 1990s similar trains with potentially deadly cargoes were winding their way through Clapham as well.

---

14 'March for our future', *The Cutlet*, no. 132, 11 February 1982, p. 5.

9

Rate-capping and the Second Front...

> It is highly unlikely that the government will make a Clay Cross martyr of Ted Knight and his colleagues
> Editorial, *South London Press*, 30 May 1979

The showdown over rates had of course been ongoing since the cut in the support grant. Whilst the main attack line in the media was against 'profligacy' the real ideological drive was to ensure that there could be no real constitutional power outside of Parliament. For all the talk of stripping away red tape, local government was being restructured to significantly increase the level of supervision and checking by unelected officers over councillors. Thatcherism was a strengthening of aspects of the state whilst claiming to be rolling it back.

The possibility of setting rates on behalf of local councils was initially raised in 1982, before being formally proposed to the electorate in the Conservative manifesto for the 1983 general election. The manifesto outlined the motivation and the means to limit the spending powers of select local councils: There existed

> a number of grossly extravagant Labour authorities whose exorbitant rate demands have caused great distress both to business and domestic ratepayers. We shall legislate to curb excessive and irresponsible rate increases by high-spending councils, and to provide a general scheme for limitation of rate increases for all local authorities to be used if necessary.

Further on they pledged,

> The Metropolitan Councils and the Greater London Council have been shown to be a wasteful and unnecessary tier of government. We shall abolish them and return most of their functions to the boroughs and districts.[1]

---

[1] Conservatve Party General Election Manifestos, 1900-1997 (Routledge 2000), p. 304.

The 1983 election victory sealed the fate of local government. Convinced that Thatcher had the absolute mandate she needed, and certainly not afraid of Labour opposition in parliament, her government was ready to end the municipal socialist experiment once and for all. An indication of how seriously she took the "urban left" was revealed in her Carlton Lecture delivered on 26 November 1984, just months after the IRA bombed Tory Party conference. Thatcher outlined her thinking on the threat to society from 'extremism': "At one end of the spectrum are the terrorist gangs within our borders, and the terrorist states which finance and arm them. At the other end are the hard left operating inside our system, conspiring to use union power and the apparatus of local government to break, defy and subvert the law."[2] Placing the local government left and Arthur Scargill along the same spectrum as the IRA demonstrated quite clearly the intensity of the Conservatives fear and hatred.

The Rate Act itself was designed to impose a limit on the powers of councils and regional bodies to raise local funds. If the Rate Act was made law then it would be the first time since 1601 that local government could not set their own rates. Instead the Secretary of State could identify 'high spending' councils and control their finances in a way that many suspected would be used in a partisan manner against Labour run councils. Like a lot of the key proposals that came to characterise the Thatcher era, whilst the bill was voted through parliament it did not command complete support from the ruling party, or their allies. It was opposed by 26 Tories, and the *Financial Times* and *The Times* newspapers both ran editorials against the proposed new law.[3] But this was a strategic consideration for the government – they had to implement it no matter the protests from the 'wets' in the establishment.

But what infuriated the Labour councils was the lack of transparency and accountability. Why had they been selected and not others? Why had the rate cap been set at the level it had been? The Environment Secretary, Patrick Jenkin, talked about formulas but none were revealed to the rate-capped authorities. It was clear that this was a politically motivated attack. Allegations of 'exorbitant rate demands' had of course been a key part of the local Tories election campaign in the 1982 local elections.

Lambeth knew it was going to be one of the first up before the firing squad. There could be a high personal cost for public opposition. The Rate Act was backed up by the 1982 Local Government Finance Act which gave District Auditors extensive powers to investigate councils, impose personal fines (surcharges), and disqualify councillors if they were deemed to have acted improperly, so-called 'wilful misconduct'. This was considered a

---

2 Quoted in Hugo Young, *One of Us: A Biography of Margaret Thatcher* (London 1989), p. 373.
3 Eric J. Evans, *Thatcher and Thatcherism* (Routledge 1997), p. 46.

'shackle' on local councillors, and to step "outside these limits brings punishment that no other elected person would tolerate."[4]

Having their rate levels imposed would remove one of the last weapons in the Council's box to maintain spending on services at the level they believed necessary. It had to be opposed by any means necessary. Now the fourth poorest borough in the country was about to go toe-to-toe with Thatcher and Heseltine.

THE IMPACT ON LAMBETH

The initial proposal for Lambeth was to cap their rates at a level that would have led to around a £13 million deficit in the councils planned budget for the year 1984/85. In some ways, however, the cuts to Lambeth's budget were not as excessive as others. Rate Capping in Lambeth would have reduced the rates by 12%, half as much as Southwark, where the rate cap would have brought them down by 25%. For that year the Lambeth proposed budget was £126 million, but if the rates were limited by central government then the budget would have been reduced to £101 million.[5]

These cuts were being imposed at a time when the structural unemployment of the 1980s had taken deep root in communities. The Council's figures showed that unemployment in Lambeth had risen from 9,000 in 1979 to 25,000 by 1985.[6] This was in areas already blighted with racist recruitment bias and generational cycles of poverty. The Labour councillors had come in promising to use their political power to leverage jobs, more funds and grants for their area, instead they were faced with never ending cycles of cuts and austerity.

The local press reported on the unemployment crisis in the borough. "More than forty people are chasing every job vacancy in Lambeth. Latest figures show that there are 23,645 unemployed in the borough – up 4 per cent on the previous month. And of all the youngsters out of work, 52 per cent have been on the dole for more than six months." Lambeth had 18 per cent unemployment – one of the highest in London and nearly 5% above the national average.[7]

It was with such figures in mind that the Labour Councillors moved into battle with the Conservative Government. Conference voted to endorse actions by the councillors to defy the law. This was a significant victory, the first time (certainly in living memory) that a Labour conference had ever endorsed illegal action by Labour Party members.

Knight and his councillors knew that they needed wider support across the labour movement to win. The rate-capped Labour Councils also saw it as

---

4 *Battle for Lambeth*, 1986, p. 3.
5 Cited in a pamphlet produced in 1984 from the Office of the Leader of Lambeth Council titled *How Much?*
6 Cited in *West Indian World*, 12 June 1985.
7 *South London Press*, 4 March 1983.

an opportunity to open up a 'second front' in the fight against Thatcher. As moves were put in place to fight the rate-capping, the national miners' strike was getting under way. Livingstone recalled how Knight pitched it: 'They can't fight us and the Miners. We can bring down Thatcher and then anything can happen".[8] The town halls would become the battleground of the second front. In an article in *Labour Briefing* in March 1985, John McDonnell, the deputy leader of the GLC, marshalled the troops: "The London Labour Party's Regional Conference on rate-capping urged Labour councils in London to take on the Government and not to set a rate. If London's Labour councils stood together in defiance of the Government's demands for cuts there would be a major constitutional crisis which would make Poplar and Clay Cross look like minor skirmishes."[9]

Thatcher was thinking the same thing. In a private meeting for Tory MPs in July 1984 her speakers notes made clear her views: "Enemies within. Miners' leaders. Liverpool and some local authorities."[10] As far as she was concerned, this was a war for the soul of Britain and the power of parliamentary authority and sovereignty.

SOLIDARITY WITH THE MINERS

As the miners walked out of their pits across the country in March 1984, it was clear that the much anticipated showdown with the Thatcher administration was finally on. Lambeth's trade unions swung into action to start to build support for their comrades in places like Kent, Yorkshire and South Wales. Fundraising was crucial; the government has sequestered the NUM's funds and assets, including their benevolence fund which was intended to alleviate suffering for elderly and sick miners. The NUM were clear that this was daylight robbery and politically motivated. The government thought this was a revolutionary war to bring them down, the miners knew it was a battle of survival.

The act of solidarity, throwing yourself into a do or die strike like that, had a profound impact on local activists. Committing yourself to that cause, dedicating yourself to it, shaped the left's outlook for a whole generation. As the strike went on and people travelled to the pit villages and lived with the families, fought alongside them on the picket lines, that was something that couldn't be forgotten. In Lambeth the local Trades Council, the various socialist groups, women's organisations, and black activist organisations all came together in a moment of unity to support the strike in any way they could.

Local black campaigners also provided forums for the (overwhelmingly white) miners. When the Brixton Defence Campaign organised an event at

---

8   Ken Livingstone, *If Voting Changed Anything, They'd Abolish It*, p. 315.
9   'Open up the second front!', *Labour Briefing*, March 1985, p. 9.
10 Cited in Andy McSmith, *No Such Thing as Society: A History of Britain in the 1980s* (Constable 2011), p. 164.

the Ritzy to celebrate the third anniversary of the Brixton uprising, among the films (*Bob Marley in Exodus* and *The Harder They Come,* directed by Perry Henzell) and poets, they hosted speakers from Sinn Fein, the Newham 7 defence campaign, and a striking Nottingham Miner. Black activists protesting police violence saw a direct connection between their struggle and the brutal militarised violence against the NUM picket lines, and the illegal roadblocks and restrictions on people's right to free movement felt all too bitterly familiar to people in Brixton. A coalition of groups organised a solidarity rally at County Hall in December 1984 alongside speakers from Sinn Fein and the Palestine Liberation Organisation:

> MINERS MUST WIN
> NO PIT CLOSURES
> NO JOB LOSSES
> AS BLACK PEOPLE WE KNOW WHAT IT IS TO BE
>   UNDER SEIGE AS A COMMUNITY
> AS BLACK PEOPLE WE KNOW WHAT STATE
>   VIOLENCE IS
> AS BLACK PEOPLE WE KNOW WHAT IS
>   UNEMPLOYMENT
> OUR STRUGGLE, MINERS STRUGGLE IS THE SAME
> MINERS COMPLETE VICTORY IS OUR VICTORY
> MINERS DEFEAT IS NOT ONLY OUR DEFEAT BUT
>   DEFEAT OF ALL WORKERS
> THE EXPERIENCE OF IRISH PEOPLE, BLACK PEOPLE
>   AND THE MINERS ARE SAME[11]

Labour Party Young Socialists (LPYS) supporters from the colleges also went out to raise money during the day, which they could only do for about an hour before being moved on by the local police. Nevertheless they regularly raised around £100. The miners were treated like royalty by most of the left. In the bar in the Town Hall they were given free beer whenever they wanted. One trade unionist felt that there was too much of a culture clash: "London was so different from South Wales and perhaps it was the wrong thing to invite miners into this environment for long periods. Some I believe never went home."[12] Others spoke about how some of the young men from the pit villages were dazzled by the bright lights: "some of them met girls and stayed in London. Especially when the strike was over they just didn't go back, they felt like what was the point?"[13]

A local feminist organisation, Lambeth Women's Support Group, and local activists within Women Against Pit Closures sought to reach out to

---

[11] Leaflet from Brixton Defence Campaign, Black Cultural Archives GUTZMORE/1, *circa* 1984.
[12] Interview with Ed Hall, October 2015.
[13] Ibid.

women in the mining communities. In an interview with *Spare Rib*, one local woman activist explained that, "what else would have brought together women from mining villages and London feminists, giving us access to each other's different ways of life?"[14]

Naturally, the Labour councillors were fully supportive of the strike. The council gave the miners an office with phone lines to coordinate local efforts. Postal worker Noel Hannon used his position as chair of the Licensing Committee to procure a market stall in Brixton where they raised large sums. They asked council workers to voluntarily have money deducted from their wages to go towards the strike fund, which many did.[15] All told, the Lambeth Miners Support Group raised around £200,000 for the strike in its first nine months.

At the start of the strike different organisations and union branches invited NUM delegates to visit them on an *ad hoc* basis. As the strike went on the NUM wanted to organise the fundraising more efficiently, so they twinned different regions with specific places. Lambeth was formally twinned with Betwys Colliery near Ammanford, South Wales. The movie, *Pride*, recounts the culture shock for the Welsh Miners as the young activists from Lesbian and Gays Support the Miners (LGSM) turned up in their villages and had to overcome quite profound cultural differences. The joint feelings of solidarity, of struggle against a common enemy, helped overcome any lingering prejudice.

The experience of coming to Lambeth affected the miners too. Miners came from South Yorkshire and Kent to argue for solidarity with the strike and raise funds. Before speaking at packed meetings across the borough, the miners and their socialist allies would head to Brixton tube station to collect money in buckets. Local folk would shake the hands of the miners whilst apologising that they were unable to contribute much to the strike fund because they were unemployed. Then they would go to the post office on Ferndale Road to cash their giros and force a £5 note into the bucket on the way back.[16] One of the Militant activists who took part in the local fundraising, Steve Nally, still felt tearful recounting the selflessness even 30 years later. Many of the Yorkshire miners were used to village life or living in small towns which were far more routine than living in a place like Lambeth. They also had well-paid jobs, their own homes and pensions, indeed that is what their strike, the defence of their communities and livelihoods, was all about. When a group of miners were taken around the Ethelred estate to raise money and saw the local kids, some of them without shoes on, it took them aback. These were men from communities who had known hardship, due to the terrible conditions of a life worked underground, but there was

---

14 Diarmaid Kelliher, Constructing Alliances: Why my Research on the Miner's Strike Solidarity Movement Matters, History Workshop, October 13, 2014. *Spare Rib* was a radical feminist publication between 1972-1993.
15 southwalesguardian.co.uk/news/18279721.end-miners-strike-remembered-35-years/
16 Interview with Steve Nally, August 2017.

something about the poverty of an inner London estate that was affected them deeply, more so how readily the long-term unemployed willingly gave them what change they had. Some sat in tears in the local pub afterward, others in a grim silence, thinking about their own lives, their families back home in Yorkshire, what it meant to be poor in inner London and still give money to striking workers from communities hundreds of miles away.[17]

A number of those miners and their wives and girlfriends also came to Lambeth, staying with the local black population, speaking at meetings organised by the Trades Council to predominantly black local workforces in local government and local industry. These miners had heard all kinds of scare stories about Lambeth, about black muggers, about the 1981 riot and alleged 'no go areas' for whites. Lambeth NALGO activist Simon Berlin recounted how he had gone with some miners to Notting Hill Carnival:

> They had never been to London before, and they said they would remember the day for the rest of their lives – because it was the spirit of unity and harmony on that day that was the urban expression of the life they knew in their own villages, and the miners were a natural and feted component at the carnival, because the miners' strike and the carnival expressed the same aspirations, a Britain that we all want but which is being denied us by Thatcher and her associates.[18]

It was also clearer after Orgreave that the police violence against inner-city young blacks was part of the same struggle as the miners faced against police violence. The government was at war with these communities; broken bones, broken heads, and mass arrests were all part of the conflict. That both the miners and the Brixton Defence Committee invoked the language of 'self-defence is no offence' was part of a shared fight against both police incursions into their community and self-defence on a picket line to preserve the integrity of the strike from scabs and their police escorts.

It wasn't just about the racism of the police, the strike also brought the question of resistance from gays and lesbians to the fore. Lambeth Town Hall hosted a meeting of LGSM in January 1985, chaired by Ray Goodspeed, with Stuart Holland MP and Ali Thomas from Dulais Miners Support Group (who Lesbians and Gays Support the Miners had twinned with) speaking. Thomas praised efforts of LGSM saying the miners "have a common struggle with lesbians, gays and other minorities… Particularly you people know about fighting."[19] There was widespread applause as he saluted the struggle of people against the state oppression that both they and the

---

17 Ibid.
18 Diarmaid Kelliher, 'Networks of solidarity: the London left and the 1984-85 miners' strike' in E. Smith (ed.), *Waiting for the revolution: The British far left from 1956*, (Manchester University Press 2017).
19 *Capital Gay*, 25th January 1985.

miners faced. Holland made links with how the police treated the gay community, including the use of 'pretty police' – young male undercover officers who would hang out at the Royal Vauxhall Tavern and other places so they could arrest homosexuals under the 1824 Vagrancy Act for 'importuning for immoral purposes'. This outdated law had been intended to stop men harassing showgirls after performances and was no longer used, apart from as an excuse to harass gay men. It wasn't just the local black community that was being targeted under obsolete laws from 100 years ago. Holland publicly argued for the right to self-organisation and defence against police harassment.

In such a highly politicised struggle, collections for the miner's were not without risk. In early 1985 there was a coordinated clampdown by the police on collections. At one point members of Lambeth Trades Council were arrested whilst collecting money and charged under the 1916 Police, Factories etc. (Miscellaneous Provisions) Act after the Council arranged for them to visit residents and local workers to collect funds.[20] In other parts of London activists were detained for begging under the 1824 Vagrancy Act and had their funds confiscated. A number of Lambeth activists went up to the large protest in February 1985 in Whitehall, where police charged the crowd, arrested 131 people and broke a demonstrators leg, some argued deliberately. "Orgreave comes to Whitehall" was how participants described it. It was clear the police were out to break the strike and break the supporters of the strike.[21]

One of the leaders of this young radical queer movement was buried in Lambeth. Mark Ashton, who helped to set up LGSM who was featured in *Pride*, a gay communist, a leader of the Young Communist League (they left that out of the film), died aged 26 of pneumonia brought on by AIDS in February 1987. He was buried just over the border in Streatham Cemetery, hundreds of supporters gathered around the grave, miners and communists and radicals of all stripes, holding red, pink and rainbow flags alongside the miners' union banners. James Somerville of The Communards, in the vanguard of out and proud gay singers in the mid-80s, wrote the song, *For a Friend*, after Ashton died:

> I never cried the way I cried over you
> As I put down the telephone and the world it carried on[22]

THE SECOND FRONT

It was the militancy and seriousness of the miners' strike that provided the backdrop to the rate-capping dispute. In July 1984, the Labour Local

---

20 Paul Charman, 'Miners and the Met', *Time Out*, 19-25 July 1984, p. 7.
21 'Orgreave Comes to Whitehall', *Commentator*, March 1985. Cited in D. Kelliher, 'Contested spaces: London and the 1984-5 miners' strike', *Twentieth Century British History*, 28(4), 2017.
22 *For a Friend* by The Communards, from the album *Red* (London Records 1987).

Government Conference met in Sheffield and planned how to resist the Westminster instructions and the inevitable cuts that would ensue. There were two principle reasons why they felt confident enough to take on Thatcher; the first was that they were meeting in the middle of the miners' strike. The miners had brought down Heath and might bring down Thatcher, now seemed like an excellent time to join the fight. The conference was held just after the battle of Orgreave, one of the key moments of the miners' strike which had been ongoing since March. Militancy was in the air. Also in attendance were councillors from Liverpool. Though they were not being capped, they were in an ongoing dispute over the support grant.[23] The Labour councillors were particularly inspired by the actions of their Liverpool comrades who had just been handed an additional grant of £20 million by central government. They did this after holding out for several months, refusing to set a rate, and demanding more money to fund urgently needed local services. In the wave of action taking place, it seemed like the Thatcher juggernaut was finally vulnerable.

Labour Councils affected by the rate-cap hammered out a strategy: "The choice before Labour councils was presented starkly – defiance or compliance. Several options for defiance were aired, including mass resignations, majority opposition, deficit budgeting (setting a legal rate but with a higher 'no cuts' budget) or refusing to set a rate."[24] The proposal by Knight was for local councils jointly refuse to set a rate and carry on with their previous budget spending plans. The question was, who would buckle first, the councillors or central government?

Militant Tendency representatives from Liverpool Council proposed putting in place a 'needs budget' – effectively an unbalanced or illegal budget. This would have allowed them, in practice, to demonstrate to voters that they wanted to spend money on their residents and force the hand of the government, effectively making them decide if they wanted social workers to go unpaid. Needs budgets would be partially based on how much money the councils could raise and how much they had in reserve. This meant that some councils would be faced with a showdown with central government before others. Lambeth and other London councils preferred a fight around not setting the rates, which was something that could be done together. The deficit spending approach was supported by the soft left who thought it bought more time, but Knight and his supporters considered it a fudge. The key issue was the principle of councils being able to set their own rates, something that had been in place since the start of the 17th century.

It was agreed that the strategy would be for all councils and metropolitan authorities to defer setting their rates and to continue budget spending at previously agreed levels, in other words with no cuts. Deferring rate setting

---

23 Andy McSmith, *Faces of Labour: The Inside Story* (Verso 1997), p. 163.
24 Stewart Lansley, Sue Goss, Christian Wolmar, *Councils in Conflict: The Rise and Fall of the Municipal Left* (Macmillan 1989), p. 35.

wasn't considered illegal *per se*, though it would, sooner or later, lead to a clash with central government, but of course that was the whole point. Whilst deferring the rate setting the councils would lobby for more money from central government. At the Labour Local Government conference in July 1984 the no-rate option of 'non-compliance' was supported enthusiastically.[25]

On 19 January 1985 there was a special London Labour Party conference on rate-capping. (Of the 18 rate-capped authorities, there was the GLC, ILEA and nine others which were London boroughs). Hackney argued for unbalanced budgets rather than setting no rate but couldn't convince the other councillors so were heavily defeated. An amendment calling for recognition for a left-wing led cross union organisation called London Bridge appeared to be passed on a show of hands, but the NUPE delegation demanded a card vote and got it defeated. Sheffield Council Leader David Blunkett was in a fighting mood at the conference: "Our authorities and the trade unions are totally united behind the stand taken of non-compliance… today we made it clear that, whatever the government says, we are not going to be divided. No authority will try and get itself off the hook by accepting deals from the government individually."[26]

Kinnock told the 1984 party conference that, "We cannot sharpen legality as our main weapon for the future and simultaneously scorn legality because it doesn't suit us at the present time".[27] This became the mantra of the Labour right. Kinnock himself had been clear that there should be no 'illegal' actions taken by the party since, as a prospective party of government, it had to respect the legislation from Westminster. As one biographer described it: "*law*-breaking was anathema to *Kinnock's* philosophy, and in a speech to *Labour* councillors in Birmingham in February 1985, he urged them not to resort to gesture politics and risk losing office: Better a dented shield than no shield at all."[28] Knight denounced Kinnock's words as "totally inadequate and out of touch with the rank and file".[29] He articulated the perspective of *Labour Briefing* and the more radical wings of the party "It has always been a principle in the labour movement that a law that operates against the interests of our class is a law we are not required to obey."[30] In the words of the Poplar struggle: better to break the law than break the poor. *Tribune*, the journal of the soft left, was more sanguine, reporting in late January 1985 that "Labour local government leaders and trade unionists emerged from meeting Neil Kinnock on Monday cautiously optimistic that

---

25 *Illusions of power* pamphlet.
26 Cited in Peter Taaffe and Peter Mulhearn, *Liverpool : A City that dared to fight*, (Socialist Books 2017).
27 Andy McSmith, *Faces of Labour*, p. 164.
28 Eileen Jones, *Neil Kinnock* (Robert Hale Ltd 1994), p. 72.
29 'Illusions of Power', *Socialist Organiser*, 1985, p. 17.
30 *Municipal Journal*, 21 June 1985.

the party leadership will back their campaign against rate-capping".[31] Yet, a few lines later, the same article commented: "There was a clash between Mr. Kinnock and Lambeth's Ted Knight and Liverpool's Deputy Leader Derek Hatton, when Mr. Kinnock warned that it would be impossible to turn back Tory allegations of illegality if councillors' call for defiance of the law for its own sake. There will be no pledge of indemnity for surcharged councillors."[32]

The level of support (or not) from the wider party would to a large extent determine whether the local government resistance could be generalised to a level that would force a constitutional crisis. Without clear support councils and councillors risked being isolated. This was a factor in convincing many local councillors, who were worried about being surcharged, to accept the option of setting a rate. The danger was clear though – Kinnock's approach to the miners strike veered between lukewarm to outright hostility and the local government hard left knew that they would face the threat of a leadership clampdown sooner or later. This fear had a profound impact on the soft left allies that they needed to rally to win the votes in the Council chambers.

Despite conference resolutions and some lukewarm words in the media, there was clearly a cool wind blowing from Labour HQ on Walworth Road. In his memoirs, the Minister for Local Government, Kenneth Baker (who had been brought in to 'deal' with the left in local government) claimed his Labour opposite, Jack Cunningham, had told him that Labour would not support people like Derek Hatton and were happy to let the 'loony left' London council leaders "twist in the wind".[33] With friends like that, the Lambeth councillors didn't need any enemies. It also gave the Tories a green light to mow down the fragile left opposition in the council chambers.

Locally the Labour Councillors encountered determined opposition from their rival Conservative Councillors. In the month before the rate setting meeting, Lambeth deployed a campaign bus to drive around the borough with a loud hailer and distribute leaflets to explain the council's position. On one occasion Hazel Smith was accosted by Tory Councillor Charles Williams who boarded the bus on Clapham Road and tried to grab the microphone from her. A tussle saw Williams sit on the floor of the bus and refuse to move. Smith described him as "extremely aggressive and totally out of control".[34] Another Tory Councillor, Bob Parker, was caught tearing down council notices throughout Clapham which asked residents for feedback on rate capping. A Council spokesperson warned that they would wire some of the signs up to the mains in the lampposts to prevent tampering; "We won't

---

31 *Tribune*, 25 January 1985.
32 Ibid.
33 Kenneth Baker, *The Turbulent Years: My Life in Politics* (Faber and Faber 1993) p. 108.
34 *South London Press*, 12 February 1985.

say which signs are live. Councillor Parker will find out when 2000 volts go through him."[35]

ILEA AND GLC ABANDON THE FIELD

A short bus ride from Brixton to the north of the borough, the rate-capping fight at the GLC was about to begin. At the palatial GLC Headquarters, John McDonnell, the deputy leader and head of GLC finance, was marshalling the troops for the showdown with Thatcher. Deferring the rate was the agreed upon strategy as McDonnell argued it. But behind the scenes the debate in the Labour Group showed that things were far from unanimous. Livingstone was concerned that, as a Metropolitan Authority, they had a legal requirement to set their rates by a certain date, whereas the councils could operate in more of a grey area. He was given a way forward by GLC Director-General Maurice Stonefrost, who sent a briefing around the Councillors outlining how they could set the government imposed rate as well as make no cuts.

McDonnell clashed with GLC leader Ken Livingstone over how to go forward. McDonnell favoured delaying the rates, referred to as 'going illegal', which was the agreed strategy of the rate capped councillors. Livingstone was unconvinced that the strategy would work and suspected that McDonnell was presenting a doomsday scenario of £138 million in cuts to force the GLC Labour group to stand up to Thatcher.

In the run up to the March budget-setting meetings, Livingstone had what he described as an "explosive row" with Knight. Livingstone knew that the GLC had a fiduciary responsibility to set a budget when it was supposed to, whereas the councils had some leeway (or so they argued). After Livingstone stormed out Knight chased after him, trying to calm the situation. He squeezed Livingstone's arm and reassured him, "Trust me Ken, we're all going illegal together. I promise you there's no backsliding. They can't fight us and the miners. We can bring Thatcher down and then anything is possible."[36]

The Labour right began a frantic campaign to pressure councillors to vote to set a rate, saying that their careers would be finished if they fell on their sword over this. Cllr Sharon Atkin got a phone call from Janet Boateng one night, very distressed that her husband Paul Boateng, a GLC Councillor and previously leader of the 'Scrap the sus' campaign, was getting leaned on and might buckle. For their part the left had its own frantic phone calls to make to wavering GLC councillors to bolster their resolve.[37] In the run-up to the budget meetings the strategy for the left councils was subtly but crucially changed, from "going illegal" and setting unbalanced budgets to only

---

35 *South London Press*, 22 March 1986.
36 Ken Livingstone, *If Voting Changed Anything They'd Abolish It*, p. 315.
37 Interview with Sharon Atkin, October 2017.

deferring the setting of the rates. This came about because of pressure from some councils who said they didn't have enough of a majority for an unbalanced budget but did for deferring. The battle lines shifted as the left retreated to a more 'realistic' position.

On the 7th March the GLC met to vote on its rate. Outside a sizeable demonstration had gathered. The day was also part of the TUC's 'democracy day' protests across the country in defence of local government financial autonomy. The meeting failed to agree a rate, much to the cheers of the people assembled in the gallery and the left councillors. However a recall meeting was agreed for Sunday 10 March, the final day before the rate had to be legally set. News had reached the GLC councillors by that time that the ILEA had agreed to set a rate at their meeting. At this point the campaign began to unravel like a cheap suit.

Despite his earlier bombastic attacks on rate-capping, Livingstone began to lose heart. He worked behind the scenes to undermine the left minority on the GLC, helping Labour Councillors Mike Ward and Barry Stead, who wanted to use creative accounting to propose a legal budget with no cuts whilst agreeing to the rate cap, to win a majority of the votes at the recall meeting.[38] The argument was that a rate could be set below the government imposed limit and no cuts would be made, which was a win for the GLC and London more generally. Livingstone led the way in arguing that the 'no rates' position was flawed at the time that the New Urban Left was trying to hold the line against wavering colleagues. It took 23 hours of meetings over that whole weekend to debate whether to set a rate or not.

McDonnell was furious. For the left it was a principle, a united front against the Tories to challenge the government. He knew that GLC councillors faced more legal pressure than the local government elected members, but the GLC was also a bastion of the left, a fortress of resistance across the river from Parliament. He knew the damage that would be done so early in the rate-capping campaign if the GLC and ILEA folded so quickly. Soon afterwards he was forced out of his job as deputy and replaced by Mike Ward as Livingstone began a *rapprochement* with the Kinnock camp. McDonnell and Livingstone didn't speak to each other for years.

Within weeks, Livingstone was interviewed in *Marxism Today*, the favourite magazine for left-wingers desperate to move right towards the "new realism." He concluded that there was simply no basis for popular support for the rate-capping campaign: "They've discussed it endlessly in some boroughs like Lambeth and Ted Knight's addressed endless mass meetings of workers. People assume if they're rushing around doing all these things that it's actually producing something, and that if you just talk to workers long enough somehow it's going to create a base that you can then mobilise".[39]

---

38 Ken Livingstone, *If Voting Changed Anything They'd Abolish It*, p. 322.
39 *Marxism Today*, interview with Ken Livingstone, May 1985, p. 8.

He also thought the left that were hanging on were deluding themselves, and only motivated by their own principles, unable to command other forces: "Phil Turner of Camden, I think it was, proposed that they should bring together all the affected councillors in London, about 350-400. Ted Knight actually argued very strongly – and I only found this out quite recently – that it would be disastrous because if they all could see where we were going they most likely will want to get out right now. And so there was a quite cynical attempt on the part of some of them to say well we don't want a debate because we know we won't hold it when the crunch comes."[40]

Livingstone concludes with a salve to his own conscience that the debate was far more nuanced than the left gave credit for: "I think John [McDonnell] and Ted's mistake was simply to perceive that what they were operating with was fear on the part of some councillors and if they just upped the ante, they'd force them to stand firm. That overlooked the strong element of principle in both wings of the party in this debate. It wasn't all the heroic people on one side, and scabs and traitors on the other."[41]

At the next Executive meeting a motion of censure was proposed against Livingstone. But McDonnell was absent from the meeting, apparently too angry to attend, and the motion fell. Knight voted for the motion but urged the comrades to "bury the rotting corpse" and move on in support of the councils that still wanted to fight.

But there was a much more serious problem looming. By February 1985 it had become clear that the nearly year long miners' strike was coming to an end and would likely go down to defeat. After so much solidarity work and political struggle to bolster their strike, the defeat was a huge strategic crisis. The miners had brought down Heath – they were the Grenadier Guards Regiment of the British working class. All hopes were pinned on them delivering the death blow to Thatcher's politics. The decline of the strike and the growing rout of miners returning to work had a huge impact on the morale of the left, but the soft left in particular. The entire campaign had been argued on the basis of 'two fronts', the local government left and the miners side by side in battle. But despite heroic efforts the first front had collapsed. Without the 200,000 miners and their huge solidarity movement behind them, the Labour councillors suddenly felt very isolated in their chambers. Perhaps if the Labour left had given a stronger lead and made it clear that they were going into the same life and death battle as the National Union of Miners then they could have bolstered the strike a few more months to really cause a crisis for the government. But as it was the miners suspected that the rate-capping dispute simply didn't have the energy or determination to win. On 3 March they voted to return to work. A notoriously dark day for the British labour movement.

---

40 Ibid.
41 Ibid.

WE WILL FIGHT THEM IN THE COUNCIL CHAMBERS...

Despite the defeat of the NUM, the Labour councillors in Lambeth knew they had to carry on the fight. There was too much at stake now to give up. On the 7 March the Councillors of Lambeth gathered for the annual budgetary and rate setting meeting. A large crowd had gathered outside the town hall waving NALGO and SWP placards: "Blame Thatcher not Knight" among other slogans. Inside the Council Chamber was decked with union banners, from the AUEW, NALGO, London Bridge and others. It was designed to intimidate the Tory councillors, to show them the breadth of local opposition. The left made their arguments clear so there could be no doubt of their intentions, the motion before the Council declared that the Rates Act was "an undemocratic means of controlling local spending by the Central Government and represents a fundamental attack on local democracy."[42] The council needed £134 million whereas the maximum resources then being made available to rate-capped Lambeth was £116.13 million – £17.89 million less than what was needed. The Tories proposed a rate which was defeated, to cheers from the public gallery. After the meeting Cllr Terry Rich went onto the balcony outside the Town Hall and gave an impromptu speech to the crowd assembled, Cllr John O'Malley recalled it had the air of a presidential address about it. The crowd reacted with cheers. This was the moment that all the promises of the left councillors would be tested.

Beside the defection of Livingstone and the ILEA, the campaign began smoothly with all the councils refusing to set a budget. The Lambeth Council meeting was rowdy, with Tories shouting at the Labour councillors as they got up to make their speeches about why they would not be setting a rate. Outside thousands of people gathered, banners from trade unions and community groups unfurled above the local residents. It was a protest showing a broad alliance of different people of the borough, the black community, young radicals, and lesbians and gays all gathered. People that were mobilised in miners' support groups saw this as the next logical step in the struggle. A young woman with a T-shirt emblazoned with the Leninist query 'what is to be done?' posing outside the Town Hall doors. Young '80s punks and new romantics rubbed shoulders.

Elsewhere the campaign began to flounder. By the end of March Thamesdown, Leicester and Manchester had set their rates. The remaining councillors were not particularly worried about these early losses, as these had been the weaker councils and not played much of a role in deciding the strategy of the campaign. Still, it established a worrying precedent that already some were peeling away and surrendering to Heseltine.

---

42 T. P. B. Rattenbury, *Public Law within Government: Sustaining the Art of the Possible* (Palgrave MacMillan 2008), p. 134.

The first serious blow was in Lewisham in south London. Lewisham was taken out of the fight by a Tory trick. In early April when the council meeting was disrupted by a trade union protest, the Conservative Councillors saw their chance and struck. As the Labour councillors left the chamber to remove themselves from the protest, they ended up in another room. They waited for an hour before returning to the hall, only to find that the Conservative councillors had convened in their absence and voted for a legal rate.[43] There was a hue and cry as the Labour members argued the decision was out of order and had no legal basis, but they were advised by Council officers that the decision was a constitutional one.

Given all the pressures from the media and the government, it was only a matter of time before strong winds blew off loose leaves on the Lambeth Labour group. So it was at the 10 April council meeting when Labour Councillor Stuart Cakebread was the first to break ranks, urging his Labour colleagues to set a rate and end the campaign. The following day the screws began to tighten further as the DHSS was the first government department to write to the Town Hall explaining that they would withhold rate rebate subsidy because no rate had been set.

Once again the Chief Executive wrote to the government appealing for a meeting. The government was clear that they were not prepared to meet with "an unrepresentative group" of councillors, but would receive deputation on issues that affected the borough.[44] From Knight's point of view the implicit message was that the government couldn't be seen to give in to left councils but might make concessions through what appeared to be the usual government-council channels of communication. Pursuing the usual channels, Lambeth asked for nine categories of expenditure to be disregarded for their Rate Support Grant, but all categories were rejected.

At the end of April, Haringey was taken out of the fight by the leader of the Labour group, George Meehan, splitting his party and voting with the Tories to set a rate. The majority of the Labour group who still backed the rate-capping fight were furious with the splitters. Meehan had to step down, being replaced by Bernie Grant. The loss of Haringey was a real blow to the campaign and the first sign in the Councils that the soft left didn't have the heart for the battle.

A turning point in the fight was the Hackney law case. Hackney Council, led by Hilda Kean, was taken to court by a local SDP activist over its public policy of not setting a rate. On the 6 March a Judge had placed an interim order prohibiting the council from setting any rate that was not the lawful rate and from using any monies from rates since 1 April, or from borrowing money until a rate was set.[45] The Labour Group defied the ruling and voted

---

43 Graham Taylor, 'Red faces as Tories pull off Rates coup', *South London Press*, 10 April 1985.
44 Letter sent to LGIU and Blunkett, 14 March 1985.
45 Martin Loughlin, *Legality and Locality: The Role of Law in Central-Local Government Relations* (Clarendon Press 1996), p. 190.

for a motion the next day in council that Hackney simply could not set any rate. When the case went to trial, the judge found against Hackney. In a ruling designed to send a clear message to other rebellious councils, Mr Justice Woolf declared that a council would be in "breach of duty" by not setting a rate by 1st April; in Hackney's case "not to make a rate by 1st April or within a reasonable time thereafter (weeks not months) would be *prima facie* evidence of unlawfulness."[46] After their appeal failed, a majority of Labour Councils reconciled themselves to setting a rate, though they were initially prevented from doing so by union members locking the doors of the town hall to prevent a meeting. Hackney conciliated on 23 May. David Blunkett's contribution to the fight had already collapsed on 12 May, as Sheffield set a rate whilst acknowledging that it may have to cut up to 2,500 staff to make ends meet – the worst of both worlds.

What the court case revealed was that the primary means for applying financial pressure on the councils was by central government departments withholding monies from councils for the duration of the dispute. The DHSS withheld the rate rebate element of housing benefit and the Treasury Valuer refused to hand over contributions in lieu of rates on Crown property. After the ruling, Hackney set a rate in May, and Hilda Kean resigned as leader.

As the retreat gathered pace and became a rout, the much hoped for wave of industrial action from the Town Hall unions to back up the remaining councils failed to materialise. Back in Lambeth the struggle ground on. Council meetings were uproarious affairs, full of high spirits alongside a sense of dread. At the Council meeting on 15th May, Knight moved his amendment the same as before, but now a split occurred in the Labour ranks. This time three Labour councillors defected; Vince Leon and Janet Boston joined Stuart Cakebread. Leon had been an inveterate wobbly, and Knight had used all of his powers of persuasion just to get him this far. Boston and Cakebread were more calculated; lawyers by training, their argument was that the Judges' ruling clarified the law. By this stage individual heroics would not stop rate-capping. Despite also being a practising lawyer, Bowring refused to go along with his legal colleagues. For him it was an issue of principle that he was prepared to face prison for. Disbarment was not enough to deter him. Boston and Cakebread proposed an amendment to set the rate and establish a mechanism to rapidly reduce expenditure to bring the budget in line with income. Their amendment was defeated but only on the casting vote of the mayor. Knight's amendment went to the vote as the substantive but lost by one vote, thus nothing was agreed. The vote was split 32-32, the mayor cast the deciding vote in favour of the Labour majority position.[47]

---

46 *Local Government Review*, Volume 150, 1986, p. 442.
47 *The Telegraph*, 16 May 1985.

The day after the council meeting *The Telegraph*[48] ran an article critical of Labour spending in Lambeth comparing it (once again) unfavourably to Tory run Wandsworth. The article argued that Wandsworth had similar demographics and social problems but had a much lower spending rate than Lambeth. Wandsworth ran at 26.44p in the pound but Lambeth was spending 122.34p in the pound with £70.1 million. Wandsworth was used repeatedly as the 'good brother' to the renegade Lambeth during the dispute.

The District Auditor, Brian Skinner, was dispatched to look over Lambeth's finances and council motions and make a decision on whether they had flouted the law or not. He was initially given one of NALGO's offices by the council, but the union made its feelings towards him known when he turned up to work one day to find it reoccupied by trade unionists with his files dumped on the floor outside. Union activists at the Department for Housing put up Wild West style 'wanted' posters for Skinner around the Tesco supermarket on Acre Lane.[49]

From this point on the mood had altered considerably from previous council meetings. A number of other councils had now collapsed and set their rates, and the advice from the Chief Solicitor was clear: the councillors would be in breach of the law if they didn't set a rate. The Lambeth left stood firm however, they argued that the officers' figures on losses incurred by not setting a rate were too pessimistic and there might well be no loss incurred. If no loss was incurred then surcharge couldn't be used against them. Ted Knight was quoted in the *Evening Standard*: "There is no alternative but for us to carry on the fight".[50] The Labour Group hit back, demanding £14 million in grants that had been withheld over the previous years by the Thatcher government.

The pressure on the councillors around Lambeth was also growing. Sharon Atkin was furious when her son at Dunraven School in Streatham was berated by a teacher in front of the class about his mother's political stance. The teacher in question turned out to be a Labour member from Camden and saw fit to shout at the son of one of the rebel councillors. Atkin's son was defended by a young Naomi Campbell, who jumped up to tell the teacher to "shut up" which caused a commotion.[51]

The opposition again demanded a recall meeting. Knight delayed it to the last possible date he could, 5 June. At that meeting the Boston/Cakebread amendment was again defeated and Knight's passed with a majority of two votes. At a key meeting of the council called on 5 June another vote was called to try and set the rate. The new mayor Lloyd Leon attended, even though he found out his mother had just died 3 hours earlier, in case another casting vote was needed. It wasn't only the Mayor who faced difficulties;

---

48 Ibid.
49 *South London Press*, 24 May 1985.
50 *Evening Standard*, 3 June 1985.
51 Interview with Sharon Atkin, October 2017.

Sharon Atkin was in hospital and could only go to the council chamber if accompanied by a doctor, which had to be arranged by Knight; Gordon Ley was in hospital for a knee operation and forbidden to travel. He climbed out the bathroom window and hailed a taxi to get to the vote on time. His wife was astonished when she saw him on TV that night: "That can't be him, he's laid up in St Tommy's!"[52] The reinforcements weren't necessary though. In the end the Labour Group won 32-30 because two of the Conservative councillors had failed to attend; one on a business trip and one was out of London to see his sick girlfriend. But support was dropping across the country, Camden set their rate, followed by Greenwich on 8 June. On 10 June Skinner wrote to the majority of the Labour Group to inform them that he was preparing to issue notices to them. It was this that triggered the defection of Boston and Cakebread, the threat of bankruptcy and possibly breaking the law was too much for them. Then news came through that Liverpool set a 9% rate budget on 14 June.

By this time Lambeth had still not set a budget. It wasn't clear what the endgame was going to be, however. The rate-capping campaign was clearly finished, the councils had folded and the cavalry charge of the mass industrial action from the trade unions hadn't materialised. At this stage it was essentially a battle of wills between Lambeth and the government to see if any money could be secured, which would offer a glimmer of hope that the fight had been worth it.

One last heave. The battered forces of the Lambeth left, abandoned on the field by their erstwhile allies, grimly locked in a battle they knew they could no longer win outright. The deadlock was broken when, on 21 June, Labour councillor Mike Bright announced that he was resigning his council seat. No one held any bitterness against Mike, certainly the remaining councillors seemed phlegmatic about it. None of them really explained why he chose to break ranks at this point, though it seems a certain amount of demoralisation had set in. His resignation letter stated that; "Martyrdom, however heroic, is usually the sign of a lost cause."[53] His resignation gave the opposition a majority of one at the next council meeting. The rate would be now be set, it was only a matter of time.

Faced with the final collapse of the rate-capping struggle, the trade unions moved into action. An occupation of the town hall on 21 June was organised by Lambeth Trade's Council and on 25 June, 1,000 NALGO members voted to support the councillors' actions and endorse the occupation.

The notices were sent on 26 June warning of an extraordinary audit to ascertain losses. On the same day the Labour NEC met and passed a motion that the party "supports the Labour councillors, and calls upon all sections

---

52 Ibid.
53 'Rate rebels are 'doomed'', *South London Press*, 2 July 1985.

of the Party to offer maximum support to those councillors, in Liverpool, Lambeth, Edinburgh."[54]

Then, unexpectedly but most welcomely, there was a ray of good news. Lambeth was informed that the formula to decide its Rate Support Grant, specifically the housing subsidy, which was being altered with a net result that they had more cash. On the eve of the 3 July full council meeting, the head of finance rushed into Knight's office and shouted "we got the money!"[55] – £5.5 million in fact. Several councillors breathed a sigh of relief for the apparent vindication of their strategy. Nevertheless, the setting of a rate would still mean that Lambeth's future would be torturous and they would, in principle and in practice, lose control of their own finances.

At the 3 July meeting the halls was once again full of banners and protestors. Knight's amendment fell by one vote, leaving the way clear for the Boston/Cakebread amendment, calling on the council to meet no later than 24th July to set a legal rate, was passed. As the vote was counted – 32 for the rate, 31 against – Vauxhall Labour unfurled a large banner in the hall behind the Conservative group, enraging one Tory who grabbed at it to tear it down. Terry Rich jumped forward to defend the banner only to be held in a headlock by another Tory Councillor Dickie Bird. Pandemonium ensued as a scuffle broke out. Labour members in the public gallery started singing the Red Flag at the tops of their voices. Mayor Lloyd Leon adjourned the meeting for twenty minutes.[56]

The rate-capping struggle was over.

When the council reconvened the Councillors heard that a significant sum of money was being provided from the (soon to be closed) GLC. Alongside changes to accountancy, it meant that the actual budget cut for 1985/86 would amount to only £2 million. Knight and his comrades felt partly vindicated – at least they hadn't made the cuts that Westminster had demanded. Despite this reprieve however, the fight was over. Lambeth was the last council to set a rate, but they had done so according to the instructions of Westminster.

One fallout from the Rate Capping dispute was the political alliance between Knight and Livingstone, now irrevocably torn asunder. Livingstone was expelled from the Editorial Board of the *Labour Herald*, replaced by his deputy, John McDonnell. Livingstone didn't mind, he had his eyes set on a parliamentary seat in North London. His ex-comrades on *Labour Herald* labelled Livingstone's new found affection for Kinnock as fake realignment, "a personal vehicle for the careers of a rag bag of the defeated and the opportunists of the old broad left."[57]

---

54 Cited in Peter Taaffe and Peter Mulhearn, *Liverpool : A City that dared to fight*, (Socialist Books 2017).
55 Interview with Ted Knight, April 2016.
56 Interview with John O'Malley, August 2017.
57 *Parliament and Politics: Livingstone Sets Seal On Rift With Far Left*, 21 May 1985.

WE WILL FIGHT THEM IN THE COURTS....

After the dust had settled and the enthusiasm of the initial campaign, as well as the doggedness of the sheer principle of standing up to Thatcherism, had passed, it was clear that the matter would turn to more legal affairs. The councillors largely relied on the fact that, under the law, there was no clear date by which a rate had to be set, (unlike for the GLC and ILEA). As such they felt that had given them sufficient wiggle room for their policy of delaying until they secured more money from central government.

The councillors waited with baited breath while the District Auditor prepared his case. They eventually received their surcharge notices on 9 September. Immediately a legal challenge was mounted alongside their comrades in Liverpool. The District Auditor's decision carried legal weight, in essence it was a verdict on their behaviour and conduct in office. Due to the nature of the offences, this was one of the those instances where you were effectively guilty, as decided by the District Auditor, so you had to prove your *innocence*. Now the councillors had to appeal their innocence, primarily by citing Councillors section 20(3) of the 1982 Act. Hiring Martin Day Solicitors, the councillors made affidavits in their defence whilst still carrying on their roles as councillors and Labour Party activists. Some of the lengthy affidavits had to be written on pieces of paper balanced precariously on knees whilst at Labour Conference.

As the court date drew near, Knight, Atkin and the *Labour Herald* crew were drinking in a bar in Streatham when Labour MP John Gilbert, the ex-Secretary of State for Defence under Callaghan, walked in. The councillors shuffled uneasily, certain that Gilbert, no friend to the left, would excoriate them for their stand. Instead he reached out a sympathetic handshake: "what is happening to you is a fucking disgrace" he told them.[58]

After Gilbert left, Atkin saw Knight struck by a rare moment of doubt. He mentioned the older councillors like Frank Quenault, or Pat Williams in her wheelchair: "did I lead them down the wrong path?" Atkin told Knight he had done no wrong in their eyes, "We're all adults and we all knew what we were letting ourselves in for."[59]

The occasion of a surcharge required Bowring to meet with the head of his Chambers, a Tory by temperament who Bowring feared would be less than sympathetic. "I'm in a spot of bother," he told his boss, "I've been surcharged and might be made bankrupt because of this rate capping business." "And?" snapped back the reply. Bowring was taken aback. His manager shrugged "have you been accused of any wrong doing?" "Not really, perhaps only political stupidity." His manager dismissed him, "only come back and talk to me if you are actually made bankrupt." Relieved, Bowring nevertheless ended up missing the trial as he was defending a client

---

58 Interview with Sharon Atkin, October 2017.
59 Ibid.

two doors down in the High Court whilst his comrades presented their case elsewhere.[60]

Outside the court there was a vigil to boost morale. Around 100 trade unionists, councillors and Labour activists gathered, parked next to them was the Lambeth battle bus, fresh from its tour of the country to raise funds and support. Draped over the fence outside the court were banners from the engineering union (AUEW), NALGO, NUPE and UCATT.

It was only upon entering the court that the situation really hit many of the councillors.

Their alleged crimes were severe, the equivalent of the kitchen sink was thrown at them by Brian Skinner. He stated that Lambeth Council's officer's own advice had argued that refusing to set a rate at all would be a clear breach of the Local Government Act 1972, and delaying setting a rate *without a legitimate reason* would also constitute wilful misconduct. In court what the councillors had to prove was that they had a legitimate reason. Skinner argued that they did not.

The defence mounted by the councillors was that they had delayed setting the rate as they still believed that the Secretary of State for the Environment might relent and make more financial resources available to the borough. In Court their delay in setting the rate was entirely predicated on, as Knight declared in his affidavit "the prospect of obtaining more money from the Secretary of State ... and thereby not having to make harmful or damaging cuts to the detriment of services in the borough needed, were sufficiently good to run the risk of the cuts which be incurred if we did not succeed."[61] He believed that "the Secretary of State was "still open to the pressure of public opinion, particularly in the face of determined action by a group of authorities."[62] As such there was no misconduct in not setting the rate as they believed that the delay was reasonable as, if they had convinced the Secretary of State, then they could have secured more money for their council. This made their conduct not willingly improper but in fact reasonable and proportionate given the circumstances.

Brian Skinner's testimony to the court curtly responded that Councillors were "not entitled to gamble with the ratepayers' money on such a prospect."[63] In essence they were accused of being guilty of wilful misconduct as they had consciously and deliberately not set a rate as an act of political defiance against the government and this had incurred losses to Lambeth's revenue. In terms of their personal liability the amount could be horrendously high, depending on what Skinner decided they were responsible for.

In calculating the losses that the councillors had incurred, Skinner didn't consider the interest on the rates that were not collected, his argument was

---

60　Ibid.
61　Judge's verdict, para 13.40.
62　Ibid.
63　Ibid, para 11. c page 7.

that this was simply too complicated to do. Instead he referred only to the interest lost on the Rate Rebate Subsidy from the DHSS and the Payment in Lieu of Rates from the Treasury Valuer. This would come to around £100,000 for Liverpool and £125,000 for Lambeth. The Councillors knew that they would be bankrupted having to pay that amount, especially with the court costs thrown in.

After three days consideration, the judges decided the fate of the assembled Labour Party members. They concluded that the councillors' purpose in delaying the rate was explicitly to force a confrontation with the government, whereby "chaos would ensue". They dismissed this as a reasonable course of action, "such pressure is not a valid reason for deferring making a rate."[64] "Each council had acted unlawfully since their objective, that of threatening chaos if the Secretary of State did not make more funds available, was an improper reason for refusing to make a lawful rate by the beginning of the financial year."[65] The ruling also disagreed with the councillors' belief that the government would provide more money, pointedly stating that "no sensible or reasonable council could believe after 1 April 1985 that government would provide much, if any, more money."[66] The judge went further and condemned the councillors for "political posturing" in their campaign for the government to do away with rate-capping.

Mr Justice Corfield described the actions of the Lambeth Councillors as the "pinnacle of political perversity" – a line in the judgement that was specifically delivered to audible gasps for the benefit of the headline writers at the *Evening Standard*.[67] He reminded the councillors of the subservient role of a borough council "a local authority is not a miniature parliament and can only exercise the powers given to it. They must obey the statute."[68]

The decision came back; Liverpool was fined £106,103, Lambeth £126,947. The cost of over £2,000 each would disqualify them from holding office. Liverpool launched an appeal to the Law Lords but, after considering their options, the Lambeth Councillors declined to do so.

Back in Lambeth, the movement knew it had a fight on its hands to not abandon the councillors that had gone to the wall in the fight against Thatcher. At the national NALGO conference, Lambeth branch proposed a motion, motivated by Anna Tapsell, which argued to

> Take solidarity action on a selective basis and in full consultation with the joint union committees of the workforce affected and, in the event of selective action having to be escalated to all out strike in Lambeth, conference would call on

---

64 Judge's summary, p. 137.
65 Judge's summary, cited in Martin Loughlin, *Legality and Locality*, pp. 192-3.
66 Judge's summary, p. 138.
67 *Report of the Labour Party Annual Conference*, volume 85, 1986, p. 41.
68 *Local Government Review*, volume 150, 1986, p. 439.

the NEC as a matter of overriding priority to trigger a national strike levy. Branches would contribute to the Fighting Fund set up to pay the initial costs of councillors and trade unionists 'forced' to fight their case for non-compliance through the courts… If we have to escalate that action… then for the sake of our community it is absolutely vital that the strike action be 100% solid and that it is won and over with the utmost speed if our vulnerable people and those who are suffering from deprivation in Lambeth are not to suffer further.

The motion concluded:

> The government is coming for Lambeth today, but, Sussex, Surrey, Berkshire, and Bromley, they are coming for you tomorrow. We are not rejoicing in Lambeth, we are very frightened and our councillors are very frightened … but we are not going to back down.[69]

Speaking in support, Tony Bado from Newcastle NALGO made the case that if the union couldn't support Lambeth then it would be seen as a sign of weakness by the government: "unless you support Lambeth, the eyes of the world, particularly this government, will simply say: 'if they cannot support Lambeth, what else can they support?'"[70] The NEC opposed the motion, arguing that it was unlikely that the union could put its members out for strike action on a 'selective basis'. Once again, when it came to action the trade union national leadership proved to be a conservative drag on activity.

Using his connections on the far left and through the WRP, celebrities, including Vanessa Redgrave, Matthew Kelly, and Frances de la Tour, were all called on to help raise funds. Labour Party members were out on the streets of Lambeth every night with buckets raising money. The surcharged councillors travelled the country to raise the cash to prevent bankruptcy and pay their legal bills. Behind the scenes three of the bigger unions had secretly promised to make sure the costs were covered in the event that the collective fundraising failed. The councillors were a little suspicious however, as they suspected that the unions might renege on their promise. But also the fundraising campaign was itself a political act, to make sure the cause was kept in the public eye.

When the surcharge was finally served on 2 April 1986, it meant the majority of the Labour Councillors would be forced out of office. This would leave the Conservatives in charge of the council for the remaining few weeks until the May election – who knew that malicious damage they might do? Now there was a race against the clock to prevent the Tories from seizing power until the May election.

---

69 *Municipal Journal*, Volume 93, Part 2, 1985, p. 1019.
70 Ibid.

At the final Council meeting before the surcharge was set and they were debarred from office, Knight led a tearful tribute to the other councillors. The gallery in the town hall was packed. Among the local residents sat Bernie Grant of Haringey, Margaret Hodge from Islington, and Tony Rich from Southwark. They led a standing ovation as Knight fought back tears, praising his comrades on the benches around him. The left then carried out a two pronged manoeuvre to prevent Mary Leigh from ascending to the leadership. With hours to go, the Standing Orders for the Council were amended to abolish all the committees and replace them with a single committee made up of the three remaining Labour councillors. As part of the plan the Mayor resigned, replaced by Kingsley Smith, a new Labour councillor who had been elected in a by-election in October 1985. Another new councillor returned in a by-election, Linda Bellos, was made the deputy Mayor. All they needed was a third person for their *ad hoc* committee, Janet Boston volunteered. To prevent the Tories overturning the new all-powerful committee, a court order was secured on the basis that the Councillors hadn't been given sufficient notice of the Council meeting on 25 April – that was Boston's idea. This stopped the meeting before it started, preventing the Tories from forming an administration and altering the budget. Leigh was startled, as she was served the court order by a left wing solicitor, Louise Christian, as she walked into the council chamber. The only thing the disgruntled Tory councillors managed was to instruct the red flag to be taken down from outside the Town Hall. When the meeting emptied, Leigh was left to bitterly remark that: "the loonies of Lambeth have had their day."[71]

But the trade unions had other ideas. The second part of the plan involved some direct action, as trade unionists and community activists subsequently occupied the town hall and temporarily took control of the building. They unfurled a 30-foot banner (designed by Ed Hall) from the clock tower emblazoned with the words, "The Council is under the control of the community, trade unions and the 31 Labour Councillors until local people vote on 3 May." There was a strong sense that the local labour movement would not allow the Tories to take charge – not even for an hour. Too much had been sacrificed already, too many people had made a stand for the principle of defending local government. The sense of a shared fight, of unity in action, was palpable – the highpoint of the united front between unions and Labour councillors against the government.

Thatcher won the war on rate-capping. Every Local Authority had set a legal rate which established the principle that central government could control their revenue raising powers, a crucial step on the road to the Poll Tax. The Labour left had to lick its wounds, survey the wreckage of the campaign, and consider how to regroup.

---

71 *South London Press*, 26 April 1986.

10

The 1985 Riot and Inner City Blues

Away from the struggle taking place in the Council Chamber, community tensions were once again running high with the police. In a tragic moment of history repeating, in 1985 Brixton was once again on fire as anger erupted from the local community against more police brutality. Urban uprisings, initiated by the oppressed black community but rapidly joined by supporters and allies from other ethnic groups, were clearly becoming a semi-regular feature of neoliberal capitalism.

There had been some efforts since 1981 to harmonise police-community relations. One of the recommendations of the Scarman report had been to introduce a system of lay visiting of police stations. The Brixton Council of Churches, which had been organising a working group on the relationship between the police and local community, proposed more regular meetings between community groups and the police. Sean Creighton, who was involved in the proposal, wrote that the plan was for regular meetings with the Commander-in-Chief and their deputy and for a schedule of "unannounced visits [which] should be made by two members of the Board who would be on duty for a week at a time, with the right to go anywhere in the Police Station, and to talk to anyone".[1] The Board charged with overseeing this would also be involved in the complaints procedure.

This new proposal was different to the prison visitors scheme or 'Help on Arrest'. This was intended to institute a board to carry out a degree of oversight on the local police force. It was hoped that it would lift the lid on unaccountable policing in the borough. The initial draft of the plan was sent to the Home Secretary to consider, as it required his signature to allow the police to take part in any meaningful way. Knowing that the question of policing was a powder keg, Home Secretary Willie Whitelaw was cautiously interested but wanted it to go through an entire national plan, involving lengthy negotiations with local authorities and the police, before it could be approved as a pilot in Lambeth. In response both John Tilley and Stuart

---

[1] Sean Creighton, 'Dignity without Liberty', Report for Brixton Council of Churches, 1991.

Holland asked questions in Parliament to try and usher the Home Secretary along.

In the run up to the 1983 election the Tories had suddenly warmed to the idea of lay visits and a scheme was suddenly announced in Greater Manchester. Lambeth was given the go ahead, the terms of reference were agreed, and volunteers were recruited to carry out their random spot checks on police stations. This was the formal launch of what became the Lambeth Police and Community Consultative Group; its organisers' aim was to provide scrutiny of police operations, whilst the police hoped it would cast them in a better light with a sceptical community. The police were also making a propaganda effort with local residents – just a couple of months before the riot the local press featured adverts and an editorial for Lambeth Police Day on Clapham Common, due on 14 July.[2] Despite these efforts, however, the experience of many working class residents in Lambeth, both black and white, was one of over-policing and under-protection.

Hence another explosion in 1985. A couple of local stories from the weeks before the riot provide some context. It was reported on 16 August that "for years police were wary of mounting major 'Front Line' operations for fear of sparking another riot. But during the 10 or so raids this year, there has never been any hint of disturbance."[3] Clearly the raids on Railton Road were still continuing apace. Yet on 23 August the *South London Press* published a special report by Chief Investigator John Twomey on the police's failure to apprehend anyone in connection with the New Cross Fire in 1981. The police had explicitly rejected the notion that the arson was caused by racists, though it was a widely held belief by black people across south London that the far right were somehow involved.

Whereas the sequences of events leading up to the 1981 riot were confused, the causes of the 1985 riot were clear. In the early morning of 28 September seven armed police, accompanied by dogs, raided a flat at 22 Normandy Road, looking for Michael Groce, who was a suspect in an armed robbery in Hertfordshire weeks earlier. Poor intelligence and a lazy investigation meant the police didn't realise that he no longer lived at that address. The police also believed the house was a squat. Instead, his mother Dorothy "Cherry" Groce lived there with her five children. As police kicked the door down, Cherry came out of her bedroom to see what the noise was. As she turned on the stairs she saw the police and began to run back to her room, but as she did so she was shot in the back by Police Officer Douglas Lovelock. At the 2014 inquest that was held after her death, Lovelock said that it was an accident, his finger just slipped on the trigger in all the commotion.[4] The accounts of what happened next paint a picture of the complete inhumanity with which community policing was conducted. As

---

2 'Police and the public working together', *South London Press*, 5 July 1985.
3 *South London Press*, 16 August 1985.
4 *The Guardian*, 1 July 2014.

Cherry Groce lay in a pool of her own blood, she looked up to ask an officer crouched over her if she was dying; "No, it's just like having a baby" came the sarcastic reply. One of Cherry's children, Lee, came running out of the bedroom screaming, "What have you done to my mum!" A police officer snapped back, "someone shut up that kid". Groce was paralysed from the waist down by bullet fragments. Lee remembered seeing his mother lying on the floor, bleeding, thinking how vulnerable she looked.[5]

When word spread the next morning, a small group of local youths went to the house to shout at the police. Within a short space of time more police arrived. Then more people came to protest. A large group marched from Normandy Road to Brixton Police Station. People gathered outside the front of the station. Petrol bombs and stones were hurled at the building. Police officers could be heard screaming racial epithets from the windows at the assembled crowd. A priest from the local community police consultation committee was produced and tried to quell the crowd but was forced to leave after a barrage of bottles. After a while the police stormed out from their bunker in the station and formed a line of shields to push the crowd back.

By the afternoon it was clear there was a second full blown riot in Brixton, a violent reminder that that none of the major issues of police-community relations had been resolved. Once again the national press descended on the area. One notable feature of the 1985 clashes was the number of petrol bombs that were distributed and used. The same image of the furniture shop on fire, the lines of police, the youths hurling stones could be seen.[6] The heat and blazes of incendiaries. The confusion over where the fighting is, who is moving forwards or backwards. More police arrived and horses and vans were brought in from across the capital. Rioters hijacked a bus and attempted to drive it at the police lines. By midnight there were a thousand police on the streets.

Fighting with the police lasted all day and well into the night. As they did in 1981, the police tried to deflect from criticism over any alleged racism by pointing out that half of the 197 arrests made were of white people. Again, as with 1981, this reveals something more profound about the community, that this was still about wider issues of unemployment and bad housing, of dispossession and alienation. The spirit of resistance in the area combined with the general hostility to the police that a working class Labour voting borough felt in the mid-1980s meant that when the black population rose up against the police, they were joined by others from the local community. This was white people who worked with, friends who socialised together, lovers who co-habited alongside the black population. An attack on the black community was seen as an attack on everyone, on Brixton itself. This wasn't simply a black issue, it was a community in revolt.

---

5 Ibid.
6 'From the archive: Riots in Brixton after police shooting', 30 September 2009, theguardian.com/theguardian/2009/sep/30/brixton-riots-1985-archive

Local reporters from the *South London Press* were also targeted by the police. Stewart Morris was hit twice around the head by batons and Lesley Johnson was dragged along the ground by police after one baton charge. They had identified themselves as journalists but were contemptuously told by the police to "get off the streets and go home." The journalists witnessed one youth beaten around the head by riot shields.[7] This was not policing by consent, it was the re-imposition of order on a community that felt terrorised by the armed forces of the state. At one stage Chief Inspector Robinson grabbed a firehose from the fire brigade and fired it at the protesters in an impromptu first use of a makeshift water cannon against civil disorder.

By the time it was over there was millions of pounds of damage, 279 police were injured, 55 burnt out cars and other vehicles littered the road, as did the makeshift barricades hastily assembled at various intersections. Nearly 30 buildings had been completely gutted by fire and over a hundred others were damaged. John Fraser MP had been caught in the riot – his car was stuck on an estate, due to traffic being blocked, when the car in front of his was set alight. The Tory Club on Effra Road (today the Effra Social) had its windows smashed and cars destroyed outside. The anarchists celebrated it as a spectacular moment of community resistance against the 'pigs'.[8] The black community was more circumspect; many felt this wasn't political, it was simply a matter of justice.

After the rioting, journalists pointed to the widespread looting that took place as a way of de-legitimising the anger that had led to the fighting. Looting is an inevitable by-product of most riots, when the powerless become powerful, when the goods in the shops that are so often out of reach, unaffordable, come tantalisingly close. When the normal economic relations of capitalism become upended and wealth doesn't matter any more; where the poorest can seize the most expensive watches and necklaces from a jeweller, where you can punish the rich for lauding it over the poor with their conspicuous consumption.

The events of 28 September have to be understood in their totality before we can accept that it was simply an act of community resistance or an outbreak of thuggery or politically motivated violence. Inevitably with a breakdown in order and the anonymity of a huge crowd of rioters there is often looting and other crimes. Anarchist accounts usually focus on damage to property without also seeing the uglier side of rioting. The police pleaded that they had 'good community relations' established in the last couple of years and it was only upset by "an unruly criminal element."[9] But the speed with which thousands of people came out to challenge the police, and the

---

7   *South London Press*, 1 October 1985, p. 3.
8   *Through a Riot Shield: The 1985 Brixton Riot*, (Past Tense Publications 2014).
9   *The Guardian*, 30 September 1985.

shooting of an unarmed black woman in her own home indicates that this was more than just a handful of troublemakers at work.

Once again urban warfare had left parts of Brixton a wreckage. But just as with the 1981 uprising, the black population was merely fighting for its right to exist, to live without fear of being shot in their own homes, to live without fear of the police terrorising them. In response to the violence the Council withdraw its support from the Community Police Consultative Committee. Linda Bellos placed the blame firmly on the police: "the people of Brixton only want peace, but I think that the police are bent on war."[10] And behind the headlines lay the unfulfilled pledges of the Scarman report, coupled with the managed decline of inner cities that Thatcher's government was steadily pursuing through structural unemployment. Nevertheless, the state had to be seen to act to quell the uprising. West Yorkshire Detective Chief Constable John Domaille was dispatched the next day, followed by TV cameras, to speak to the family. The police used dogs to break up an open air meeting of a Groce group called the Cultural Awareness Programme where Cllrs Irma Critchlow and Ameldaa Inyang, (just back from Nicaragua), were speaking.[11] Home Secretary Douglas Hurd rejected calls for a public inquiry, citing the need to prioritise rebuilding relations, and that "young blacks" did not feel a sense of community "that is partly their fault and partly ours."[12]

But the tragic wounding of Cherry Groce in 1985 didn't reduce the instances of police intimidation or roughhouse policing strategies. Less than a week after the Brixton riot, a black woman called Cynthia Jarrett died of a heart attack after police pushed her over whilst searching her flat on the Broadwater Farm Estate in Tottenham. More rioting resulted in the death of a police officer and further rounds of recriminations and media attacks on the black community. It seemed that the death rate for black people coming into contact with the police was increasing significantly in London, further eroding any of the supposed gains that had been made since 1981. The violence of the police and their unaccountability compared to the over policing of the black community was a central point of the Cherry Groce Campaign:

> OUT OF CONTROL OUT OF ORDER
> ONE LAW FOR BLACK, ONE FOR BLUE[13]

The issue didn't go away for many people. In 1990 Black History for Action organised a picket of Brixton police station, calling for justice for the three black men sent to prison for the Broadwater Farm riots whilst no police were charged with the numerous beatings and violence meted out against the black community. The police and the justice system seemed to fail

---

10 *Hansard*, Volume 112. Cited in Parliament by The Parliamentary Under-Secretary of State for the Home Department Mr. Douglas Hogg on 20 March 1987.
11 *South London Press*, 1 October 1985, p. 2.
12 Ibid.
13 Brixton anti-racist campaigners leaflet, Black Cultural Archives, EPHEMERA/77.

black people on a daily basis. After the shooting, the Groce family was offered very little money to take care of Cherry and no legal aid to pursue the matter. Detective Lovelock was put on trial in 1987, causing a number of armed police to hand in their guns in protest. Lovelock was acquitted of all charges after a short trial. Cherry Groce's family had to wait until 2014 for the Met Police to issue an apology, three years after she had died.

TRANQUILITY

The period this book covers was one of intense hardship and political and social turmoil that, for some, required determination and bravery to survive. It was quite a violent time, and inner city areas like Lambeth were no exception. According to the Crime Survey England and Wales and police figures, violent crime escalated in the 1980s, peaking in 1995 before beginning a general decline. There were inevitably different responses to the question of how to tackle criminality; Scarman in his report had made the decidedly liberal point that sometimes it might be better to turn a blind eye to small crimes in order to keep 'tranquility' in a given area. What did a little cannabis possession matter if the consequences of zealous enforcement of drug laws just led to potential upheaval? Alternatively in the US an article in *The Atlantic* in 1982 by James Wilson and George Kelling, "Broken Windows: The police and neighborhood safety" introduced the argument that any sign of social decline or lack of rule enforcement (in this example, a broken window in a residential area) was a scratch that led to gangrene.[14] A smashed pane of glass creates the impression that the ordered nature of society is breaking down, giving license to vandalism, theft and violent crimes. Ultimately the police had taken the view that more repressive measures were needed, not a light touch.

Of course the issue of crime in Lambeth was always highly racialised due to the large Afro-Caribbean community. Two academics, Louis Blom-Cooper and Richard Drabble, examined the Metropolitan Police submission to the Scarman inquiry's claim that there was a "unique" and specific violent street crime situation in Brixton that may require extra policing.[15] In their view the reporting of crimes was racialised. Two categories were highlighted, "Robberies and other violent theft" and "other theft and handling". They found that comparing 1980 with 1976 the violent theft category had increased by 773 whilst the 'other theft' category had decreased by 836 counts. They concluded that there was a bias towards reporting crimes in Brixton as 'violent' to make the figures look worse – otherwise why would there be such a huge decline in the more mild sounding category? The bias in recording of crimes was related to the racist stereotype of black street

---

14 George L Kelling and James Q Wilson, 'Broken Windows: The police and neighborhood safety', *The Atlantic*, March 1982.
15 Louis Blom-Cooper and Richard Drabble, 'Police Perception of Crime: Brixton and the Operational Response', *British Journal of Criminology*, vol. 22, April 1982.

crimes as being fundamentally more violent than any carried out by non-black perpetrators. The popular cultural image of the Black mugger, deployed by the the far right as part of their racist campaigns in the late 1970s, was also how police themselves perceived policing in the borough. Stuart Hall's book *Policing the Crisis*, outlines the political nature of the 'mugging' moral panic, a term first coined in 1972 that was intended to describe a new and dangerous form of violent crime, usually carried out by 'feral youths' who cared nothing for people's safety or their property.[16] Indeed there was no actual crime of 'mugging', it was a journalistic phrase that politicians began to repeat until it became common currency.

Alongside imagined crime statistics there *were* real problems for the local community. Black people were in fact more likely to be victims of crime than white people, and they had to deal with an uncaring or biased police force.

There was serious crime against women in the borough. Scanning through the local press archives you are struck by how regular and shocking the reports are of serious sexual violence against women. Of course a historian has to be careful relying on the local press, they can often lead with salacious accounts of crime to sell copy, emphasising some criminal activities over others, but nevertheless the regularity with which women were being abducted, raped, tortured and murdered appeared startling. No wonder that in the classified section of the *South London Press*, nestled among the adverts for Kiss-a-grams and porn magazines, there appeared adverts for 'personal shrill alarms':

> FEEL SAFE – FEEL PROTECTED
> Used by council workers, approved by the police. Price £1.95[17]

One report into crimes against women makes for hard hitting reading. In the context of the violence being committed, the contribution by the Women's Rights Committee pulls no punches: "The usual image of rape as depicted by the media and the police is that of a 'pretty', young, white woman being attacked by a stranger in a dark alley. In reality, this sort of attack constitutes a minority of the incidents of sexual violence, as most occur within the home in the form of husbands raping their wives (not at present a criminal offence), incest and men raping women known to them as friend, acquaintance or relative. This also belies the media stereotype of 'the rapist' as a Black man as, by definition, same-race rape is more common than Black men raping white women."[18]

The primary concern was that most rapes were not reported to the police. The indication that this was widespread was the disparity between the number of rape accusations the police recorded in a given month and the

---

16 Stuart Hall, Chas Critcher, and Tony Jefferson, *Policing the Crisis: Mugging, the State, and Law and Order* (Macmillan, 1978).
17 *South London Press*, 21 March 1986, p 28.
18 Policy Committee Support Unit report, 1977, Lambeth Archives LBL/94.

volume of calls that the London Rape Crisis Centre received. Simply, a lot of women were being attacked and not reporting it. The police's attitudes reflected, in a concentrated form, the views of the majority of society, that sexual violence is the only crime where the victim is commonly and persistently disbelieved. Women reporting rapes or assaults were often interrogated by male police officers and treated as if they were lying, with police picking holes in their stories and looking for inconsistencies.

Lesbians were vulnerable to sexual assaults and even rapes by men as a form of 'punishment' but they were found to be less likely to report sexual assaults by men. Because of the anti-lesbian attitudes by the police force, they feared becoming a target for harassment or simply being mocked by officers. And it wasn't just a question of sexual violence against women. The T&G union published a report in March 1986 highlighting the 'terror routes', where physical assaults were most common for bus drivers and passengers. The union cited 1,211 assaults in 1985, 413 in South London alone. Brixton topped the list for the year with 72 attacks on bus crews, 27 in Streatham and 26 in Clapham.[19]

The violence of inner-city life has to be seen in the context of the massive unemployment of the 1980s, caused by the Conservatives monetarist and proto-neoliberal policies. It effectively ripped the heart out of social welfare and the intricate and complex webs of support and safety that can exist in a community. The view of those on the right, of course, was that the inner-cities were crumbling because of the moral decay of the people living there, the disgusting and grimy streets and estates inhabited by a criminal underclass.

These Neo-Victorian attitudes were prevalent and damaging, blaming the victims of economic deprivation and social alienation for their own condition. It saw Lambeth as being divided between the upright Tory-voting working-class in Streatham, the yuppies crowding into Clapham, the wealthy old money in the lavish houses of Kennington and the black underclass around Brixton. All of these were stereotypes that were grafted onto a complicated inner-London community, one where many people struggled during the 1980s. It formed the background rumble to a city in transit from the post-war era to the post-industrial space, the estates and commercial districts at first facing redevelopment and then gentrification. The music coming from the club halls, squats and basement parties was an inner-city blues, increasingly turning to the loud, repetitive beats of a city being transformed.

---

19 *South London Press*, 21 March 1986, p. 6.

11

The Left Regroups

The period that opened up after the fall of Ted Knight coincided with the increasing moves by Neil Kinnock to carry out what was euphemistically called the 'modernisation agenda' within the Labour Party. Kinnock had started off as a left winger, talking about abolishing the House of Lords and quoting the Italian Marxist Antonio Gramsci. But he was to rapidly become the pioneer of the 'reformers'. From the Labour leader's point of view the goal was to transform the Party into a respectable party of opposition as a means of becoming a serious contender for government again. This was in large part a backlash to the perceived 'leftism' of the 1983 manifesto. This perception was driven by intellectuals around *Marxism Today* and the journalists in the media who trumpeted a move to the right in British society and lambasted Labour for being hopelessly out of touch with aspirational well off working class people. People like Peter Mandelson were firmly on board, having resigned as a Lambeth Councillor, he gravitated to the new order, claiming his experience "of Labour lunacy in 1980s Lambeth [convinced me] that our party had to change or die."[1]

As such, the aftermath of the 1983 electoral defeat convinced many in the party that it was the left that was to blame. The 'suicide note' of the 1983 election manifesto, (which in many ways was not as left as the 1974 election manifesto), the notoriety of Tony Benn as the figurehead for the left inside and often outside of parliament, combined with the prominence of organised far left currents like Militant Tendency, were all blamed for the poor electoral performance of the party. The 'loony left' label was so ubiquitous by this time that it even started to be used in internal Labour Party discussions about their own members. The media put huge pressure on Labour to purge the New Urban Left due to their supposedly embarrassing focus on lesbians and gays, or their obsession with the red flag flying above town halls. A crucial moment in the war against the left had happened before the 1983 election at the Bishop Stortford conference of 1982 where the trade union leaders demanded that the left around Benn stop their attempts

---

1 Peter Mandelson, *The Third Man* (Harper Collins 2010), p. 214.

to reform the party and get behind the leadership or risk another damaging split worse than the SDP defections.[2] The line of attack was clear during the 1980s, the left were the problem and 'moderation' was the solution.

The process of modernising the party meant isolating the far left and foregrounding the more moderate voices in the party. From Kinnock's point of view it meant making Labour a party 'fit for government' in a period where everything was moving rightward. The ideological basis for this was provided by figures such as Stuart Hall and Eric Hobsbawm, both of whom theorised the scent of the hegemonic New Right and the way in which Labour's forward march had been supposedly halted. In this great moving rightward show, a number of figures who had started on the left were rapidly shifting their ideological positions. One such organisation that now pursued the modernisation agenda with the passion of the newly converted was the Labour Co-ordinating Committee (LCC). The LCC had started off in the Bennite sphere of politics, backing the left wing Alternative Economic Strategy of the 1970s. However, as the 1980s wound its painful way through Thatcherite victory after victory, the LCC became convinced that only the leadership of Neil Kinnock and a ruthless war against the left could deliver another Labour electoral victory.

Naturally, the left's perspective was radically different, namely that it was the swing to the right by the leadership and the failure to adequately *fight* Thatcherism in a bold and decisive manner, as opposed to capitulating to key tenants of it which left the party unable to challenge the establishment of the new right hegemony. The Party's failure to properly back the miners or the rate capped council's now left it looking bereft of energy, too concentrated on the Westminster bubble, too obsessed with spin.

After the miners' defeat Thatcherism increasingly seemed unstoppable, though in 1986 some hoped that there could still be a Labour victory at the next general election. Although the party and class had suffered a defeat, the Labour Party in Lambeth felt confident because it had at least fought and built a reputation for resistance. From their perspective they had fought Thatcher to a standstill. But the regime established at Labour's HQ on Walworth Road, just across the border in Southwark, was in no mood to indulge left wing rebels from renegade local authorities.

What the councillors saw as a principled stand against Thatcherism and for local democracy was derided by the Labour machinery as 'gesture politics'. What the left saw as a struggle against Westminster autocracy was dismissed by Labour officials as vote-losing antics by the loony left. The modernisers around Neil Kinnock had no time for the kind of activism that Lambeth's left felt was simply bread and butter political work. Although Labour has always been a party that united the left and right of social democracy, the pressure cooker of 1980s politics and the high stakes game

---

2   Key players from the TULV were Moss Evans of the TGWU, Clive Jenkins of ASTMS, Bill Keys of SOGAT, and Larry Whitty from GMWU.

of challenging Thatcherism meant that these different approaches to politics were simply too contradictory, the lines of divergence too extreme. Something had to give.

KNIGHTFALL

With almost the entire old Labour council group barred, there was a desperate search for fresh members. Labour held selections in the Town Hall almost round the clock, interviewing as many applicants as they could in exhaustingly long sessions, with only weeks to go before the election in May 1986. Linda Bellos described it afterwards: "There was an almighty scramble to find people willing to stand, and it has to be said that they scraped the barrel."[3] Who she thought was bottom of the barrel was as yet unclear.

There were also some concerns locally that the councillors lacked support. A poll had found 46% of local voters (across all parties) didn't think the stand against the government was worthwhile. At the 22 public meetings called across the borough to outline the nature of the cuts and the council's stance against them only a handful of people turned out. One meeting had only five members of the public present. Knight argued that the low turnout was because of the sizeable support locally; if people were angry with him then they would go to the meeting to voice their opinion (as they had done during the rate increase controversy in 1982).[4] Despite the brave face, there were some nervous twitches in the local Labour parties.

On 8 May 1986 the voters of Lambeth spoke. Labour was returned to power with an increase of eight councillors, with 62.5% of the vote. In 22 wards where Labour won seats they significantly increased their share of votes, doubling it in some cases. The Tories lost six and the SDP-Liberal Alliance coalition lost two. Labour gains in Thornton, Clapham Town and Herne Hill were cheered as Mary Leigh stood crestfallen. Knight joked with local party members that Labour's triumph meant that he did not have to join the Tories to carry on his political ambition of becoming an MP. For the Labour left, the local elections vindicated their stand; if the surcharged councillors had been so unpopular then that would have been reflected in a reduced Labour vote.

After the removal of nearly the entire group, only three serving Labour councillors survived. The new group had to elect a leader. Speculation was rife that Lesley Hammond, a friend of Ted Knight, would waltz into the role. Other possible leaders might include Janet Boston, or Joan Twelves (described as "left wing but with no council experience.")[5]

---

3   Linda Bellos, 'Who really wrecked Lambeth?: Savaged budgets and bans on councillors were a recipe for scandal, says the borough's former leader', *The Independent*, Wednesday 27 January 1993.
4   Interview with Ted Knight, November 2015.
5   *South London Press*, 7th March 1986, p. 3.

One name that was not mentioned was Linda Bellos. She was an emerging campaigner for black rights in Lambeth Labour, making a name for herself especially in the establishment of the local Black Sections. At the start of the 1980s she was involved in the *Spare Rib* collective but was also close to the Poale Zion tendency in Labour, the Zionist Jewish group. She didn't come from the same socialist left background as her predecessors. At the Labour Group AGM it was Bellos who was elected leader by a crushing 33-1. She appeared to have overwhelming support from the councillors, but her political leadership of the group was as yet untested. Unlike Knight, she was not in charge of a disciplined force of councillors forged together as a fighting unit over many years. There was tension and factionalism among the councillors that had been absent during Knight's day. A number of new councillors were members of the Labour Coordinating Committee which was by now loyal to the rightward moving Kinnock regime and very critical of the 'hard left'. On the opposite end of the spectrum a number of councillors were either in or had been members of the Fourth International's British section the International Socialist Group. Greg Tucker and Steve French were current members, Joan Twelves had been a member of the ISG's predecessor organisation, the IMG. Other councillors had been in or around the far left in the early 1980s. The jockeying for position focused on the election for chief whip; Joan Twelves for the left contested the leadership position against Dick Sorabji of the Labour Coordinating Committee standing for the pro-Kinnock right. Twelves won the election 22 to Sorabji's 15, the left had dominance but wasn't hegemonic.

For Labour locally this was a real shift in leadership, an openly gay, black woman with something approaching a national profile would lead Lambeth Council. For Bellos, it was a challenge to get to grips with the machinery of local government in the middle of a historic confrontation with Thatcher. She was one of three black council leaders at the time, alongside Bernie Grant and Merle Amory, who were in charge of Haringey and Barnet respectively.

Alongside being in the forefront of the advancement of race politics in the capital city, LGBT political issues had exploded into public consciousness only a few years earlier with Peter Tatchell standing for Labour in a by-election in Bermondsey in which he had been subject to violent abuse and discrimination for his sexuality. Bellos would be the first 'out' council leader at a time when Labour was very cautious about making itself look unpopular by being associated with LGBT issues. She describes how, "The day following election results, the Labour Party sent us a PR person to help advise us on handling quite a lot of media attention. I recall making a statement to her and others in the rooms that I had chosen not to mention my sexuality, but that if the matter was raised by the Press then I would not deny it. This seemed to go down well, I had outed myself to some of the new Councillors who did not know me and made clear that I would not be defensive on the issue."[6]

Another new councillor that caused a stir was Rachel Webb, a transgender woman and long distance lorry driver by trade. The local newspapers delighted in referring to her as 'sex-change Rachel Webb', 'sex change lorry driver' or simply 'transgender Rachel Webb' – often referring to her name before she transitioned.[7] Webb had a background in revolutionary politics having been active in the Militant for a while and had been in the TGWU in King's Lynn, where she faced discrimination due to being transgender. When she moved to Lambeth in 1981 she was living her life as a woman. She was something of an idiosyncratic character however, and even some of her comrades on the left felt she was a little too radical sometimes. The local press reported that upon being elected she was whisked away by Labour Party handlers to prevent journalists asking questions.[8]

With so many new councillors, the Labour Group's lack of experience in running local government became apparent. Whilst some of the surcharged councillors stuck around in local Labour Parties and on the Local Government Committee (LGC), many of them, exhausted after the two year long fight which consumed so much of their energy, disappeared from the scene with amazing speed. There was also the thorny question of the legacy of Ted Knight himself. The council reforms of the early 1980s and the sheer muscle required to get Lambeth to oppose rate-capping had produced a culture in which Knight had achieved a lot through sheer force of will. Writing in the mid-1980s, Livingstone cast a critical eye on Ted Knight's leadership style. Knight abolished the policy committee and ruled through a series of *ad hoc* committees with different personnel in terms of officers and councillors. This favoured a "strong, competent leader developed a close working relationship with the Council bureaucracy and also controlled the flow of information to the rest of the Labour Group."[9] The problem for the incoming leadership was that the last experienced leader was now gone, replaced by a new and relatively inexperienced crew. Bellos had to live up to Knight's legacy whilst also overcoming it – they were two totally different types of leader from different backgrounds and the left needed to regain its footing after the bruising rate-capping struggle.

Within a few weeks of forming the new administration, there was a clash with the old guard – in this case involving alleged nepotism. Fred Taggart, the new chair of the housing committee, came to the Labour Group to inform them that, in his opinion, Ed Atkin (Sharon Atkin's husband) was not a competent choice for Director of Housing. Bellos investigated and thought that the other candidate Gurbux Singh had been better qualified.

---

6   Bellos' website, *Some History*, lindabellos.co.uk/some-history.
7   For example, 'The return of left-wing lunch', *London Evening Standard*, 8 March 1991.
8   *South London Press*, 13 May 1986, p. 4.
9   Ken Livingstone, *If Voting Changed Anything They Would Abolish It* (Pluto1987), p. 125.

She also suspected that the appointment had been a favour to Sharon Atkin by Knight for her support. Confident in her position, she moved to get Ed Atkin's position terminated at the end of his 6 months' probation. Twelves recalled the event: "It was a real baptism of fire for us – most of us had never sacked anyone before. Greg, Steve and I were totally united with Linda over sacking him. Ted was furious. Denounced us all for selling out, accused us of racism and so on... I remember a heated packed meeting of the Left where he subjected us to a full Ted rant. It was the first real breach with the previous administration."[10]

The Bellos era did, however, try and make moves to clamp down on corruption and financial irregularities. Steve French was elected chair of Construction Services and took steps to shine a spotlight on areas of the council that so far had enjoyed carrying out some of their work in the dark. Over several months an inquiry team, headed up by two ex-council chiefs and Bill Rankin, an ex-senior NALGO and TUC member, looked into allegations of misconduct. The ensuing report ran to 240 pages. The inquiries in 1986 and 1987 into the DLO and housing found serious problems with overspend, mis-management and poor quality repair work being done. The report concluded that there were areas where there were "no accountability procedures, where workmanship was poor and where there were a serious lack of procedures designed to ensure the Council obtained value for money."[11] The report identified several of the corrupt practices that had plagued the DLO for years, as well as the increasing prevalence of contractors who fleeced the system. It was a tricky task for the new and inexperienced administration to make the necessary improvements.

Just as new Labour councillors attended the council chambers, so too did new Tories, including people who had been leading figure of the Monday Club Immigration and Repatriation Committee.[12] The aims of the committee were the end of Commonwealth immigration, voluntary repatriation and repealing the Race Relations Act. In short it was a charter for the kind of policies the far right were peddling, only under the supposedly respectable guise of an establishment drinking society like the Monday Club. The secretary of the committee was one John Bercow, a student activist in the Federation of Conservative Students at the time that they were producing posters that said "Hang Nelson Mandela". Joan Twelves knew Bercow from Essex University where they were contemporaries; Twelves had chaired a 'Troops Out' [of Ireland] meeting on the campus when Bercow and his Monday Club allies led an invasion to disrupt the

---

10 Interview with Joan Twelves, February 2016.
11 Report into Lambeth Council Construction Services, 1986, Fred Taggarts papers, Lambeth Archives.
12 The Monday Club was a right wing Conservative pressure group, notorious in the 1980s for its extreme right wing positions.

meeting waving giant Union Jacks. Twelves remarked of the incident "stuff like that certainly teaches you how to chair a meeting!"[13]

Bercow went on to become the Speaker of the House of Commons and inclined more towards liberalism, but in his youth he was a firebrand nationalist zealot and a leading member of an organisation that advocated removing black people from Britain. It must have been quite a surprise to his critics when he was elected as a Conservative Councillor for Lambeth in 1986. In the mid-1980s Bercow was a fierce Thatcherite dogmatist and scourge of the left on the council, a period that he later described as "utter madness".[14]

Much like Ted Knight before her, Linda Bellos was subjected to a furious tirade in the press. They delighted in referring to her as a militant, black, feminist lesbian – hints of salacious sexual and racial radicalism in Lambeth sold newspapers. Bellos was defiant however, she revelled in being presented as the stuff of nightmares for *Daily Mail* readers. At a Labour fringe event in 1987 Linda Bellos described Thatcher as "leading Britain down towards the gas chambers" which Roy Hattersley described as "ridiculous".[15] The *South London Press* castigated her for "launching herself at targets with the unwavering aggression of an Exocet missile."[16]

The first budget meeting for any new council is often a tricky one. For Bellos, only having been a councillor for a year, it must have been nerve wracking. The position agreed by the LGC and in the manifesto was for a standstill budget, but due to various other financial factors there would still be a cut of £3.4 million. The proposal was to cut the housing repairs budget in order to ensure that no jobs would be lost. The majority of the councillors backed this proposal but Steve French, as head of construction services and a man opposed to any cuts on principle, made clear his intention to vote against. In a circular to Labour Party members he explained his reason for rejecting the budget: "Only 10 months after the surcharge and disqualification of 31 Lambeth Councillors, the new leadership have capitulated to the first obstacle placed in our way." Furthermore, "we will not be throwing [the manifesto] away after the elections... we will be fighting to see that it is implemented, whatever obstacles placed in our way."[17] At the council meeting eight councillors voted against the cuts, Steve French, John Harrison, Bill Houghting, George Huish, Jonathan Oppenheimer, Greg Tucker and Rachel Webb. This was the beginning of a ferocious battle among the Labour group at the council.

---

13 Interview with Joan Twelves, February 2016.
14 'The racist and gay hate past of Speaker John Bercow – who's now the hero of the right-on MPs who are battling to block Brexit', *Daily Mail*, 20 March 2019
15 *Illustrated London News*, Sunday 1 November 1987.
16 *South London Press*, 2th October 1987.
17 Report to Lambeth Local Government Committee, October 1987 [private papers of Joan Twelves].

THE TOWN HALL SOCIAL

It is impossible to underestimate the centrality of the Town Hall in the political life of the borough. Centred in the heart of Brixton, the building was the focal hub of the local government unions as well as the left councillors and the Labour Party. But it was in the basement of the Town Hall that the politics really happened.

The Lambeth Social Club was formed in the wake of the formation of The Lambeth Workers Joint Trade Union Committee and was opened with the patronage of Knight, who gave the Club the old court room in the Town Hall basement. Originally it was split level; the upper dais was where the magistrate had sat with the royal coat of arms. Trade unionist Jim O'Brien, the first Chair of the Club, had been tried in the court as a juvenile. Initially just for trade union members and guests, the entry requirements ended up being slightly loosened as councillors, staff, protesters and various local figures would retire there to drink and chat after a protest or a lengthy council meeting. People would head there for a drink after any Brixton demo and regularly bumped into other local lefties. The more right wing council staff would drink in the Trinity, a couple of minutes walk away from the council premises, so the left had the run of the place. Kitted out with a jukebox, dartboard, regular bridge and cribbage sessions, a folk night on the second Tuesday of every month, and live Jazz on the first Thursday, the bar was a popular and cheap haunt. During long council sessions, members of the public would leave the gallery, get a drink or two and then go back up to heckle the councillors. The drinks were a modest price too – 86p for a lager, 95p for Guinness and 80p for Tartan Bitter.[18]

Ed Hall remembered the venue fondly: "In its heyday it was very popular with sell out Saturday events. Trade unionists and elected councillors mixed in a way not seen before or since. Louise Garret of the *South London Press* was a regular visitor, anxious for stories."[19] The social club was run by a management committee and held an AGM. The committee had to deal with disciplinary issues; the volatile mix of adrenaline and alcohol during the intense political battles of the 1980s was a recipe for fist fights. One alteration involved Steve French and John Bercow. Bercow was apparently barred for a time, though some considered the evidence against him 'shaky'.[20]

The social club was popular with Tory councillors but less so with the Liberals, who attempted to get it closed down. Even the Council objected in court to the renewal of the alcohol license but this failed as no evidence of misconduct was presented to the licensing magistrates.

---

18 86p in 1987 is equivalent to £2.54 in 2019.
19 Interview with Ed Hall, October 2015.
20 Interview with Joan Twelves, February 2016.

Scottish anti-Poll Tax leader Tommy Sheridan would occasionally attend the Council's sessions in the late 1980s, commenting that the quality of the heckling from the gallery and the visceral hatred of the Tory and Labour Councillors for each other made the Town Hall the "best free entertainment in London."[21] After 1986 a special room adjoining the bar (the red room) was covered with photos from the recent rate-capping struggle. The famous banners that Hall made for the protests were also stored safely away there behind glass cases to shield them from spilt beer.

Some Council workers criticised the culture in the town hall social, feeling that it was the kind of place where union leaders would mix too readily with the councillors and all manner of backroom deals were cut. Concerns over collaboration were matched by a feeling that the alcohol helped create loose lips, the local journalists undoubtedly picked up a story or two from the inebriated left wingers hanging around the bar.

Away from the political machinations and manoeuvres of the Town Hall, Lambeth was facing even greater economic problems. The closure of the GLC near Waterloo was going to hit many local residents hard, as thousands of jobs would be lost. The West Lambeth Health Authority had just been beaten in a bruising dust-up with the government, the result of which was that two hospitals had to close, threatening more unemployment. The public sector cuts followed hot on the heels of the deindustrialization of the north of the borough where factories like the Unigate milk processing plant (closed in 1978) and British Vinegars Ltd's bottling plant (closed 1982) were being replaced by retail; the first Sainsbury's supermarket built in London was opened at Nine Elms by Margaret Thatcher in 1982. Along with the rest of the country, Lambeth was changing.

---

21 Interview with Steve Nally, August 2017.

12

Queer in Lambeth

Lambeth in the 1980s was much like any other inner London area for lesbians and gays – a cultural and political battle ground. Whilst the borough had a relatively healthy night life and some places where homosexuals could go without being accosted by bigots or the police, it was still on occasion a dangerous place. Homosexual relations between men had been legalised by Labour in the 1960s and Stonewall and the Gay Liberation Front, among others, had been fighting prejudice and bigotry in the ensuing decade. Lambeth had a very active LGBT community, many people were active in politics as well as cultural events. Out In Lambeth was one particularly popular event, an art festival with a series of plays. The Oval Theatre was doing some pioneering work, putting on plays written and performed by gays and lesbians. One play, *The Risk*, was written Nigel Young and Stephen Gee, both of whom had gone on a City Literary Institute course on 'Existentialism, Surrealism and Marxism' which inspired them to delve deeper into new dramatic forms and representations of social and political relationships on stage. The flyer was emblazoned with a pink triangle and solemnly declared "those who talk about changing the world without changing themselves talk with corpses in their mouths."

But as homosexuality moved out of the closet and the less salubrious venues into the mainstream the backlash grew stronger. It was a time where lesbians and gays had to fight for their rights to be in public, to defy those who insulted them or attacked them for 'flaunting' their sexuality.

If the black community was under siege and threatened with ghettoisation, the gays and lesbians could, with no hint of irony, say they felt the same. This was the middle of the AIDS epidemic. A leaflet warning people of the dangers of infection was being delivered to every house in the country – the first time such a feat had been attempted since the war. On TV screens and in cinemas before the main feature, the government had put out a terrifying advert; John Hurt's booming voice about the dangerous new disease as a black monolith was being carved with the words, "AIDS. Don't die of ignorance".

But ignorance was everywhere. Despite the official government line that HIV and AIDS could strike you whether you were gay or straight, the popular view was that this was a gay disease. The more fanatical believed that possibly this was even a plague from God sent to the sodomites, a sign of the end times.[1] The US Reverend Jerry Falwell set the agenda, proclaimed on national TV in the US that "a God who hates sin has stopped [homosexuality] dead in its tracks by saying, 'Do it and die'".[2] But the homophobia spread to all corners, compounding the view that gay men in particular were engaged in heinous acts that now spread physical as well as moral sickness. Some firefighters were refusing to give the kiss of life to gay men due to a perceived risk of contracting AIDS. Inmates at Wandsworth prison were threatening to kill gay prisoners in case they spread the virus. The *South London Press* published articles by local doctors appealing for calm but misinformation and suspicion was everywhere. The fear spread to drug users. A heroin addict died in a flat in Kennington and there was community hysteria about it in case he had the virus.

In Lambeth the LGBT scene was struggling to come to terms with the new threat. For many young gay men it seemed a bitter homophobic irony that just as they were coming out and getting loud and proud a new blight was being cast on them. Of course, for the bigots it all made sense; promiscuous, unnatural gays were getting what they deserved. As such the essential issue facing LGBT people was the same as it had ever been: widespread homophobia, both of a casual nature on the street but also the official homophobia of the state. As the Conservatives had always claimed to be a party of 'traditional' family values, many of them saw homosexuality as either a sin, if they were religiously inclined, or a perversion, associating it with paedophilia or other scandalous paraphilias. The LGBT movement had struggled hard in the 1970s, especially after Stonewall, to not be afraid of violent attacks from either the far right or the police. When straight people complained that the concepts of 'pride' in your sexuality or being 'out and proud' were just a bit too ostentatious, with a patronising *couldn't you just tone it down a bit* – they fundamentally misunderstood how the oppressed must often express themselves in proud, unabashed ways precisely in order to carve out a legitimate space in any society.

Lambeth Council in 1985 was the first council to propose prioritising some housing schemes for people with AIDS, to ensure they didn't become homeless and could get proper support for something that was effectively a death sentence in the mid-1980s. Mary Leigh, leader of the local

---

1 Anthony Michael Petro, *After the Wrath of God: AIDS, Sexuality, and American Religion* (Oxford University Press 2015), pp. 31-4.
2 Peter L. Allen, *The Wages of Sin: Sex and Disease, Past and Present* (University of Chicago Press 2000), p. 121.

Conservatives ridiculed the proposal as "another example of a load of left-wing loonies desperate for electoral support who believe that they will attract the homosexual vote by such a move."[3] Such views were not uncommon at the time, and the charge of 'courting the homosexual vote' was also one thrown around by the right wing of the Labour party.

The AIDS crisis and generalised homophobia saw tragedy strike when Anthony Connolly, a young gay man who frequented the Prince of Wales pub, was found dead, having been beaten and then stuffed into a railway shed near to Brixton train station. The police initially refused to process the body or order an autopsy; when it was suspected that Connolly was gay they suddenly become especially wary, worried about possible infection. Rumours flew that he had been picked up at the Prince of Wales and murdered by a homophobe. The fear struck home; the Prince was one of the LGBT success stories, a gay friendly pub right smack bang in the middle of Brixton, opposite the cinema and the town hall. Police still hung around late at night because of the raucous parties and steady stream of gay men that they could scowl at, but it was a safer place than most of the dive bars and some of the seedier pubs in south London.

Connolly's murderer had killed before and would kill again. He was named Michael Lupo, a Brazilian man who had been diagnosed with HIV. His diagnosis had driven him into a murderous rage, blaming gay men for his infection, hating them for what he perceives as promiscuity and recklessness, even though it was similar behaviour on his part led to his condition. Wanting cold, calculating retribution he decided to kill as many gay men as he could. Connolly had been unlucky when he agreed to leave with Lupo that night. After one of Lupo's victims escaped he some time later later spotted him in the Prince of Wales. The victim reported the crime to the police who agreed to organise a stake-out of the pub to catch the 'gay killer' striking London. They seized Lupo the following Saturday. He confessed to the killings of four gay men after police found a torture chamber in his flat.

People in Lambeth didn't take such violence or the threat to life lightly, there was a real sense that people needed community as a form of solidarity. Although by the 1980s the activists who made up the Brixton Fairies (who ran LGBT local theatre) had moved on to other things, new militant organisations like the Radical Dykes, operating out of Railton Road, had replaced them. The initial battles over the right to hold hands or kiss in pubs with bigoted threats, the fight for public displays of affection, hadn't led to widespread acceptance, but had led to some gay run or gay friendly pubs in prominent locations, like the Prince of Wales. The Fridge Bar had also been a central hub of the gay scene since the early 1980s when punk scene veterans Andrew Czezowski and Susan Carrington (two founders of the Roxy Club) opened it up. The Fridge replaced the old Ram Jam Club on 390

---

3 'Move to house Aids victims', *Glasgow Herald*, 11 December 1985.

Brixton Road, which had played soul and reggae and hosted Otis Reading and Jimi Hendrix. In the 80s it was a hub for the New Romantics and other fresh-faced kids experimenting with gender, sexuality and synthesisers. When the ACE cinema next to the Town Hall caught fire and was closed in 1985, Czezowski and Carrington moved Fridge there.

Famous Lesbian and Gay venues like the Royal Vauxhall Tavern also had to regularly fight off the redevelopers and occasional police raids. Since the Stonewall protests the police found it harder to target the gay community directly for their sexual activity so they would use the excuse of raids looking for drugs associated with the scene. One raid in 1986 saw police wearing rubber gloves (to protect them from HIV) storm the venue, seizing amyl nitrite and arresting the landlord and several staff members. A month later another raid saw 35 police storm in. Finding little of interest they arrested a dozen men for being "being drunk on licensed premises," making them sign statements back at the police station before letting them go.[4] It was this kind of harassment which still blighted the LGBT scene. One incursion saw Lily Savage, who was the performer that night, arrested for loud protests against the heavy-handed policing and the obvious targeting of men who were just out having a good time.

The left run Council prioritised joining the fight for LGBT rights. Whilst they had only limited resources, they would at least help combat the criminalisation of gay culture. For instance, they instructed park attendants who managed public lavatories not to call the police on cottaging gay men. One enraged Kennington resident fired back: "If lavatory attendants are going to 'call time' on calling the police, who spend time catching those committing offences, lets hope the attendants also throw out the homosexuals seen hanging around these lavatories. Surely with their Gay pubs, clubs, centres, etc. homosexuals need not clutter up the lavatories as well."[5]

It was the efforts of the Labour left in local government to promote LGBT rights that drew so much ire from the right and the newspapers. Anti-gay cartoons appeared regularly in the press; one particularly offensive one portrayed Neil Kinnock as a soldier inspecting his troops, caricatures of gays and lesbians, and a racist depiction of a black person. Each one was emblazoned with a badge, GAY POWER, LESBIAN POWER, AIDS POWER, ANTI-RACIST POWER.[6] The cartoonist Michael Cummings, had received an OBE in 1983 and rejoiced in mocking progressive causes and the left all of his career. Other cartoons by Stanley McMurtry (Mac in the *Daily Mail*) also drew some particularly obnoxious cartoons and was criticised throughout his career for racist depictions, or depicting refugees as rats.

---

4 gayinthe80s.com/2015/12/1987-police-londons-gay-pubs/
5 Letters page, *South London Press*, 2 July 1985.
6 Michael Cummings, *Sunday Express*, 8 Feb 1987.

The view that local Labour Councils were wasting resources and time on 'gay seminars' or 'parenting tips for lesbian parents' was a common one in newspapers.[7] In a regular column starting in 1983 in *Gay Times* magazine, called "Media Watch", Terry Sanderson documented the mainstream homophobia in the British press, including *The Sun*'s infamous headline of "Perverts are to blame for the killer plague".[8] The entrance into public life of discussions on LGBT issues and experiences sent shockwaves across an emotionally fragile and reactionary middle England. Anonymous posters went up in East London declaring:

> My name is Betty Sheridan. I live in Haringey. I'm married with two children. And I'm scared. If you vote Labour they'll go on teaching my kids about GAYS & LESBIANS instead of giving them proper lessons.[9]

With an openly lesbian leader of the Council, Lambeth was particularly subjected to reporters looking for a scandal. It was rumoured that lesbian and gay books were displayed in two play centres in the borough – children being exposed to 'gay propaganda' was a regular feature of right-wing moral panics at the time.[10] Bellos suffered another national scandal when the council decided to prioritise homeless people with AIDS getting council flats. The argument was totally understandable; they were some of the most vulnerable and had the most complex needs, housing was essential to create the conditions to help those people, but that didn't stop the tabloids from indulging in their usual outrage at political correctness going mad..[11]

Such was the anti-gay onslaught in the press that the Labour apparatus also began to cave in. Patricia Hewitt wrote an internal memo in 1987 declaring that "the gay and lesbians issue is costing us dear among the pensioners, and fear of extremism and higher taxes is particularly prominent in the GLC area."[12] In her memoirs, *The Witchfinder General, A Political Odyssey*, Labour apparatchik Joyce Gould repeated word for word the (false) claim by Tory journalist Peter Jenkins that Lambeth London Borough Council banned

---

7 'Gay Rights at 50: the British Media are still guilty of the same homophobia', *The Independent*, 26 July 2017.
8 *The Sun*, 12 December 1987, for this and more examples see gtmediawatch.org/.
9 Advert paid for by the Committee for a Free Britain and placed in *The Sun* and *Evening Standard* on 8 June 1987.
10 Anna Marie Smith, *New Right Discourse on Race and Sexuality: Britain 1968-1990* (Cambridge University Press 1994), p. 192.
11 Anti-gay stories continued to proliferate around the lifestyles of the LGBT community and the 'revulsion' that straight people might feel for them. The continued criticisms around spending for LGBT services by left run councils took on an even more sinister dimension during the AIDS plague during these years. See Matt Cook, "Archives of Feeling': the AIDS Crisis in Britain 1987', *History Workshop Journal*, Volume 83, Issue 1, Spring 2017.
12 Colin Hughes and Patrick Wintour, *Labour Rebuilt: The New Model Party* (Fourth estate 1990), p. 19.

the word "family" from council literature because this was "discriminatory".¹³

Riding the homophobic tide, the government decided to take action to please the bigots in the Home Counties. In 1987 the introduction of Section 28 of the Local Government Bill which sought to ban the supposed 'encouragement of homosexuality' forbade councils and their staff from any "publicity, teaching, funding, other help (e.g. room and premises use) and all local authority 'promotion' of lesbians and gay men."

Furthermore,

> Local authorities shall not
>
> (a) promote homosexuality or publish material for the promotion of homosexuality;
> (b) promote the teaching in any maintained school of the acceptability of homosexuality as a pretended family relationship.

This came in the context of a wider Conservative agenda to 'preserve moral values' and attacking liberal and left wing teachers. Thatcher gave a conference speech condemning "extremist teachers from hard left authorities" who were "teaching anti-racist mathematics".¹⁴ The entire ideological basis of section 28 was that homosexuality was a perverted lifestyle, a debilitating sickness that could be taught or caught through exposure to the very idea of homosexuality. Thatcher was clear: young children should not be taught they have "an inalienable right to be gay."¹⁵ The fear was that local councils were bulk buying copies of *Jenny Lives With Eric and Martin* by Susanne Bösche, (a translation of a 1981 Danish book which told the story of a little girl living with her two dads), and using this to indoctrinate children in primary schools.¹⁶ The problem was how you classified 'promotion'; was telling someone about something promoting it? As the Duke of Norfolk put it: "The clause does not contain a word to curtail the publishing of books, plays, films or videos, which stand on their own artistic merit provided that they are not used as a cover plan to *hide the primary aim* of the *sinister* corruption of youth by promoting homosexuality."¹⁷ The idea of corruption of youth was quaint, bringing to mind the trial of Socrates and his subsequent suicide by hemlock. Lord

---

13 Joyce Gould, *The Witchfinder General: A Political Odyssey*, (Biteback Publishing 2016), ch. 9.
14 Speech to Conservative Party conference, Blackpool, October 1987.
15 'Section 28: What was Margaret Thatcher's controversial law and how did it affect the lives of LGBT+ people?', *The Independent*, 24 May 2018.
16 Adam Mars-Jones, 'The book that launched section 28', *Index on Censorship*, Issue 8 1988, pp. 37-40.
17 *Hansard*, 2 February 1988, House Of Lords.

Mason of Barnsley was undoubtedly the most honest: "Many people believe that permissiveness has also gone too far."[18]

The introduction of this legislation, which campaigners feared would prohibit local authorities from providing any LGBT centred services in the middle of the AIDS epidemic, demonstrated just how little the government cared for the health and safety of that community. As Lambeth NALGO pointed out, gay and lesbian people were around 10% of the population and paid their taxes but would be denied local services tailored to their needs, just at a time when they most needed it. Young people needed to be educated around sexuality so they could be safe. Section 28 came down like a tonne of bricks on progressive education. Hundreds of gay people were dying because of HIV and AIDS, there was a literal fight for survival. Section 28 was also a bigot's charter, an excuse for whipping up violence against homosexuals. When the offices of *Capital Gay*, (a free weekly LGBT newspaper), was firebombed things escalated.[19] Tory MP Dame Elaine Kellett-Bowman defended the attack, declaring, "I am quite prepared to affirm that it is quite right that there should be an intolerance of evil."[20] Across the country homophobic attacks increased.

The Labour Party leadership shamefully put up no opposition. Dr Jack Cunningham, the scourge of left Labour councillors, confidently informed parliament that "I speak on behalf of the Labour Party when I say that it is not, and never has been, the duty or responsibility of either a local or education authority to promote homosexuality… The Labour Party does not believe that councils or schools should promote homosexuality…"[21] Clearly the point was to challenge the notion of 'promotion' itself, because the moralist conservative right were conflating promotion with simply teaching about or even potentially providing services for.

The opposition was left up to people on the ground, and it was extensive. A mass movement erupted in Manchester with a demonstration of around 20,000 people. Similar numbers marched in London in April 1988, from Embankment to Kennington Park. Lesbians invaded ITV newsrooms during a live broadcast and abseiled down the walls of the House of Lords when the bill was being debated. Despite the law being passed, no council or teacher was ever prosecuted under its provision, though one teacher in Labour controlled Bradford was almost sacked for telling his students he was gay, a threat that was rescinded when the National Union of Teachers threatened to strike.[22] However the damage was done in the sense that many

---

18 Ibid, speaking on the Local Government Bill.
19 *New Scientist*, 29 July 1989, Volume 123, p. 45.
20 Colin Clews, *Gay in the 80s: From Fighting our Rights to Fighting for our Lives* (Troubadour 2017), p. 135.
21 David M. Rayside, *On the Fringe: Gays and Lesbians in Politics* (Cornell University Press 1998), p. 30.
22 Interview with Jonathan Blake, February 2019.

teachers, healthcare professionals and librarians self-censored, nervous of ending up sacked or imprisoned.

One personal story perhaps sums up a lot of the opportunities as well as the problems at the time. Like many people, Jonathan Blake remembered being unemployed and out of work in 1985 (the distinction is important, some people were officially unemployed but working in various cash-in-hand jobs or signing onto the dole whilst also working on being a musician or an artist for example). The GLC had just launched a scheme to tackle unemployment whereby you paid £1 and you could attend any class at a London college. Jonathan had a background in theatre so when he found out that two of his friends were doing a trouser-making class he tagged along to see if he could retrain as a tailor to make costumes. At the trouser-making course at Morley college they were taught by an elderly Jewish tailor called Harry, who instructed them to sit up on the table (as tailors do when cutting cloth). As Jonathan settled, cross-legged on the table, he remembered, "it was heaven! My father sold furniture and I was never allowed to sit on the tables." During the class there was a discussion on designing patterns, someone piped up "they do that at London School of Fashion." Jonathan was intrigued and decided to venture up into town to check out the course – he had paid his pound so it was time to see what he could get. He was told it was a three-year City and Guilds diploma and was initially sceptical. As he had been diagnosed with HIV he wasn't sure he would live to see the end of the course. But life with HIV was often about displacement activity, keeping yourself busy so you didn't think about other things.

Deciding to go on the course he went to Lambeth Council to get a £3,000 grant, guilt-tripping the Council officers by telling them "if you don't then you are condemning me to a life on the dole." Jonathan retrained as a tailor, specialising in costume design. He tried to get a job at the English National Opera but struggled as the ENO was locked in negotiations with the union BECTU, and said they couldn't hire full-time employees. Jonathan was insistent however, he was worried that the HIV would incapacitate him and he needed the sick pay. Despite being one of the first people diagnosed with the virus, Jonathan survived and still lives in Brixton. He went on to be involved in Lesbians and Gays Support the Miners, eventually being played in the movie *Pride* by Dominic West.

Jonathan and his partner helped organise the 'gay commune' on Mayall Road, a collection of houses with the garden walls knocked down to create a communal space. Because so many people were involved in the creative arts there was a blurring of the line between homes and performance spaces; Ernst Fischer famously put on plays in his front room at 148 Mayall Road. In order to move beyond precarious arrangements, these homes evolved into the Brixton Housing Co-op, a legacy that remains to this day of the once vibrant housing activist scene east of Brixton underground station.

13

Anti-Racism and Anti-Apartheid

Brixton-Soweto: under attack, we fight back![1]

Although Lambeth was often associated with religious sects and preachers outside its tube station, there was also a highly politicised and radical tendency in the community. The ideas of Garveyism and Rastafarianism, as well as the strength of the Labour Party in the local black community was clear. There were also forms of black socialism in the borough which were based on specifically African left-wing ideas, such as Ujamaa and Ubuntu. Ujamaa was a system of village co-operatives based on equality and sustainability which was made popular by Tanzanian president, Julius K Nyerere. Ujamaa was rooted in a particular view of national development, the idea of self-reliance, nationalisation and communal ownership of the land. Ubuntu is the philosophical view that "I am because others are", that no-one is an island, and only through unity and collaboration can positive change come. It too was rooted in African ideals of humanism and decolonialisation, but from South Africa rather than Tanzania.[2]

One of the political issues that dominated international politics in the 1980s was the struggle against apartheid in South Africa. The oppressive Whites First legislation in South Africa had been controversial for many years, but there was a renewed push by the African National Congress and other organisations to destabilise the regime through a variety of tactics, including non-violent direct action, mass demonstrations, withholding taxes, mass strikes, and so on. The aim was to divide the South African whites and fashion a movement that could inspire international support from even the

---

[1] Gavin Brown, 'Brixton-Soweto: contours of solidarity', nonstopagainstapartheid.wordpress.com/2011/09/23/brixton-soweto-contours-of-solidarity/
[2] Christelle Terreblanche, 'The Climate Crisis: South African and Global Democratic Eco-Socialist alterntive', in Vishwas Satgar (ed), *The Climate Crisis: South African and Global Democratic Eco-Socialist Alternatives* (Wits University Press 2018).

most mainstream forces and institutions. The key instrument to achieve this was the international boycott. The boycott had been around since the late 1950s but it had really begun to gain serious momentum in the late 1970s.

Scenes on television of the violence in South Africa, of police beating black people, of a national liberation struggle in real time, struck home, especially for people in Brixton. It looked like a more extreme version of what was happening in their own communities, as if that is how the whites in power would treat you if they could get away with it. The fact that the ANC was considered a dangerous terrorist organisation by the Tories underlined that legitimate representatives of oppressed people were being vilified.[3] A lot of people were making connections between the nature of imperialism and colonialism abroad and at home. The reggae band, Steel Pulse produced an album in 1988 with the song, *State of Emergency*, exemplifying the kind of internationalist outlook for many at the time:

> Forever, we will strive.
> The whole wide world is burning.
> Forever, we will strive.
> Ring, ring, gun shot, ring.
> From Brixton to Cape Town,
> Unrest all around.[4]

This feeling of a global unrest against structuralised, violent racism led to frustrations when the British wing of the ANC solidarity campaign, the Anti Apartheid Movement (AAM), founded in 1959, blanket refused to do any anti-racist campaigning in Britain. The aim of AAM was to put pressure on the Thatcher government to stop dialogue with the apartheid regime and join the International boycott, for them engaging in a critical argument about racism for black people in Britain was a dangerous diversion that would have muddied the waters. This position caused some controversy and soul searching in the AAM when they were debating why there were so few black people active in their organisation.[5]

For those looking for more radical politics than the liberalism of the AAM, there were huge debates on the nature of the struggle in South Africa. Whilst some saw it merely as a kind of anti-colonial struggle to establish a liberal democracy, others saw in the mass strikes the possibility of a more radical socialist future. Within the black community there was a debate between the politics of the ANC and the Pan-Africanists. Generally, there was unity around the need to support the anti-apartheid struggle, but that was only a question of practical unity with people in struggle; the question was, should it go further? This was also a time of armed movements – the

---

3   'Margaret Thatcher branded ANC 'terrorist' while urging Nelson Mandela's release', *The Independent*, 9 December 2013.
4   Steel Pulse, *State of Emergency* (MCA Records 1988).
5   For more on this issue, see Elizabeth Williams, *The Politics of Race in Britain and South Africa: Black British Solidarity and the Anti-Apartheid Struggle* (Bloomsbury 2015).

Symbiose Liberation Front, IRA, Red Army Faction, Italy had recently had its 'years of lead', the ANC had its own armed wing Umkhonto weSizwe (Spear of the Nation). Many people felt that the British state was heading towards fascism, that the deep state would never tolerate a left wing government or a militant black movement. One local anti-racist activist remembered: "Those forces were present in the debate too. Looking back on it the African Liberation movement didn't take up arms in the UK, Barclay's wasn't bombed, but who was to say it wouldn't be at some point?"[6] It was during this time that some of the armed groups from abroad were making approaches to the black liberation movement. Frankly, some of the young activists were tempted to go down the urban insurrection route. The violence of the British state against the black population, the violence of the South African apartheid state, wasn't it all part of the same struggle? In the end though, the road of armed insurrection wasn't taken, the wise-heads won out against the hot-heads, arguing that armed confrontation was not the stage the struggle was at. The feeling was that the state would be only too happy to shoot and kill more black people if there was any hint of bringing some of the more violent forms of resistance to areas like Brixton.

When it came to the international campaign around the South Africa boycott, Lambeth Council also took practical solidarity action, for instance banning Tarmac from building contracts and moving the council bank account from Barclays.[7] In May 1984 the Council adopted a statement against apartheid that pledged an active boycott of all trade and cultural links with South Africa and also to rename streets and buildings after famous opponents of apartheid.[8] Prior to this there had been a dispute with the residents of Rhodesia Road when the Council proposed to rename it to Zimbabwe Road. The eight affected residents petitioned the sub-committee responsible to keep their original name, only for their current street name to be dismissed by Cllr Terry Rich as "Imperialist Trash".[9]

By the time the proposal came to the Civic Amenities Committee in 1986 to rename parks and libraries in Lambeth after prominent Black people, including South African revolutionaries, there was uproar. The Chair of the committee, Sharon Atkin, had proposed a list of 28 parks and other amenities, like the Streatham swimming pool, to be renamed; Brockwell Park was to be called Zephania Mothopeng Park and South Lambeth Library would become Angela Davies Library.[10] The plans were leaked to the *South London Press*, who had a field day, whipping up all manner of complaints ('MAD MAD WORLD!' read the headline). Inevitably, their letter page was

---

6 Interview with Neil Williamson, March 2019.
7 As reported in Lambeth NALGO's journal, *Lamb*, April 1983, p. 6.
8 Lambeth Council Annual Report, 1985/86, p. 1.
9 *The Observer*, 11 November 1984.
10 Stewart Lansley, Sue Goss, Christian Wolmar, Councils in Conflict: The Rise and Fall of the Municipal Left (Macmillan 1989), p. 128.

full of enraged missives from local residents complaining about how ridiculous the foreign names sounded: "imagine asking the way to Shapurji Saklatvala Park (Myatts Fields)" wrote the head of the Herne Hill Society.[11] The fact that Saklatvala had been a south London Labour MP in Battersea in the 1920s (and had been arrested for speaking at a mass open-air rally of workers in support of the 1926 general strike) was lost on people – there was only moral outrage over foreign-sounding names. One person suggested renaming the borough Zongolapopo-m'belebele, after an old African king. One letter stated that "the true racists of Lambeth are in the Marxist element in the council. Viciously anti-English."[12] The *South London Press* helpfully produced a 'diary of a citizen of the new look Lambeth' which described how "We walked from Zimbabwe Road but it was a cold day so we caught the bus from Shapurji Saklatvakla. We had thought on taking a dip at the Mangaliso Sobukwe pool but decided instead to kick a ball about in Zephania Mothopeng Park…."[13] The fevered story goes on. Where Lambeth did successfully change names with no backlash was with their own buildings. Various offices housing different directorates were renamed after prominent black people, for instance Paul Robeson House, Mary Seacole House in Clapham and Olive Morris House.[14]

There were some legitimate concerns; the councillors had tried to pass the new names without any consultation with local residents and it was clearly going to be a contentious issue. For a council that pleaded democracy and socialism it was not a good look to simply impose changes on local people. But behind the complaints about process and transparency there were clear, strong currents of racism running through the jokes made at the expense of 'difficult to pronounce African names'. For her part, Atkin remained defiant, pointing out that Britain had a colonial history of exporting English names abroad.[15] The level of hostility and resistance to having African and Asian names imposed on a community should have perhaps given some residents pause to think about Britain's own imperial past which was so relevant and often painful to the local immigrant black population.

Despite the outrage, in her final weeks as a councillor Atkin did succeed in renaming a handful of locations in Lambeth. Atkin's particular love of Jazz musician Max Roach led to an Angell Road Park being renamed after him, there is also Francis Barber Close (Barber was a servant to Dr Johnson) and various council houses in SW8, bordering Wandsworth, were named after prominent black athletes, such as the javelin thrower Tessa Sanderson

---

11 *South London Press*, 4 March 1986, p. 20.
12 *South London Press*, 14 February 1986, p. 6.
13 Ibid.
14 Of those three only Mary Seacole house remains, Olive Morris House was demolished in 2020.
15 *South London Press*, 14 February 1986, p. 2.

and decathlete Daley Thompson. However, the more radical proposals regarding Brockwell Park were dropped by the Labour group under pressure from the local Constituency Labour Parties after the tirade of abuse from the local media and some residents.

Other anti-racist activists set their sights on the legacy of Henry Tate in Brixton Oval. A bust of his head was displayed in front of Tate Brixton Library. Some argued for the statue's removal as Tate's fortune was made in the import and refining of sugar, a commodity intricately linked to slave labour in the Caribbean. Several of Lambeth's libraries were funded by Tate. Activists saw cruel irony in the fact that the descendants of those battered and enslaved on sugar plantations now borrowed books from buildings commissioned by the sugar magnate. Tate was neither slave-owner nor slave-trader but prospered in an industry constructed on a foundation of slavery. The campaign was unsuccessful and the proposal to rename the library was rebuffed, though David Warner from the Brixton Society did suggest that the reference section and reading room be named after CLR James, which was agreed to.

Ultimately Tate's head was left where he was, though Bellos did have a memorial to the 1960 massacre at Sharpeville erected in the square only feet away. The massacre at Sharpeville was a notorious moment in the legacy of South African racism. A protest march on a police station was fired on by the police. When the guns fell silent there were 69 dead and nearly 200 injured. But the memorial was not uncontroversial, even within the left. The demonstration had been called by the Pan-African Congress (PAC), a different party to the ANC. Such was the hostility, putting the Sharpeville memorial up in the centre of Brixton led to angry exchanges with the representatives of the ANC in London. Bellos was a member of Black Action for the Liberation of South Africa (BALSA), a different group to the official Anti Apartheid Movement. BALSA activists criticised AAM for being too white and too middle-class. Bellos had been to the local Lambeth branch of AAM and told them in no uncertain terms that the AAM had to do more to attract black people.[16] Even in the anti-apartheid struggle there was competition for leadership between different ideologies and factions.

Lambeth trade unionists were also the centre of controversy at the time. Both Lambeth and Birmingham Trades Council issued statements condemning the TUC's inaction on apartheid. The TUC had passed a motion in 1985 supporting the boycott but some on the left felt that not enough was being done to make it a living campaign. Lambeth Trade's Council called a lobby of the TUC on 23 July 1986, demanding a TUC fronted campaign of all trade unions for a blockade and workers' sanctions. The TUC launched a funded advert to promote the boycott, which was shown in cinemas. Not to rest on their laurels, Lambeth joint trade unions committee followed up with a further criticism, calling on unions to "push

---

16 Interview with Marc Wadsworth, November 2018.

the TUC beyond adverts in newspapers and into encouraging direct action in the workplace. Individual action by consumers [was] not enough. Collective action in the workplace is long overdue."[17] They called a conference, alongside the City of London anti-Apartheid group (also left critics of the AAM) but the meeting was denounced by the AAM as divisive and sectarian. All of these activities put the Trade's Council on the wrong side of the TUC one too many times. One ex-participant remembered that "we kept on being shut down by the TUC all the time for passing motions calling for the arming of the South African black working class."[18]

Many of these efforts were of course dismissed at the time, with the first appearance of the now familiar 'political correctness gone mad' label. They were viewed as uppity blacks who dared to rename parks and streets, who dared to build monuments to the shared struggle against racism, the anti-colonial and anti-imperialist struggle. Naturally, attempts at remembrance of a black culture that speaks to itself and for itself were derided by the media and many white politicians. By this logic, a memorial to World War One is essential and cannot be questioned but a memorial to anti-colonial resistance by black people in South Africa was a scandal. The battle to reaffirm memory, to defy the master's narrative and say that, yes, these things happened; yes, blood was shed; yes, history is real and lives in us and through us – not the safe history of a local writer getting a Blue Plaque (important though that is) but to establish an absolute truth, that the history of black people under capitalism was a bloody and dangerous thing, marked by resistance and a fateful complicated relationship to the nations that inflicted that suffering on them.

For the Tories' part, the MP for Streatham, Bill Shelton, attended a ceremony in Namibia in 1985 to inaugurate the instalment of a new South African backed transitional government.[19] Namibia was controversial as it had been handed to South Africa in 1922 by the League of Nations, against the wishes of the local population. The Multi Party Conference explicitly refused any participation by SWAPO, the armed nationalist organisation that many of the local black population identified with. The Anti-Apartheid Movement had condemned the Multi Party Conference as an unelected puppet of the South African regime. When Hazel Smith wrote to Sir Geoffrey Howe, the Foreign Minister, asking the government to cut links with the South African regime, he rebuffed the councillor arguing that "such a policy would only serve to weaken the South African economy, thus creating greater Black unemployment, and increase the polarisation of opinion within the country."[20]

---

17 Roger Fieldhouse, *Anti-apartheid: A History of the Movement in Britain: A Study in Pressure Group Politics* (Merlin 2005), p. 405.
18 Ibid.
19 12 July 1985, p 4.
20 'Apartheid Snub for council', *South London Press*, 14 February 1986, p. 15.

The overlapping terrain and interests of the radical left and a highly politicised black population provided a rich example of how campaigns and communities of resistance can emerge and struggle for a common aim, despite political or even social differences. The issue of Apartheid was central to the anti-Thatcher struggle because it showed fundamentally a difference of values; whether to support a country that practised constitutional and institutional violent racism or whether to oppose it. It is no surprise that many black people felt an affinity of struggle with the black population of South Africa; it wasn't just a question of shared ethnicity, they felt that Thatcher's Britain was engaged in systemic oppression against them also.

14

Reflections on the Housing Battleground

By the late 1980s housing remained the epicentre of the local social and political crisis. Complaints to the council were increasing and the general mood of residents was despondent that the huge backlog of repairs could be fixed. The waiting list had spiralled out of control again, 400 families were homeless by 1987, housed in bed & breakfasts at the cost of £4.2 million a year. Linda Bellos decried the Shire dwelling government ministers' policies, "All in all, municipal privatisation and systematic napalming have similar effects The government's housing policy will make thousand of people homeless and infrastructure will suffer at the hands of cowboy contractors."[1] However, Lambeth's go-slow policy and regular propaganda discouraging council house sales was having some effect. After seven years only 1,794 homes had been bought by residents, compared with 4,492 in neighbouring Wandsworth.[2]

Whilst the number of squats had declined, by the mid-1980s the short-life housing was still in full swing. The squatters of the 1970s had (mostly) become semi-legal as short-life tenants in an arm's length arrangement with the Council. Hundreds of homes across the borough were by this time run by co-operatives, the buildings managed and renovated by the residents that lived there. The Council was generally happy for this situation to continue. People would sign up with six year tenancies and end up staying for twenty.

The co-operatives were also a fascinating cross section of people. Many of them had some kind of aspirational creative dream, actors, singers, writers. Most were on the dole and many got extra money on the side — some cash-in-hand work, sometimes selling marijuana. The co-op set the rents during residents' meeting so the cost was usually negligible. Even by the mid-1990s it was often only £25-£50 a week. The most important thing was to be able to afford repairs. A lot of the houses were very cold in the winter. In the summer the wood would warp making doors hard to close and floorboards creak, but it was a home and a community.

---

1 *South London Press*, 25 September 1987, p. 6.
2 *South London Press*, 2 October 1987.

It attracted alternative living and lifestyles, radicals, vegetarians and environmentalists. Some were idealistic, seeing it as a template for future living, others were just enjoying the cheap (or non-existent) rent. Some were full time revolutionaries or anarchists, others were writing their breakthrough novels. Because of the politicised nature of the community it could get factional within the co-ops, mostly centred on rival claims for allocations when properties became available. Political living occasionally degenerates into personal grievances. Everyone wanted to move in their mates, or if you were a member of a political tendency or some kind of activist group then you wanted your comrade to move in. People would slip into arrears regularly – it was awkward to collect rent from your mates. One co-op called Coronation which was based around Hubert Grove and Tasman Road was dealing with huge rent arrears. The chair, an Irishman named Eamon, explained how they eventually had to evict a guy after he didn't pay his rent for years. They had to impose some kind of discipline on the co-operative otherwise no one would pay any rent at all, all things said it was "Not easy to be a ring master of that particular circus."[3] Eamon himself was an actor on occasion, mainly in the theatre but with a few TV appearances. His strong Cork accent gave him an opportunity to play Irish assassins in a period when TV dramas were keen to culturally reflect some of the 'The Troubles'.

The short life tenancy, an evolution of the squatting scene, in essence preserved a lot of the Victorian housing that the architects of the 1970s wanted to demolish. Bonnington Square was one such community – previously dilapidated housing, ear marked for redevelopment. The short life community preserved those houses, renovated them and then – thirty years later – they were worth millions. People that started off squatting out of desperation ended up sitting on a small fortune decades later.

There were also struggles over the council getting people housed. Abibat remembered moving to Lambeth in the early 1980s.[4] Like many young newly arrived people, she and her friend went to the housing office to find somewhere to live. The housing officer said they could move into a flat in Southwyck House, just east of Brixton. The only condition was they had to move in that same day. The Barrier Block was considered by some a neobrutalist nightmare, others felt that its imposing lines and austere veneer made it a local landmark. It was rumoured by locals that the architect had killed herself after the project was finished it was so hideous. Untrue of course, but the gossip added to the mystique of the building. There was a front page article in *The Guardian* in the 1990s implying the development was a "grey sullen wasteland, robbing people of self-respect" and blaming John Major for the development because he was chair of Lambeth Housing commission in 1970 when it was commissioned.[5] As was common in

---

3 Interview with Eamon Maguire, September 2019.
4 Interview with Abibat Olulode, July 2018.
5 *The Guardian*, 27 April 1995.

Lambeth at the time, various problems with construction had left the Barrier Block uninhabited for several months after it was completed. Inevitably the empty flats were a honey pot for squatters.

A number of people though weren't squatting the flats themselves. Imbued with the entrepreneurial spirit of the Thatcher era, they were renting out the flats to people, many of who were not aware that they were being accommodated illegally. To combat this the Council was desperate to get people into empty flats before they had to grapple with evicting people who were unsuspecting squatters. When Abibat showed up with her friend they found the flat door open and two large men showing around some people as if they were estate agents. After a short and sharp conversation the men left with their prospective tenants, leaving Abibat and her friend to sleep in the flat that night, no furniture or bed, to secure the property.

To make up for the unsightly architecture of the estate, the actual flats were quite nice though, loads of storage and two toilets, with a kitchen big enough for a table. The downside was the crime. Some women would never carry a proper handbag in case it was nicked. Abibat would walk back home with her bank cards stuffed down her socks to fool any potential thieves of muggers. There was also a few people who operated protection rackets. You would get a knock on the door and a request for money to look after your possessions. If you refused then later that week you might return home from work to find your door open and all of your furniture and white goods gone. Then you would end up paying to get your stuff back.[6]

When the police raided the estate, as they often did, it was done with such theatrics that people often simply stared at the operation in disbelief. When a raid occurred, two or three police vans would scream onto the estate, the back doors flung open to disgorge a small battalion of men in full riot gear, helmets, shields and large battering rams to get the doors open. As soon as residents heard the commotion, windows were flung open and packets of drugs would fall from the sky like narcotic rain, landing on the grass and concrete below. Usually the cops would bust a door down and drag a gaggle of young men out into the vans, hauling them off to Brixton station to be interrogated.

ANGELL TOWN ESTATE AND THE HAT

Often in working class communities the struggle over housing, rights, jobs and amenities – as well as basic dignity – can produce local leaders who come to symbolise a spirit of resistance. The estate of Angell Town had one such person in Dora Boatemah, a formidable woman who died young in 2001 but dedicated her life from the late '80s to fighting for her estate.

Angell Town had a bad reputation in Lambeth during the '80s, one of several notorious estates that occasionally appeared in the national press as scare stories of inner city life. The Council had started construction in 1974

---

6   Interview with Abibat Olulode, July 2018.

but even before it was finished in the early 1980s it was being written off as pit of crime and deprivation. Its architectural planning failed at a kind of modernist vibe but essentially was a 'pack 'em in' rabbit warren, the local press wrote off its "council blocks standing as miserable monuments to the town planning failures of the 1970s".[7]

This also has to be seen in the context of the wider housing problems in the borough. Raid reductions in the Housing Investment Programme during the 1980s and the constant squeezing of local government finance meant that there was less money to deal with housing problems. By the late 1980s 43% of residents in the borough lived in council homes but 70% of them were in need of major renovation. The scale of the problems was simply overwhelming. But this was also a deliberate move on the part of central government to foster disillusionment with council housing and encourage people to buy their homes. This philosophy in ruling circles meant that many of the people in charge saw estates like Angell Town and concluded that the only way to properly deal with them was to take them out of the withering hand of the local council and put them into the hands of the private sector which faced far less restrictions on capital expenditure. Perhaps a few highly motivated, socially mobile individuals, flush with cash, could resolve the complex social needs instead of the bureaucrats at the Town Hall?

Dr Dora Boatemah had moved to the estate in the late 1970s and rapidly become a dissenting voice against the urban decline she and her family were condemned to. She had come from a ruling class family in Ghana, whose mother had worked for the national liberation leader Kwame Nkrumah. With a background in radical politics she recruited local residents to resist the sense of terminal inner city decline, not to allow Angell Town to be branded with the dreaded term "sink estate" or referred to in the press as "notorious". The important step was to build community, a sense of social solidarity, of people caring for each other but also for the place in which they lived. Most anti-social behaviour is carried out by people alienated from community, people who, for whatever reason, are struggling personally and have little time or inclination to be 'good neighbours' or able to provide much structure for their children. Boatemah was adept at securing some money from different places to fund community projects and services. A number of disused garages were converted into shops which breathed life into the area and provided some much needed space for black owned businesses. Such was the attraction of the area that it convincing famous people like Chaka Khan and Naomi Campbell to pay a visit.

As is usually the case, people come together through struggle. They are bonded together by fighting a common enemy – it could be poverty, racism, a hated politician or a law. Struggle provides a platform for individuals to emerge, their talents to be put to use, from organising to public speaking, to engaging new people to raising money. A campaign forges people, allows

---

7   *The Guardian*, 6 February 2001.

them to play to their strengths and forces unity of common purpose. A successful campaign anyway.

Such an event was the struggle against the Housing Action Trusts (HATs). The Housing Act 1988 was being piloted through Parliament by the arch-Thatcherite Nicholas Ridley, who was also intimately involved in the looming Poll Tax saga. The proposed law allowed central government to take entire estates that were suffering from serious social or housing problems out of the hands of local authorities and place them under the auspices of a private landlord as a HAT. A HAT came with extra money to improve the housing stock and other bribes for local communities to swallow the pill. The HAT would last for five years, at the end of which the entire estate could vote on whether to go back into Local Authority control or move into a housing association or in to private hands. But the vote was rigged – not voting was counted as a YES vote meaning anyone not engaging with the process and voicing their opposition was making privatisation easier.[8]

Two estates were identified in Lambeth, Loughborough – which also had its fair share of problems – and Angell Town. The Local Council were not consulted by the government – for obvious reasons. Instead consultants were dispatched to the borough to speak to the residents directly, including local figures like Boatemah. Angell Town was picked partly because of the high number of single parents and elderly residents – the rumour was that the government believed they would offer the least resistance. Boatemah and her neighbours were less than impressed when the Consultants in their suits showed up. She excoriated the proposals; "Firstly we object to people coming in and taking over our houses without asking! Secondly it is clear that the rents will double – well we can't afford to pay market rents; thirdly we are going to have most of our rights and security taken away!"[9]

These concerns would become perennial fears as the 'regeneration' projects of the 1990s and 2000s kicked in an entire estates were hauled down and replaced with expensive flats for investors to make money from. The Lambeth residents welcomed extra money, but they knew that it came with strings attached, that homes would be torn down and replaced with more expensive dwellings that might be sold or let to yuppies not the local population. They were worried that black people in particular would lose out. One community activists referred to the HAT as 'asset stripping' of council property to feed the Thatcherite agenda.

What caused serious unease was the government's top down, autocratic approach. The initial proposal was that parliament would decide if an area got a HAT, not the local residents. Even more worryingly a HAT only had to announce its plans for the estate after it had been launched – leaving residents lumbered for five years with an unaccountable board that could

---

8 *Labour Local*, Vauxhall Labour Party's Newsletter, Autumn 1988, No 16.
9 Norman Ginsburg, 'The Housing Act 1988 and its Policy Context: A Critical Commentary', *Critical Social Policy*, Vol. 9, Issue 25, p. 73.

tear down their entire estate and potentially leave many residents homeless. Residents were not enamoured of the council's track record — in fact they had very harsh words for the people at Town Hall over the extent of disrepair and the long waiting lists to get jobs fixed. But they trusted the Tories even less and they knew the Council wouldn't sell their homes from under them.

A national campaign the National Organisation of Tenants Opposed to HATs (NOTOHATs) was launched with delegates from estates across the country affected (all but one were Labour controlled of course). Boatemah went in her capacity as chair of the local Tenant Association. As a confident black woman with a firm grasp on politics and a passionate public speaking voice, she quickly became a prominent spokesperson of the campaign. She was on the platform of the national rally for council tenants held at Central Hall in Westminster the day that the Lords debates the Housing Act 1988 and went with residents affected by other HATs to Downing Street to hand in a petition.

Such was the success of the campaign and the clear issue that Ridley was having with imposing a HAT on an estate that didn't want it, that representatives of the campaigns were invited to a tea and biscuits meeting with the Secretary of State for the Environment and his colleagues. The meeting did not go well, Mary Clerk the chair of Loughborough Road TA recounted how "Ridley was as nice as could be at the start of the meeting. We could have coffee, we could have tea, we could have biscuits. But when we asked for a ballot, we could get stuffed! We then asked if we could get the money he was offering without the HAT. When Ridley said 'No', Dora Boatemah, the Angell Town chair, banged her fist on the table and said 'Meeting over' and we all walked out."[10] After the meeting Ridley complained that he couldn't find out what people thought of the HATs if they just kept 'walking out of meetings' — as if the act of walking out of the meeting didn't send a clear enough message.

After sustained pressure the government rehired consultants in 1989 to go back to the estates and look into the implications of running an official ballot and how they could drum up support to win it. They decided to ballot estates in Sunderland first - their intelligence reports indicated that those estates were the most likely to support a HAT. They didn't reckon on local campaigners however who mobilised a decisive rejection at the ballot box — 80% voted no. A MORI poll on the estates in Lambeth commissioned by the Council had also found that there was 72% opposition to the plans. Clear that their concession of an estate ballot meant that they would lose, grudgingly the Tories admitted defeat and shelved the plans. Instead money was granted to the Loughborough and Angell Town estates and the HATs were scrapped.

---

10 *Community Action*, 1988c, p. 25.

THE CARDBOARD CITY AT WATERLOO

It was in the north of the borough that the most visceral and painful example of the complete failure of the 1980s social and housing policies of the Conservative government could be found. Around Waterloo station hundreds of homeless people had gathered to build a makeshift community, which became known as Cardboard City. London wasn't the only city to have a large temporary community built by people who had found themselves vulnerable and lacking support under a market-driven economy, similar gatherings occurred in New York as well, another city undergoing huge social problems due to right-wing economics and Conservative social policies.

Described as a 'lost civilisation', the underpasses, nooks and crannies around the Bullring, between Waterloo Train station and the Thames, were filled with "Bashes", the name for the sometimes elaborate dwellings made out of cardboard, canvass, string and tape.[11] It was the largest concentration of homeless people anywhere in London. In the heart of this property-owning democracy, not more than a short walk from Westminster, were the living symbols of the failure of Thatcherism to provide a life for everyone.

These weren't only homeless men, there were also families living there, hunched under the concrete overpass which was so low in places that you couldn't stand up straight. Many residents defended their community, angrily denying that it was unsanitary and dangerous. But the derelict nature of the area meant it was prone to problems, in 1988 a sewer pipe burst, disgorging a colony of rats over the people living there.

The place was full of people with mental health problems, drug addicts, ex-soldiers struggling to readjust, people who had just had too many knocks in life and didn't that the support system to keep them on their feet. But at Cardboard city they could at least find company and some degree of support. Inevitably a place where an 'underclass' begins to develop attracts the attention of the authorities. The Bull Ring was the site of regular police operations throughout the late 1980s, including one raid called Operation DropOut that told you all you needed to know about the attitudes of the police to the homeless people living there. At one point in the 1988 the police and fire brigade went to the Bull Ring and literally washed away the Bashes with water cannon. The residents protested and lodged claims with the council for the loss of their possessions and homes... the total compensation came to only £60 per person.

An effort was made to finally clear the Bullring of its homeless residents in May 1990 when civil engineers noticed that Waterloo bridge was losing its structure due to the nightly fires lit under it. Whilst a mix of coercion and

---

11 'The legacy of Cardboard City, and Britain's grim renaissance of homeless encampments', *The New Statesman*, 18 February 2020.

support moved most people on within a year, they started to congregate there again. The social and community services were simply not strong enough to handle the blight of homelessness in people's lives. The people who had been rehoused and managed to get their lives back on track were just replaced by new rough sleepers with nowhere to go. It would take years to undo the legacy of the Thatcherite housing policy and social programmes, and the huge increase in homelessness after 2010 would show that for some people a Conservative government always meant destitution and social misery.

15

Lambeth Isolated

> Lambeth is one of the last bastions
> Martin Jacques, *Marxism Today*

There was more of a sense of hope about the 1987 general election. Labour was behind in the polls, but they had a new leader and a more 'moderate' manifesto than in 1983, so the belief was that the impediments to victory at the previous election had been removed. Kinnock projected an air of competency and that seemed good enough for most. Labour members repeated the mantra that the country was sick of Thatcher, that her hate-fuelled attack on the miners had made her unpopular, and that people would not put up with continued long-term, structural unemployment any more. It was such whispered dreams that kept people going. In the run-up to election day there was the national *Red Wedge* tour, fronted by Billy Bragg and Paul Weller, which was a series of gigs across the country designed to mobilise the youth vote. Various musicians joined the tour, including Tom Robinson, The Beat, Bananarama, Elvis Costello, Sade, and even The Smiths, before Morrissey became an alt-right mouthpiece. The tour arrived at the Brixton Academy in 1986, leading to something of a carnival of left-wing stalls and campaigns outside on Stockwell Road. Many people in Lambeth had a lot riding on a Labour government, even one led by Neil Kinnock. That was even more true for the council.

Labour Councillors up and down the country had their fingers crossed for a good result in the 1987 general election. They desperately needed to keep to their election pledges of no cuts, but realistically that could only come about with the relief of a Labour government. Councils like Lambeth were basing some financial decisions, at least *partly*, on the hope that Thatcherism had run out of steam and Labour would win the next election, or at least produce some kind of hung parliament.[1] This was the basis of a strategy that became unofficially known as *mortgaging the future*, a series of

---

[1] Interview with Joan Twelves, June 2016.

creative accounting decisions that put the council into debt in the hope that relief was just around the corner.

The strategy proved to be a mistake, an error of perspectives that led to a very deep round of cuts that would hit many councils in 1988. To the shock of many, Thatcher was returned to power for a third time, a post-war record. No one had achieved what she had done. Sure, Labour had secured an extra 20 MPs (enough to save Kinnock from a resignation) but Thatcher and her *ideology* were still dominant. In fact, 1987 proved to be a turning point. The defeat of the miners in their historic clash with the government had signalled a strategic shift in industrial and class relations in the United Kingdom – the beginning of a long downward spiral and collapse of the kind of trade unionism that had originally given birth to the Labour Party and sustained it for years. The GLC was dead and buried. The defeat of rate-capping had convinced people like David Blunkett to give up on resistance and focus on securing a Labour government, even if it meant collapsing long held principles.[2] This type of view impacted on Labour, driving it further to the right, towards accepting the siren call of 'New Realism'. Closer to New Labour. The yuppies were the most obvious sense of things changing, that life was different now, that *Greed Was Good* and financial deregulation was going to give that steroid injection straight into the economy. The middle classes of London – furthest away from the industrial heartlands – were looking towards the Tories.

Despite the national defeat, there was some good local news in Lambeth. The vote in Norwood and Vauxhall held up handsomely and Labour halved the Tory vote in Streatham where NALGO activist Anna Tapsell stood as the candidate. Tapsell had secured the nomination after months of lobbying by the Black Section and left in the CLP. Tapsell fought a terrific campaign against William Shelton; her left credentials motivated many Vauxhall activists to cross the constituency border and invest a lot of hours in her campaign. But behind the scenes the NEC had tried to remove her before the election, only failing to do so because the CLP (including the right) was reluctant to run their whole selection process again so close to an election.[3]

The dislike of Tapsell by Kinnock was clear. During the election campaign, Tapsell found out that he was doing a photo opportunity at St Thomas's hospital in the north of the borough. She and her election agent raced up there in their car to get a photo with the leader, but when Kinnock saw them he jumped into a car and drove off at speed. Tapsell followed him through London for a few minutes, beeping her horn to make him stop the car, which he studiously ignored.[4] After the car chase came to an end, the left candidate gripped the wheel of her car, clenching her teeth in frustration

---

2 See Simon Hannah, *A Party with Socialists In It* (Pluto 2018), Chapter 5.
3 Interview with Anna Tapsell, December 2017.
4 *South London Press*, 30 January 1987, p. 21.

at how Kinnock was acting. Tapsell increased the Labour vote by 4,000 but couldn't make a dent on Shelton's command of 46% of the vote.

Holland's re-election was pretty inevitable given how staunchly Vauxhall voted red. But, even as he celebrated with his comrades, he was brooding on a thought that he couldn't share, that he had hoped for a position in the shadow cabinet worthy of his intellectual prowess, but the party's remorseless slide to the right meant that his opportunities were becoming far more limited and that someone so closely associated with the AES in the 1970s probably did not have much of a future in Labour's upper echelons.

Away from parliamentary concerns, for the Labour councillors in the Town Hall the re-election of Thatcher was a disaster. They had been counting on a Labour government to save them from having to make massive cuts. Now that the Tories' assault on local government would continue for another term, panic descended on Labour-run councils across the country, in particular London. Bellos, sensing what was coming, wrote to every Labour Council leader in July of that year, calling on them to stand firm and unite to save jobs and services. She waited for responses in the hope that a new campaign could be struck against future cuts, banking on the chance that a united front of councils across the capital could deliver a blow to Thatcher. But each council was now turning inwards, factional disputes began to dominate as the local parties despaired at ever ousting Thatcher from power. Lambeth would be left alone to handle the looming budget deficit.

When finance officers met with the committee chairs and informed them that the cuts would be substantial in 1988 there was only stunned silence to fill the room. Silence and a sense of dread about what was to come.

SPLITS IN THE LABOUR GROUP

Faced with this looming crisis, the summer of 1987 saw an inevitable and devastating split start to foment in the Labour group. This set in motion a series of events that led to breakdown and a tough factional struggle that would last until 1990, when Kinnock finally intervened to finish the left. The communication Bellos sent out to local residents on behalf of the council in 1986 had been resolutely against cuts: "You have my pledge that the new Council will safeguard services and jobs. With the support of the trade unions and the community we will continue to say No Cuts Here".[5] But a year later the government announced the rate-cap for 1988: a spending limit of £152 million was set for 1988/89, compared with £210 million in the previous year. This meant cuts of around £60 million. This was the largest cut Lambeth had faced in generations, far more than the rate-cap limit imposed during Knight's time. Bellos proposed £60 million of cuts as the only viable solution to the financial black hole. From her perspective the

---

5   Lambeth Council, *Who's who on the council*, 1986.

previous means of avoiding cuts, such as creative accounting, GLC borough stress grants, and using cash reserves, had run out.[6] All that was left was to sell off buildings and acquire capital from assets in the hope that the finances would improve soon – the 'mortgaging the future' strategy in action'.[7]

Bellos argued she was going to target them at services that, from her perspective, middle-class people used, in order to shield the more vulnerable residents.

As this was done without consulting the Local Government Committee, it caused consternation and disarray in the Group as well as the wider Labour Party in the borough. Chairs of committees that opposed the cuts were excluded from important meetings. Instead decisions were made by a smaller caucus of councillors who had supported her earlier attempt to sack the Chief Executive.

The far-left were caught in a difficult situation – they were in charge of important committees and, with Twelves as the whip, were responsible for getting support for the budget cuts through the Labour group. Twelves demonstrated a pragmatic side to her politics during the fight over the budget cuts by lobbying support for Bellos, on the basis that it was more strategically important to keep Bellos in charge than allow an LCC take over. The fear was that letting in Sorabji's followers would no doubt speed up out-sourcing of services and mean there was not even the possibility of soft opposition to the cuts. Others on the left demanded a harder line.

The right and the centre ground around Bellos were intransigent from the start: the cuts had to be made. Their view was that without a movement similar to the rate-capping fight, it was hopeless to not set a balanced budget. The left pointed to the manifesto commitments and the importance of standing up to the Tories – if Lambeth wasn't going to do it then who was? Bellos saw herself as ploughing a moderate furrow between what she described as the "Trotskyite wing" and "the Right Wing who seemed to be arguing that they would make more cuts and that they would all be painless"[8] The vote was close however, the Group instructed the leader to set a balanced budget by only 16-13.

The 5½ group, calling themselves Labour Action, placed themselves in the tradition of the radical left, but argued that the rate-capping struggle had exhausted the possibility of non-compliance with the law. Now the choice was simple: either leave office to the Tories and carry on in glorious socialist isolation or make the best of a bad deal and "provide the best services we can within the law, recognising that building mass support against the Tories needs a longer term strategy."[9] They called for a vote for Benn and Heffer,

---

6 lindabellos.co.uk/some-history [Accessed September 2019]
7 Interview with Joan Twelves, June 2016.
8 lindabellos.co.uk/some-history [Accessed September 2019]
9 Labour Action briefing, undated, early 1988.

even though some councillors like Fred Taggart saw themselves as being on the more traditional right wing of the party.

The Council responded by planning cuts and putting forward controversial plans for a Redeployment Scheme. This was to involve cutting posts by freezing recruitment when they became vacant and then moving people from other jobs to cover them. Basically people could be forced to change jobs within the Council and potentially sacked if they refused. The policy was launched but never implemented – six months later not a single member of staff had been redeployed but no-one had been recruited either, leaving large vacancies in housing and social care. This was in part due to NALGO's position of not covering vacant posts, which Taggart had pleaded with them to abandon at mass meetings of the housing directorate workforce. Some areas of housing had estimates of 25-30% unfilled posts. NALGO chair Allan McPherson described it as "like working on the Titanic".

In the face of left opposition, the right openly called for them to be removed, not only from their positions on the council, but from the Labour Group altogether. Their primary target was the chief whip, Joan Twelves. A sensible move on their part, as having a left-winger in the whips' office would make implementing the cuts and ensuring group discipline very challenging, if not impossible. Twelves and her allies were indignant at the move to sack her. In her role she had loyally built support for Linda's budget even though she personally disagreed with it.

At a Labour Group meeting in July 1987 a resolution was moved, proposing, "in response to a third term of Thatcherism, this group resolves to reject the tactics of illegal defiance, mass resignation or majority opposition."[10] The Kinnockite wing were angling against what they called gesture politics, the notion of public opposition that was tokenistic and ultimately damaging. The left opposed the motion, proposing an alternative: "to base our strategy on a commitment to the principles of the 1986 manifesto, i.e. no cuts in services, no redundancies, continued recruitment, no privatisation, no rent rises, and defend jobs and services with a practical and flexible approach to campaigning and the tactics we develop jointly with the Parties, the trade unions and the community." Councillor Rachel Webb proposed (seconded by Steve French) a short motion stating that the Group is "committed to an illegal budget if it is necessary to defend jobs and services."[11]

A spokesperson for the Ministry for the Environment ironically stated that "the government's attitude is that local authorities should be left to run services without too much interference."[12] At a borough conference on 12 September the Orange paper was rejected by 62-16 showing huge support

---

10 Lambeth Council minutes, 24 July 1987.
11 Ibid.
12 *South London Press*, 13 May 1988, p. 8.

from the membership to oppose the cuts. However, less than a week later, on 17 September, Vauxhall General Committee (the CLP's leadership) voted to support a balanced budget. The following week Norwood CLP and the LGC rejected the proposed cuts.

By October 1987, Bellos and the LGC were at loggerheads. Bellos wanted to submit a motion of no confidence in the left councillors, but the leadership of the LGC intervened and persuaded her to drop it.[13] Instead, the LGC submitted a motion calling for the decision to be suspended for proposing such extensive cuts, but the Labour Group voted against 14-21. For their part, the LCC submitted a motion to the LGC against the left councillors, but it was rejected on the grounds that the rebels were only carrying out party policy as contained in the 1986 manifesto and therefore could not be subjected to disciplinary action. In response, the left on the LGC pushed for re-interviewing all councillors, asking them if they still agreed with the manifesto commitment to no cuts. The councillors who were prepared to vote for cuts saw this as intimidation, as the LGC leadership were associated with the anti-cuts wing of the Group through being chaired by Greg Tucker. Then the eight left-wing councillors around Twelves resigned their positions in order to oppose the direction of the Labour group from their back benches.

COUNCILLORS AGAINST THE CUTS

In the run-up to the budget meeting in March, the left councillors, now free of any obligations and responsibilities in the Labour Group, launched a new organisation called Lambeth Councillors Against the Cuts. The opposition was based on the belief that implementing cuts would only signal compliance with the wider Tory agenda of decimating local government and opening the door to further privatisation.[14]

It wasn't possible to plug the holes in the budget by moving money around, the scale of the cuts year on year was just too much. Their demand focused on the councillors using their position to mount a political challenge to the Tory government. They rejected the argument that passing cuts budgets at least allowed Labour to stay in political control. "But we are not in political control. Not only is the leadership being led by the nose by senior officers, but they are doing exactly what the Tories want... We are doing the Tories dirty work for them. They get the cuts they want and – as a bonus – they get to blame Labour for making them."[15]

The alternative was to increasingly act like Tories in dealing with the council work force – the cuts and recruitment freezes that triggered strikes and the lock out of AEU members were not conducive to good industrial relations. Instead Labour had to "use the Council as an effective platform on

---

13 Interview with Joan Twelves, June 2016.
14 'Why we resigned', statement dated 8 December 1987.
15 Lambeth Councillors against the Cuts, Bulletin 2, February 1988.

behalf of the working class, unite all sections of the workforce and community and fight back."[16]

This was an attempt to keep alive the *Labour Briefing* municipal socialist strategy of the early 1980s – using the council as a platform to promote both an alternative vision of society but also as a tool to mobilise the community. Their alternative financial arrangements, however, were vaguer, they did believe it was possible to construct a short-term budget that involved no cuts, but the specifics of how that might work were not elaborated on. The Labour right were sceptical that calls for more activism would solve the problem – would a march on Downing Street really secure the £60 million worth of funds that had been lost? A principled stand of mass resignation rather than vote for cuts or a strategy of confrontation that might end up with the Tories in power locally.

The LCC criticised the budget for the way it was handled, namely that a small clique of councillors had worked with a small group of 'trusted' council officers to produce a financial plan which, inevitably, provided more money for the selected officers fiefdoms whilst cutting money elsewhere.[17] They also accused Bellos of making cuts essentially at random across the council, something that Bellos stringently denied. Bellos believed her budget was a class-based budget that targeted the cuts at service provision for the more affluent middle-class Lambethians whilst protecting the poor, ethnic minorities, and so on.

As a 'stop the cuts' leaflet from 1988 argued: "Instead of a political campaign against the government's attacks on local democracy, the Council has gone into confrontation with its own workforce."[18] The main concern from the left wasn't that you could simply ignore the budget cuts but that a political campaign involving the unions and community was needed to put pressure on the government. The danger of just pressing ahead with the cuts is that it would sever the link between the Labour Council and the local government unions.

CLASS WAR AT THE COUNCIL

> They came for the temporary workers,
> But I didn't do anything, because I was't a temporary worker.
> They came for the 'inessential posts'
> But I didn't do anything because I wasn't an 'inessential post'
> They came for the redeployees,
> But I didn't do anything because I wasn't to be redeployed,
> They came for the privatised jobs,
> But I didn't do anything because my job wasn't privatised (yet)
> They came for my job

---

16 Ibid.
17 LCC leaflet handed out at 1988 budget meeting, Joan Twelves papers.
18 Lambeth Councillors against the cuts Bulletin, 3 March 1988.

> But nobody would do anything for me,
> Why?
>
> *A verse for '88*, Lambeth NALGO[19]

Back on the Council shop floor there was serious trouble brewing. In the run-up to the 1986 election, the Tory councillors had pledged a full investigation into NALGO, accusing them of ballot rigging and intimidation. Mary Leigh made a great play at being tough with the union: "It is a tragedy that NALGO in Lambeth has fallen into the hands of extremists. Unless we stop this, the union will constantly thwart council policy."[20] It's true that the Town Hall unions were very strong in Lambeth, fostered in part by their on-off working relationship with Ted Knight and links to the left in the CLPs. But they were also trying to navigate ideological inclement times, with national union leaderships that were tied to the moderate wing of the Labour Party and therefore hostile to rank and file action.

But by 1986 the fighting unity between the unions and the councillors built around the rate-capping struggle had come to an abrupt end. The council's finances were in a mess and the political battle with the government had meant there was little focus or direction on many departments. NALGO instructions to not cover for vacant posts and the Council's recruitment freeze meant that there were huge gaps across the Council. Due to workload pressures, NALGO banned staff from answering phones in the housing department. At one stage they were receiving thirty calls a minute, with complaints which led to some staff simply walking away from the phones in distress and going home. The union instructed members to set up an answer machine message telling residents to contact their local councillors directly.

A ban on ordering supplies saw a complex bartering system emerge among staff for stationary, with officers desperately exchanging items to keep their departments running: "just tell me where I can exchange some three year old badges saying 'no cuts' for some A4 pads!" sardonically begged one council employee.[21]

In the libraries the council had sent a communique to staff to tell them not to handle the News International newspapers, in solidarity with the Wapping dispute. When the council was threatened with legal action they dropped the boycott, though NALGO members continued it unofficially for some time afterwards, leaving *The Sun*, *The Times* and *The News of the World* in a pile on the floor of the library. The town hall unions got a petition together when the tea trolley service was suddenly stopped in November 1987 as part of cut backs. A NALGO convenor, Kai Pokawa, argued that the cuts lead to workers wasting time because they had to walk up flights of

---

19 Lambeth NALGO AGM booklet 1988.
20 'Lambeth's Tories plan probe on NALGO. Inquiry planned into allegations of ballot-rigging by union extremists', *Sunday Times*, 6 April 1986.
21 *South London Press*, 11 December 1987.

stairs to the canteen to make tea. What about the health and safety implications of split liquids on floors?[22] The combination of tea with health and safety concerns made this perhaps the most quintessentially British of trade union issues.

Trade unionism was much more a part of working life in Lambeth. It wasn't just the density of the unions in the workplace, it was their combativity and their public profile. In 1986 the Lambeth Trade Union Resource centre was set up, initially in the Bon Marché building in Brixton, but then moving to Thornton Road in Stockwell. Paid for by the Economic Activity and Employment Committee of Lambeth Council, it was a place for printing leaflets, placards and newsletters on their photocopiers and offset litho printers, it had a full time crèche and meeting space for local campaigners and workers. It eventually merged with the Lambeth TUC Unemployed Workers Centre, itself a space for campaigning and organising among people without work. The unemployed centre doubled up as a drop-in advice centre for people with work or welfare related queries, as well as holding seminars on the history of social security and unemployed movements. Its work publishing various left journals had led to it being fire bombed in the early 1980s by persons unknown, but presumed to be the far right.

The battle over the 1988 budget was a serious one for the town hall unions. The cuts were unlike anything they had seen before. As the dispute rumbled on, the left councillors criticised what they termed the "Murdoch style union busting", such as withdrawing union facilities and locking out workers instead of negotiating.[23] The fight over budget cuts caused significant splits and divisions in the local NALGO branch. The branch AGM, on 23 November 1987, adopted a position of complete opposition to the cuts and non-co-operation with the Council. This mandated NALGO officials to refuse to attend meetings with senior management or councillors when cuts were being discussed.

A week before the Policy and Resources Committee met to vote on the cuts, NALGO had called a one-day strike which pulled out over 5,000 members of staff.[24] Bellos wrote to the workforce telling them that striking was not going to change anything as there was no financial alternatives to the cuts. Cllr John Bercow went further, calling for all the strikers to be sacked: "In the current financial crisis these people should be deemed to have dismissed themselves if they strike."[25]

That evening the trade unionists attempted to block the entrance to the Town Hall, delaying the meeting by some time. When the councillors eventually started there was a huge ruckus in the public gallery. Amid the

---

22 Ibid.
23 Lambeth Councillors against the cuts, Bulletin 1, January 1988.
24 *South London Press*, 19 January 1988.
25 'Sack the strikers', *South London Press*, 15 January 1988.

shouts, chants and general mayhem, councillors were forced to communicate with placards that had been expressly made for them, holding up signs indicating they wanted to "move the amendment" or "oppose" or "I second it". Councillors also had to dodge flying chips and eggs as food based missiles hurtled across the chambers. Eventually the fire alarm was set off and the building was evacuated.

There was a sense that if it was a choice between fighting the Tories or fighting the local council unions, that Labour councillors had opted for the second, easier route. The sense of being given a kicking by councillors ostensibly from their own side was a bitter feeling.

An opposition emerged in the branch around Allen MacPherson and Jon Rogers, who felt that this attitude was too hard-line and it was better to fight the cuts but maintain a working relationship with the council leadership on other issues rather than blanket non-co-operation. The AGM was reconvened on 29 January and a different policy adopted. This led to the resignation of Mike Waller and a defeat for the SWP wing of the union. Instead new, younger activists like Rogers took charge. Rogers was a health and safety officer at the Council who had been working on the nuclear free zone policy and active in *Labour Briefing* circles. It marked a distinct shift in the balance of power in the branch, from the revolutionary SWP towards the Labour left.

The NALGO bulletin produced after the AGM heralded "the momentous day for the branch". The AGM had overwhelmingly agreed to oppose the council's cuts and redeployment strategy "whilst negotiating real improvements and positive alternatives." The new leadership wanted to reiterate that "far from being capitulation or abandoning our opposition to cuts, this is the means for us to build support and solidarity, negotiate from strength."[26] The first thing the new leadership had to do was build support amongst the workers in the depots who had been locked out by the council in a dispute over unfilled cleaning posts.

The depot strike meant that there were few bin collections and transport for the elderly and those with disabilities were disrupted. Many vehicles, like petrol tankers, were turned away by the pickets. After several weeks most of the demands of the strikers were met, more learners were hired and the drivers were given a flexibility payment. Disabled residents had occupied the offices of the Councillors in solidarity with the strikers, which helped pile considerable pressure on to resolve the dispute.

Another flashpoint was the installation of a new £2 million computer to process housing benefits and rent collection. The Council was desperate to make progress on clearing the backlog of rent arrears and had proudly announced that the new computer would help raise millions of pounds within a few years. The unions put up anti-computer posters across workplaces, poking fun at how managers could use their fancy new word-

---

26 *The Lamb*, Lambeth NALGO, April 1988 p. 2

processors to type your redundancy notices Of course, looking back this might look like an anti-technological attitude, but at the time the typist pool in an organisation like Lambeth Council was large and the unions were seriously concerned about job losses.

RESIGNATION OF BELLOS

As the cuts budget loomed, Ted Knight reappeared in the media, making highly critical remarks against Bellos and her administration: "we [the rate capped councillors] don't feel betrayed but I would consider the party has been betrayed."[27] At a mass community meeting in September 1987, attended by Labour Party members, trade unionists and community groups, called to discuss the cuts budgets, Knight gave a thunderous speech: "Her references to 'realism' are language we have become used to in this movement." Embattled Bellos hit back, arguing that she was "faced with the same difficulties that Ted was faced with in 1981 when he himself had to make unpalatable decisions."[28]

At the Vauxhall GC, with two weeks to go before the budgetary meeting, Tucker gave a report to the assembled delegates on the choices facing the councillors:

> Two strategies are being discussed – fudge or fight. Comrades argued that if we could fudge then we should do so. Whilst accepting that next year we would have to fight they argued that conditions were not right this year – the Party was still defeated after the failure of the rate-capping struggle, better to wait and regroup our forces. Unfortunately that is not what experience shows to happen. Where other boroughs have attempted to put off the struggles all that happened is that further demoralisation set in. What will comrades argue next year when they find things are even worse? Of course we have to mobilise our support. No one was saying it would be easy, particularly at this late stage, but we had no other choice.[29]

By the time the annual budget meeting rolled around in March 1988 the battle lines were drawn, the arguments were had out in committees and party meetings from Gipsy Hill to Bishops ward. Whilst they were backed by many party members, the left were a minority on the council, and they knew it. What was particularly galling was the symbolism of the event. The council meeting began with the unveiling of a copy of a banner to commemorate the thirty-one surcharged councillors, (Lloyd Leon had been expunged from the roll of honour at this point). To applause from the public gallery and the

---

27 'Ted hits out at Tory links', *The News*, 18 September 1987.
28 Ibid.
29 Report to the LGC Committee February 1987.

Labour councillors, as well as stony silence from the Conservatives, Bellos spoke glowingly of the struggle of the previous administration.

Then the budget was introduced, containing £60 million worth of cuts. The cuts would primarily be achieved by scaling back repairs, replacing equipment less regularly and slowing down recruitment. Again it was hoped that the council would not have to actually lay off any staff. Lambeth Workers Joint Trade Union Committee addressed the meeting and urged them to reject the cuts, arguing that a recruitment freeze would only undermine services and leave them vulnerable to calls for privatisation from the Tories and Alliance. Outside NALGO had called a noisy protest.

Greg Tucker bitterly summed up the mood from the left during the meeting: "On 27 March at the start of Lambeth Council's Ratemaking meeting Linda Bellos unveiled the banner of the surcharged Lambeth 31... Just after midnight she brought down the curtain on their struggle..."[30]

Eight Labour councillors voted against the budget; Steve French, Lesley Hammond, John Harrison, George Huish, Jonathan Oppenheimer, Greg Tucker and Rachel Webb. Thirty-two Labour councillors had voted for it, but three of them, Alison Higgs, Joan Twelves and Julian Lewis, had only done so because they felt mandated to support the budget by Vauxhall GC, which had itself only narrowly agreed to back the proposal by two votes. Higgs wrote to Vauxhall GC arguing that "it was vital that the parties exert pressure on the Group so that no cuts from this budget are implemented... I can only say that when we face setting the budget next year there will be no more room left for creative accounting fudges, and it will be more critical than ever that the Parties support Group into standing firmly behind our manifesto." For Tucker it was about a point of principle, the "budget flies in the face of the promises made only a year ago in Lambeth Labour's manifesto of no cuts in services."[31]

In a sign of the tensions in the Black Sections, ex-councillor Sharon Atkin accused Linda Bellos of "playing the 'racist' card" to divert attention from the compromises over cuts. "The split that occurred is not one of 'white left against black left' but one of the right white holding and maintaining a grip on the black leader." One thing was clear, the focus on the fight over cuts consumed the Labour group, Bellos later recounted, "[o]f course, there was heated and passionate political argument about such a vast and daunting task [of £60 million of cuts]. How could it have been otherwise? And other issues went on to the back burner."[32]

Despite getting her budget passed, the effects of the intense faction fight on the council's leadership took their toll on Bellos. In the run up to the

---

30 *London Labour Briefing*, April 8-21 1987 number 73.
31 Ibid.
32 Linda Bellos, 'Who really wrecked Lambeth?: Savaged budgets and bans on councillors were a recipe for scandal, says the borough's former leader', *The Independent*, 27 January 1993.

Labour Group AGM, Bellos' group felt that they lacked the support of other councillors or the LGC to be able to carry on. Crucially for their plans for re-organisation of directorates and redeploying of staff they were being bitterly opposed by NALGO. The size of the vote against her budget, whilst not enough to sink it, was desperately undermining. She articulated her view of the split not as a traditional left/right one but of a white left and black left split. "I have no intention of lying to black people in Lambeth about what we are doing or plan to do."[33]

Whilst the fight was on to stop serious budget cuts, there were some critical voices that were raised about a deeper problem that the Council was struggling to get to grips with. Chris Ramsey argued in *Lambeth Labour Left Bulletin* that "[t]he central slogan in Lambeth – "services worth defending" – just didn't ring true. Starved of government money over years, chronically short staffed and badly managed Lambeth services were and *still are* in crisis. Not setting a rate offered no prospect of improving the services or working conditions in the short term, and limited the campaign to defending the admittedly inadequate provision."[34] The tension between defending the services that existed or accepting the cuts and focusing on improving the remaining services was one that dogged the 1980s. It wasn't until the war against local government came to an end in the 1990s that the councillors that came afterwards could focus on picking up the pieces.

From their perspective, the strategy of the Bellos group had been to oppose the government by providing well run services – all the better to undermine Tory accusations of incompetence. In this sense the balanced budget was a necessary condition for carrying on. Clearly the councillors didn't see their role as outright opposition, but rather to implement something approaching Kinnock's dented shield. Bellos pointed to the lack of a mass movement opposing the cuts – what use was it for the Labour group to go down in a blaze of glory, or as Knight had put it years before, expending good people on "kamikaze actions." Their message to Labour Group members equally blamed the "hard left group standing on a no cuts position" and "the right wing Labour councillors" who had "abandoned basic socialist principles." In fact "the process of agreeing a balanced budget was very painful and led to splits in the parties which are reflected in the local group."[35] In the run up to the AGM, only five out of twenty-two local branches backed the current leadership.

Then, prior to the AGM, Bellos called a press conference, informing the local Labour Parties after the fact that they were standing down. They had decided not to alert the CLPs or the LGC in case it was seen as somehow coercing or blackmailing party members. Instead it was better to just go; let

---

33 Linda Bellos memo to all members of the Labour Group, 30th March 1987.
34 *Lambeth Labour Left Bulletin*, Number 2.
35 'Lambeth Leadership steps down', 21 April 1988 statement from Linda Bellos, Dave Morgan, Fred Taggart, Peter Mountford-Smith, Phyllis Dunipace, Steve Whaley, Carol O'Donnoell.

the party sort out their strategy by backing councillors that could implement the no-cuts strategy that the rank and file demanded. In their parting comments they reserved considerable fire for the right of the Labour group around Sorabji: "whilst we have many criticisms of the politics of the no-cuts position, they do at least understand the meaning of socialism. It is very difficult to discern the politics within the latest edition of the gospel according to Poland Street,[36] and absolutely impossible to find the socialism. Socialism needs efficiency, that is true, waste and corruption do not serve the interests of working class people, but to believe that efficiency in the name of socialism equates to socialism is a philosophical falsehood of epic proportions."[37]

In the subsequent AGM, twenty-nine-year-old Dick Sorabji won; a victory of the moderate Kinnockite forces grouped around the LCC. Sorabji offered Bellos a compensatory role as chair of the Police Committee "No thanks, Bwana" was her firm rebuff.[38]

DICK SORABJI'S REIGN

Under Sorabji the order of the day became 'service delivery'. But despite their apparently pragmatic approach to the council, not much was achieved. As the deadline for the launch of the Poll Tax loomed closer, Lambeth was well behind with preparations. No computer or furniture was bought for the collection office. Fixing the issues in housing quickly seemed to be beyond almost everyone's capability.

The immediate vexed issue was the impending implementation of the Community Charge – the Poll Tax. There was also clear opposition from within the Labour Group on the Poll Tax question. On 18 November 1988 the Group passed a motion affiliating to London Against the Poll Tax, to cease implementing Poll Tax legislation. The motion was passed, nineteen votes for and only ten against (with six abstentions), revealing a clear majority for a campaign against the tax that was willing to 'go illegal'. The position of the left organised around *Lambeth Briefing* was for complete opposition, not to 'implement it sensitively'; "The tax is a kick in the teeth – and you cannot kick in the teeth sensitively."[39]

But the fractious nature of the Labour group, and the fact that the Bellos grouping and the hard left usually had a slim majority of votes, left Sorabji lacking political authority. He resorted to using various administrative measures in the constitution to get decisions through. The ruthless drive for 'efficiency' was displeasing to both the 'no cuts councillors' and Bellos' grouping who saw the direction of travel as being too far to the right. The Labour right's perspective was that socialism was unpopular and that

---

36 9 Poland Street, in Soho, was the headquarters of the LCC.
37 Resignation statement from Bellos and her allies.
38 'Take me to your leader', *City Limits*, 28 April - 5 May 1988.
39 *Lambeth Briefing*, Issue 6.

Thatcher had won the culture war; the task now was to roll with the punches but soften the blows. The mood amongst local Labour members was still combative however; the General Committees of Norwood and Vauxhall passed motions of no confidence in Sorabji's leadership. Within a year it was clear that the situation was untenable. After a four-hour Council meeting voted to reverse opposition to the Poll Tax where Sorabji's grouping were backed by the Tories to get the vote through, a motion of no confidence in his leadership was brought by the left, backed by many centre ground councillors. The vote of no confidence was the end to a turbulent political year, and Sorabji stepped down. He was replaced by Joan Twelves, who enjoyed the support of the local party members in the Local Government Committee.

Twelves was described by one journalist as "charming but manipulative... Clever and hard-working, but not an orator or charismatic leader like Ted Knight."[40] From her perspective there were four major challenges facing the council: Privatisation of services; selling off of estates; the abolition of the ILEA; and the imposition of the Poll Tax. Twelves saw her role as professionalising the council and shedding the image of incompetence that was projected by the media. Her oft-repeated mantra, "There is nothing socialist about inefficiency", was often heard from her offices in the Town Hall. One of the key reforms was to clarify the policy remit of councillors, that they shouldn't be substitutes for senior managers. Where Knight had kept the senior officers close, Twelves wanted to create distance.

The pledge of the new left slate that took power at the 1989 AGM was for a strategy of non-compliance with the Poll Tax, reversing privatisation and building a "united front which brings together tenants, Party members and the community." Their perspective, as opposed to the LCC and Sorabji, was simple: resistance not compliance.[41]

But there were inevitable problems. Due to the nature of the Compulsory Competitive Tendering laws, attempts to keep some services "in house" proved to be impossible. In order to secure the contract for road sweeping and refuse collection in 1990, the council had to submit a bid to itself with huge budget cuts, necessitating a reorganisation of routes and a closure of depots. The first six months of the new service delivery were chaotic, making the newspapers as a further example of the much maligned "inefficiency" that the new administration was desperate to avoid. The council reduced the pay and working conditions of estate cleaners, many of them low-paid women, in order to secure the contract.

But the pressure of being council leader had an immediate impact on Twelves when it came to the budget. Having to identify nearly £4 million of cuts, Twelves lobbied for support for a cuts budget among the CLPs. In a heated exchange at Norwood CLP, the proposal to remain in power and

---

40 *The Telegraph*, 20 February 1991.
41 Leaflet handed out to the 1989 Labour Group AGM.

minimise the extent of the cuts was passed with a majority of only one. Once again the dented shield became the *de facto* strategy for the council. Joan believed that her previous anti-cuts arguments were still valid because she felt that Bellos and Sorabji hadn't pursued all the available financial alternatives before opting for implementing cuts. By the time she sat in the leader's office, the options seemed far more limited due to the changes in law and the constant stripping away of council money since 1980. But with one of the previous leaders of Councillors Against the Cuts now making cuts, the left opposition on the council was isolated. A motion opposing the cuts secured only four votes in the Labour Group.

Fallings out with her previous comrades wasn't the only headache for Twelves; a motion by Rachel Webb to the Labour Group which suggested that local residents use IRA style "punishment shootings" to defend themselves from criminals also (inevitably) hit the headlines. The proposal received no support in the Group, but it gave the right a new stick to beat the left with and was leaked to the press, who had a field day with mocking the idea. Tucker then proposed a motion calling on the council to invite Sinn Fein councillors to visit later that year. Little did Tucker know that his motion would be one of the damning pieces of 'evidence' from the NEC against the left.[42] Effectively the LCC members in the council were keeping every leaflet, every motion and made notes of speeches all for the purposes of passing them over to the NEC.

In the run-up to the 1990 election, the Local Government Committee, chaired by Greg Tucker, was closed down by Labour HQ after accusations that they had broken local standing orders. The claims of impropriety were rejected by the lefts.[43] Tony O'Neil, a Labour member from Streatham, indicated what the right demanded: "[It is] evident to those of us on the pragmatic and significant left of the party that the LGC has long ceased to play any useful role in Lambeth politics. Enough is enough. It is about time that this absurd committee was laughed out of existence".[44] Cllr John Mann backed up the attack on the LGC, decrying what he described as "Stalinist show trial tactics."[45] Shortly after these attacks, Joyce Gould wrote to the LGC, suspending it indefinitely and explaining that the Lambeth manifesto for the 1990 elections would be written by Walworth Road, not by local members.

Despite the behind-the-scenes power struggles and the increasingly proactive intervention of Labour HQ, the Council elections in 1990 returned forty Labour Councillors, unchanged since 1986, though with a higher share of the vote. Some councillors chose not to stand again. In the 1990 intake

---

42 Richard Heffernan and Mike Marqusee, *Defeat From the Jaws of Victory* (Verso 1992), p. 289.
43 Lambeth Briefing December 1989.
44 Windmill Town Hall ward newsletter, September 1989.
45 Ibid.

there were twenty new councillors, a number of councillors previously couldn't stand due to the recent Widdicombe ruling and ILEA transfers, though some quit due to their frustration over the limited powers of councillors. After the 1990 election, Joan Twelves stood for re-election as leader. She was opposed by Steve French on a left platform. Bellos did not stand as a councillor again, going for a senior role at Hackney Council, though she almost lost her job when the Labour right wingers on the council vindictively tried to block her appointment.

16

The Vauxhall By-election

A major opportunity for the Labour leadership to defeat the left in Lambeth presented itself when Vauxhall's MP, Stuart Holland, suddenly decided to resign his seat to pursue an academic career in Europe. As there was no danger that Labour would lose the seat in a by-election because Vauxhall was one of the safest Labour seats in the country, this meant the real question was, who would be presented to the Labour voters of Vauxhall as the next MP – someone of the radical left or the 'New Realist' right. It was a coveted prize for both wings of the party. The left obviously wanted one of their own to replace Holland, who was a stalwart of the Bennite era. The right wanted someone in who could help with their campaign to dismantle the left of the party locally.

Given the social and ethnic composition of the constituency, many in the local party wanted a black candidate to stand. Martha Osamor was supported by the local Black Section, but there were several other credible BME candidates as well who intended to stand: Russell Proffitt, a Lewisham councillor who had been selected to fight Battersea North but had then lost out to Alf Dubs after boundary changes; Linda Bellos, who had retained a significant degree of support locally; Marc Wadsworth, Vice Chair of the CLP; and Wesley Kerr, a Newsnight journalist who secured the nomination of only a single affiliated trade union branch.

Many believed that Martha Osamor was a shoe-in, but this view was not universally held: "It is widely considered that Osamor would have easily won. This isn't true. I mean she had support but it was still a minority of the local delegates."[1] Nevertheless, the Labour machine could not allow some wildcard to get elected to parliament. Certainly Bellos and Osamor were considered as totally unacceptable to a leadership trying to distance itself from the left. The fear was that anyone with the support of the local Black Section might be someone inclined to the radical left. As Anthony Bevins argued in *The Independent*, Kinnock felt it "necessary to keep the blacks in

---

1   Interview with John O'Malley, August 2017.

line."[2] The NEC feared a repeat of the Greenwich by-election in 1987 when the local party selected left-winger Deidre Wood, who was subsequently mauled in the press, leading to a huge swing of Tory voters to the SDP to keep a 'loony' Labour out. There had also been a disastrous by-election in Glasgow Govan where a left winger from the print workers' union called Bob Gillespie had been defeated with a 33% swing to the SNP who took the seat.[3] Since that was a safe Labour seat, it sent shockwaves through the party apparatus and the party's media guru, ex-Lambeth councillor Peter Mandelson, saw it as a sign that there had to be even more centralisation to ensure media savvy and 'on message' candidates stood who could connect with the voters.[4] In essence they had to get with the New Times, the new spirit of the age, as Thatcher moulded the country to the image of a post industrial neo-liberalism. Kinnock and Mandelson ensured that the NEC had more power delegated to itself to draw up the short list for the local CLP to pick a candidate, and the leadership demanded a reliable candidate that wouldn't get into hot water with the press.

After a period of reflection, Vauxhall put forward its list of the preferred candidates to the NEC, which was duly noted and then totally ignored. In what became a national scandal in the party, Osamor was banned from standing by the NEC who also leaked malicious lies to Patrick Winter of *The Guardian* that she was being investigated by the Fraud Squad. Instead, the NEC subcommittee (chaired by doyen of the Labour right, Roy Hattersley) proposed a list of four reliable moderates, Glenys Thornton, Kate Hoey, Pat Moberley and Nick Raynsford. All were white, which produced an angry backlash in the CLP. At the meeting where the local members were due to decide who to support there was uproar and an outright rebellion when the meeting voted by thirty-three to eight to abandon the procedure and write to the NEC in the strongest possible terms that the short list was unacceptable. Tired of dealing with recalcitrants in the local environs, the NEC subcommittee instead simply imposed Hoey on the local party.

"It was outrageous what happened" remembered Steve Nally. "Vauxhall was a well organised General Management Committee. There was no reason to impose a candidate. Having someone imposed was considered an insult and outraged local members."[5] This was even truer considering that Vauxhall was one of the safest Labour seats in the country and it was effectively giving a seat in the House of Commons to someone with no input from the local party. Bernie Grant MP gave an impassioned speech in Parliament when the writ for the by-election was moved on 22 May, pointing to the

---

2   'Confrontation looms on the black issue', *The Independent*, 27 March 1987, p. 17.
3   A key contributing factor to Gillespie's defeat was Labour's position on the Poll Tax, which was to pay it once it became law, whereas the SNP was proposing non-payment. This is a notable example of a left-winger being defeated in an election because of the Party's right-wing policies.
4   Simon Hannah, *Can't Pay Won't Pay: The Fight To Stop The Poll Tax* (Pluto 2020) pp. 38-9.
5   Interview with Steve Nally, August 2017.

history of black immigration to Lambeth and Brixton in particular (a large part of which was in the Vauxhall constituency). He lambasted his own party leadership in the strongest terms: "If President Gorbachev had imposed candidates during the recent elections in the Soviet Union, everybody would have been up in arms. In the United Kingdom however, political parties can impose candidates without qualms."[6]

The local Black Sections members were also furious. Marc Wadsworth saw Kinnock's actions as a direct attack on black women candidates: "Kinnock had personally taken charge at the NEC of axing Sharon Atkin as the Nottingham East's PPC in 1987. That was two black women denied a place next to Diane [Abbott] in the House of Commons. We had to wait till 2005 before another black woman was selected by Labour and became an MP."[7]

It was widely rumoured that in her younger days Hoey had been in some Trotskyist group or other, some people said the International Marxist Group, others the International Socialists (which later became the SWP after 1977). Some had it on good authority she was in People's Democracy, an Irish revolutionary organisation. She had also once been arrested in 1970 on an anti-internment protest against the actions of the British Army in Northern Ireland. But that was a long time ago. By the time of her appointment as the candidate in Vauxhall she was a councillor in Southwark and clearly associated with the Kinnock wing of the internal party battles. Local party members knew she had been picked as a way of undermining the left, a pro-Kinnock moderate in the middle of their ranks, now speaking for their constituency. A safe pair of hands for the leadership. In this she was a far cry from the reliable left lineage of Stuart Holland. She had wanted to stand in Dulwich, but the Labour Coordinating Committee there hadn't backed her, instead plumbing for Tessa Jowell.

The campaign itself demonstrated the problem that Labour had made for itself through imposing Hoey. A large number of activists had to be drafted in from outside the borough, as local party members protested with their feet and refused to canvass. Party officials lambasted the local members, telling them to put their feelings to one side and secure the election of a Labour candidate. But to many locals it sounded like the crowing of a dubious victor, demanding they bend the knee to the NEC.

The Tory election candidate, Mike Keegan, knew he had an uphill struggle to win over the working-class voters of Vauxhall with a 9,000 strong Labour majority. His campaign was blighted by attacks on his campaign HQ – a disused hairdressers salon that had been rented by the Tories, had its windows smashed with bricks and an ashtray, and then a week later a crude, unexploded petrol bomb was found outside the office. "We will not be

---

6 *Hansard*, 22 May 1989.
7 Interview with Marc Wadsworth, November 2018.

intimidated by the attacks" said a clearly shaken local Tory spokesperson.⁸ Keegan's campaign had been launched by the Defence Secretary George Younger at a press gathering where journalists were met by four young police officers in uniform drinking from Conservative party mugs.⁹

In addition to the candidates from the main parties, there were two black candidates standing in protest at the actions of Labour's NEC in not selecting a black candidate. One was Rudy Narayan (from the Brixton Defence Committee). Narayan garnered some press attention when he interrupted a photo opportunity between Hoey and Kinnock at a community centre. He also made noises about a civil disobedience campaign against the upcoming Poll Tax. Revolutionary Communist Party candidate Don Milligan went one further, burning his poll tax registration form outside a Kate Hoey press conference. The other black candidate was Hewie Andrew, a Methodist minister, selected as the 'People's Candidate for Electoral Justice'. Spotted at the public selection meeting was Marc Wadsworth and Linda Bellos, leading to salacious rumours that Black Sections activists were going to be canvassing for Andrew, and not Hoey. Wadsworth rejected this claim, accusing Labour of spreading "Goebbels-style propaganda."¹⁰

Hoey caught some flak whilst out on the doorstep, as black residents and local party members were furious about what happened to Osamor. Many locals believed that the party had prevented her from standing because she did not have wide enough appeal as a black, working-class woman. That was no doubt part of it, but it was also the internal factional concerns in Labour that motivated the decision, not that many people on the doorstep on estates across Vauxhall cared too much about that. "They threw her out because she was black" remarked one local woman, before her teenage daughter – first time voter – added "it means they think if you are black you have no hope."¹¹ Bernie Grant had defended Osamor's alleged 'controversial' background; "If one is a black politician worth one's salt, one has to be controversial, because this is a racist society. Any black person who attempts to represent black people and put forward black issues properly will be torn apart by the media."¹²

On the Studley Estate a black man named Michael (who was actually a member of Labour living in Brixton) denounced the 'racist Labour party' to Hoey's face.¹³ On another estate she was accosted by a construction worker, named Jonathan Tanburn, who told her he was "disgusted with the Labour Party for throwing gay rights out of the boat as soon as you think the

---

8   *The Guardian*, 5 June 1989.
9   Ibid.
10 *Sunday Times*, 4 June 1989.
11 'Vauxhall's siege election', *Asian Times*, 2 June 1989.
12 Ibid.
13 *City Limits*, 8 June-15 June 1989, p. 6.

balloon is dropping. How can you possible pretend to be socialists?"[14] Hoey replied rather meekly that "things move on – we haven't abandoned any of our principles." Others were more positive, one manager of a local laundrette dismissed the concerns around racism, "I think you've got some shit stirrers and that's it.[15]

There was some solace for the left wingers on the council – both the Tories and the Liberals stood candidates as an unofficial referendum on the loony left and were resoundingly defeated. Of course, Kate Hoey herself immediately made it clear that she had no truck with the local party leaders and was bitterly hostile to the left councillors in her own party. The antagonism between her, Twelves' grouping on the council, and even her own CLP was palpable. Within a week of being imposed, the General Committee of Vauxhall CLP wrote to the NEC asking them to open up reselection proceedings immediately to ensure they could change their candidate for the next general election. In an effortless move, Joyce Gould merely changed the rules to prevent MPs elected in by-elections from being deselected before the next general election. The Vauxhall Labour Party members were furious.

Twelves had other things to worry about at the time; the council had attached a giant 15ft condom onto the flagpole at the Town Hall to mark World AIDs Day and she had to arrange getting it removed in case the 'prodigious prophylactic' blew away and caused a traffic accident on the streets below.[16]

---

14 Ibid.
15 Ibid.
16 *South London Press*, 28 November 1989.

17

Fighting the Poll Tax and the Gulf War

A poll tax? Try collecting that in Brixton!

After many of the militants in the council chambers across the country had been tamed or driven out, and the principle of local government control over council spending had been firmly disabused whilst profit making enterprises were now operating in areas where previously the public sector had monopolised, the Conservative government now turned to the vexed question of the rates themselves.

The rates system was notoriously unpopular with Conservative activists across the country, but the wider public as well often complained about the amount of the local tax they paid.[1] The issue of local government revenue was not new, but the proposed method to resolve the problem was certainly unique to the political context of the time. The primary concern of the New Right was the principle that everyone must contribute to the services they use. Since poorer people were more likely to use local services but they contributed less towards their maintenance, this could create a politically unbalanced system where disadvantaged people voted for high taxing, high spending Labour administrations. This view saw rates as a disproportionate burden on businesses and the middle class to pay for services that they were least likely to use. It was seen as a subsidy for the poor, something that the Tories detested.

Although initially rejected in a government green paper in 1981,[2] the idea behind the Community Charge was part of the same financial philosophy that led to the rate-capping and the use of the RSG as a fiscal disciplinary tool against local councils. Throughout her government, Thatcher rejected any financial proposals that would give more autonomy to local government, which could only lead to a centrally imposed dramatic shake up of the entire financial system.[3] The Community Charge was the culmination of this

---
1 Simon Hannah, *Can't Pay Won't Pay* (Pluto 2020).
2 David Wilson and Chris Game, *Local Government in the United Kingdom* (Palgrave MacMillan 1998), p. 186.
3 Hugh Butcher and Ian Law et al, *Local Government & Thatcherism* (Routledge 1990), p. 47.

centralising tendency, the final end of the principle that local authorities should set their own levies for services.

It was proposed during the 1987 election that the rates system be entirely scrapped and replaced by "a fairer" Community Charge. This will be a fixed rate charge for local services paid by those over the age of 18, except "the mentally ill and elderly people living in homes and hospitals."[4] The Community Charge was depicted as a way of creating "fairness" since everyone (with few exceptions) would pay towards local services, with poorer people earning a rebate to soften the blow.[5] But its opponents labelled it as a 'Poll Tax' similar to the one that sparked the 1381 peasant rebellion. In a form of history repeating, the working class 600 years later in 1980s Britain saw it as profoundly unfair that "a widow in her flat pay the same as a lord in his castle".[6]

If local authorities wanted to increase their funding for services, they would have to increase the tax which everyone would pay, thus resulting in possible electoral punishment for high spending (Labour) councils.[7] The proposed tax was initially trumpeted as costing only £120 per head so long as the councils spending was not too excessive. In addition, the Conservatives took local business rates out of the hands of the authorities and imposed a Unified Business Rate, decided from Whitehall.

The political nature of the Poll Tax was clear, it was to punish voters for voting in high spending Labour councils. Conservative Minister Chris Patten visited Robertson Street in Clapham, one side was in Tory-controlled Wandsworth where the Poll Tax was £144, whilst the other was in Lambeth with a hefty £548. "No I am not being provocative," he smirked as journalists swarmed around him, "Anyone who votes Labour in Lambeth next month as a passing protest would be making the most expensive protest of his life."[8]

The tax was also part of a package of reforms to Local Government, all due to come in on 1 April 1990. As well as the tax, they included the ring-fencing of the Housing Revenue Account, which would place restrictions on what housing money could be used for (ring fencing meant you could no longer subsidise rents for poorer tenants with the rates) and the implementation of Compulsory Competitive Tendering, closing the "Lambeth Loophole" that had allowed some councils to escape from mass privatisations.

Protests against the tax were inevitable and a plethora of campaigns emerged. A number of experts had advised the government not to go ahead,

---

4   Conservative Party Manifesto 1987.
5   Edgar Wilson, *A Very British Miracle: The Failure of Thatcherism* (Pluto Press 1992), p. 109.
6   Keith Laybourn, Christine F. Collette (eds.), *Modern Britain Since 1979: A Reader* (I. B. Taurus 2003), p. 11.
7   Earl Aaron Reitan, *The Thatcher Revolution: Margaret Thatcher, John Major, Tony Blair, and the Transformation of Modern Britain, 1979-2001* (Rowman and Littlefield 2003), pp. 87-8.
8   *The Scotsman*, 12 April 1990.

one civil servant famously once commented on the tax "try collecting that in Brixton!"[9] In Lambeth there were three primary organisations, Lambeth Against the Poll Tax, Lambeth Anti Poll Tax Unions, and Community Resistance Against the Poll Tax (CRAPT). The first campaign was effectively the broad coalition, whereas Lambeth Anti Poll Tax Unions was run by Militant and their allies. Both called on Lambeth Council not to implement the tax. CRAPT organisers felt that demands on Labour Councillors was largely a waste of time and only grassroots community action could deliver victory. The other campaigns also debated whether calling on workers to implement the tax or not was worthwhile. What they could all agree on however was the boycott campaign, that if the anti-Poll Tax movement was a new peasants' revolt then the peasants should refuse to pay up. The anarchist squat at 121 Railton Road became a hub of activity as direct action campaigners and local residents formed new coalitions of resistance to central governments predations.

In fact, the English left had been preparing its campaign for several years already, learning from the battle against implementation in Scotland the year before. The experience north of the border pointed to a mass community campaign as the way forward, not relying solely on trade union action to block the tax. Indeed, the national unions were incredibly slow off the mark in mounting any kind of resistance. Instead it was going to be up to solidarity organisations in estates and communities to lead the charge; providing support networks for people to stand up and say 'No', to provide moral support, legal advice and a campaigning strategy. Before the tax was launched in Lambeth there were nineteen local anti-poll tax unions, many of them based on estates like Moorlands, St Martins or Kennington Park. They began to organise telephone trees so if any bailiffs came knocking to collect the unpaid tax then the entire community could come out and block them. Graham Lewis, a Militant supporter living in Streatham, ended up as something of a legal mastermind for getting cases adjourned or thrown out of court. With a keen mind for the law, he started off as a McKenzie friend,[10] attending court with friends or relatives. When the Poll Tax roll-out came around, he provided free legal advice every Monday evening from a room in the Town Hall. His comrades pointed out he had studied law but was not a qualified lawyer, nevertheless "he was bloody good."[11] He later qualified as a legal solicitor. Years after he could be found in pubs across Lambeth, often approached by locals needing a bit of help, dolling out advice in his thick Derby accent: "best thing is to tell your brother he wasn't there", things like that.

---

9   An unknown civil servant, cited in Simon Hannah, *Can't Pay Won't Pay*. p. 15.
10 A McKenzie friend is a term given to someone who is allowed to attend a trial in order to give legal advice to a defendant but cannot address the court directly.
11 Interview with Steve Nally, August 2017.

Back at Walworth Road, the Labour Party NEC advice note on "preparing for the Poll tax" stated that campaigning against the Tax should be an absolute priority, but they expected every elected politician to comply with the law. Since Labour still ran so many councils across the country, they were effectively instructing their councillors to implement the tax, albeit regrettably.[12] Writing to her comrades in Bishops Ward, Twelves explained her reasoning for opposing the Poll Tax: "The Labour Party will not be thanked, and will reap electoral disaster, if it is not seen to be actively opposing it at every level and in every way possible."[13] On 18 November the left successfully submitted a motion to the Group calling for affiliation to the national Anti Poll Tax campaign and to cease implementation of the tax and consider all forms of non-cooperation that the council could pursue.

With less than a year until it was due to come into operation on 1 April 1990, Twelves put forward a radical proposal for a programme of "rolling opposition to the Poll Tax", starting from the position that the tax could only be defeated through mass opposition, and Labour councillors had a role to play in galvanising and organising the resistance, including refusing to register or pay the Community Charge.[14] During the fight with Sorabji's leadership, a large number of the Labour group had publicly spoken out against the tax – Rachel Webb and Twelves refused to pay it outright, Bellos stated she would only pay the tax at the level of the current rates. She would face prison if necessary.[15]

The motion to the Group proposed resisting implementation by refusing to allocate further resources (for instance, a computer to process the charges) until the point when surcharge became a possibility, at which stage the opposition would move to not fining people who have not registered. The contradictions inherent in a council led to an approach that was described as 'schizophrenic' – the council was sending out forms for people to register for the Poll Tax whilst also running a campaign against it.[16] With only three weeks to go, one in five households had not filled in their forms, however, upon investigation, it turned out that the situation was even worse, as a number of the returned forms were "abusive, questioning or not serviceable".[17]

One of the first large protests against the tax in Lambeth was on 9 March, when the amount of tax for Lambeth would be set. Everyone knew it would be high, more than the rates. The atmosphere was febrile. The day

---

12 Blunkett: "may I say unequivocally that we have made it clear on innumerable occasions to every Labour party member and elected representative that we expect them to pay the poll tax. We have made that clear in our resolutions and in our conference statements." *Hansard*, 3 June 1991
13 Report to Bishop Ward.
14 June 1989.
15 *South London Press*, 18 November 1988, p. 8.
16 *The Independent*, 14 November 1989.
17 *City Limits*, 6 July 1989.

before thousands had gathered outside the Town Hall in Hackney and a fight had broken out with the police. Nottingham Council chambers had been occupied by hundreds of protesters, some dressed as Robin Hood. Back in Brixton electrifying energy zipped through the crowd as a sense of people-power, of popular resistance and defiance to a hated government began to coalesce on the streets. People burnt an effigy of Thatcher to great cheers from the crowd. Scuffles saw people throwing paint at the police. Protesters marched from the Town Hall, down round the Academy, and up Stockwell Road before encountering a determined line of riot police near Brixton police station. An almighty fight broke out with police horses charging the crowd and a police car getting overturned. Running battles occurred with the police along Stockwell Road as UB40 played inside the Academy. The disturbances were broadcast live on the news that evening.

When the time came, Lambeth set its Poll Tax at an eye watering £559.25 per person, although that was based on an implausible 100% collection rate. The national and local press poured opprobrium on the Council, unfavourably comparing them (yet again) to Wandsworth, who had set their Poll Tax at zero for the first two years. Twelves and several other left councillors issued statements saying they would refuse to pay the tax, alongside many other Labour politicians like Livingstone and Jeremy Corbyn. One MP, Militant supporter Terry Fields, was even jailed for non-payment. But as the pressure from the Walworth Road HQ mounted and threats of disciplinary action began to circulate, Twelves and some allies called a surprise press conference and announced they would pay it. Greg Tucker and others on the left were still refusing and weren't consulted on the *volte-face*, which caused a fair amount of friction. From Twelves point of view it was untenable to be involved in a non-payment campaign while she was charged with *implementing* the tax, particularly as nationally there were so few Labour Councillors refusing to pay and the Party was breathing down her neck. Some on the left were merciless in their criticism. The council's strategy document on the Poll Tax was dubbed a "sell out", the rolling programme condemned as a "roll over programme". Jon Rogers scornfully labelled Twelves a "former left winger" in *Labour Briefing*. The eventual strategy from the leaders of the Labour group was to merely frustrate the implementation – they couldn't 'go illegal' and refuse to do it – they felt there simply wasn't the support to do that. Instead they slowed everything down to a crawl.

For their part, the anti-Poll Tax campaigners organised a deputation to the Council. Cllr Anne Hollifield suggested that the delegation to the meeting should be six local women, all recounting one after the other why they couldn't afford the Poll Tax. Helen Shaw was one of the delegation: "I remember that night well – I was part of the 6 person delegation addressing Lambeth Council from Lambeth Against the Poll Tax with the then chair of Lambeth NALGO – we managed to get into an office upstairs and hang our banner outside (or as they call it now do a banner drop!) to cheers from the crowd assembled in the street."[18]

Later that month the movement garnered international press coverage when 200,000 anti-Poll Tax campaigners marched through Trafalgar Square on 31 March 1990 and were subjected to a frenzied police attack. The night before, local anti-poll tax groups organised a benefit gig at the Academy performed by the Wee Pappa Girl Rappers. The next day the Poll Tax was due to be introduced and all anyone could talk about was The Demo. The Demo (as it was called) was due to start in Kennington Park, in tribute to the massive Chartist demonstration that had gathered there in 1848. The same place where William Cuffay, a black man and a trade union leader who lived in Lambeth, had helped organise the mass march. Cuffay, an ex-slave who became a tailor, had been deported to Australia for treason for his role in the Chartist protest and died in poverty in Tasmania. The Chartist march had been surrounded by soldiers and cannon, and the demonstrators had been threatened with obliteration if they marched on parliament, guns and sabres in hand. Without a lead from their paralysed leadership they had drifted home, the revolution postponed for another year.

Back in 1990, the organisers were more determined to march. Kennington wasn't the most convenient gathering point for the five hundred coaches from across the country, parking around the largely residential streets was hard for the sixty seater coaches, but the venue held symbolic value for the protest organisers. This was a rebellion against tyranny with as much purpose and righteousness as the Chartist cause all those years ago.

Around 200,000 people gathered (though police estimated 90,000) more joining them along the route once they knew what it was about. On the day lots of football grounds across the capital saw attendance significantly reduced, instead lots of the fans had gone to "The Demo". The numbers that flooded central London were the most that anyone had seen; it would not be matched until the march against the Iraq war in 2003. Northumberland Avenue and Whitehall were packed. A large number stopped outside Downing Street to shout at Thatcher, refusing to move on. Police charged down from Charing Cross and the Strand and poured out from the South African embassy, which was under heavy protection in case of any anti-apartheid actions that took place. A scuffle broke out as police began to manhandle protesters. Some people grabbed bricks and sticks from a nearby building site with which to defend themselves from the police. As the fighting spread riot police, some on horseback, attacked the protest. Groups of protesters broke away, some burning cars on St Martin's Lane. By the end of several hours of ferocious fighting, forty-five police officers had been injured, alongside 113 protesters. 340 people were arrested.

---

18 Interview with Helen Shaw, August 2017.

The backlash from the Central London riot sent shockwaves across the establishment. But it wasn't just the riot that killed the tax. It was the wide-scale local opposition to the tax and the fact it was so unpopular, it was essentially uncollectible. Naturally, Lambeth was a well-organised borough with several leading well-organised estates and communities. Local resident, Steve Nally, chair of the tenant association of the Ashmole Estate, became a leading figure at the first national campaign of Anti-Poll Tax unions in Manchester in 1989. He remembered that "Lambeth had a particularly strong campaign, the left councillors who publicly opposed it and a legacy of fighting the rate-capping, the riots etc. It left a borough where putting two fingers up to authority and not paying was part of the social culture that existed in Lambeth then."[19]

The 'go slow' policy at the council certainly played a role in helping to undermine confidence in the Poll Tax locally, though it also provided more ammunition for the Council's enemies. When Lambeth sent out the first batch of poll tax demand letters, a large number of the addresses were wrong. The team charged with managing the tax locally were hopelessly understaffed, the one solitary Poll Tax computer running over time just to keep up. The computer itself had been the site of a bitter battle between Twelves and her Chief Finance officer, Peter Maxstead, who had to issue a compulsory purchase under Section 114 of the Local Government Finance Act against his own councillors to force them to pay £1 million of the £2 million cost. The wider campaign also adopted a strategy of just slowing everything down, gumming up the works at every level. After some months, when so little Poll Tax had been paid, a number of people were summonsed across the borough line to Southwark Crown Court. On the day that the first set of people were being heard, 2,000 protesters showed up to observe from the public galleries. They literally packed the court so barristers, clerks and lawyers could barely get to the court room. After a while someone called the fire brigade as the building was a fire hazard. The fire-fighters showed up and promptly closed the building. By August over £18 million remained unpaid.

Another demonstration, called for 2 June 1990, saw several hundred campaigners gather in central Brixton outside the library, across from the Town Hall. The space was not as large as it is today, a large portion of what is today Windrush Square (then it was called Brixton Oval) was taken up by a used car lot called Kellet Cars. Just down the road several fridges dangled precariously from ropes at the front of the Fridge Bar, a sight that would send a local government health and safety officer into a frenzy. Feeder marches from nearby estates wound their way down to the protest, though members of the Tulse Hill Anti Poll Tax Union found time to stop off at the George Canning pub[20] before arriving in Brixton Oval. People lined up to burn their Poll Tax registration forms, letters and court summonses.

---

19 Interview with Steve Nally, August 2017.

Twelves and her allies in the Labour group had done their best to slow down the tax implementation, but as the unpaid bills began to pile up, the vexed question of using bailiffs to collect the tax was inevitably raised. A decision had to be made. The crunch meeting at the Council was on 25 June. The evening before in the Labour Group, a proposal had been brought to reject the council officers' recommended implementation plans and to oppose the use of bailiffs in collecting arrears. In the council meeting all but two Labour councillors backed the refusal to use bailiffs (two councillors abstained) and the motion was passed. For some of the Labour councillors, the threat of bailiffs was a reminder of poorer upbringings, their parents terrified of the knock on the door because of unpayable debt. Twelves herself had been involved in community campaigns against poverty in the late 1970s. The principle of not sending anyone to prison for lack of payment was an important one for the left. The meeting was filmed with a live feed into the Assembly Hall downstairs for the local community and campaigners. Outside there were between 6,000 and 7,000 protesters filling the intersection causing traffic to jam until the police re-routed cars.

Charged with energy, the protest marched down to Brixton police station and then back again, cursing Thatcher and the Tories. The ubiquitous placards emblazoned with "can't pay, won't pay!" were hoisted high above people's heads. After some time of marching back and forth around central Brixton, one protester, Eamon Maguire, remembers leaving with his friend to go to the Trinity Pub. Rounding the corner he found Trinity Square packed with police, in vans, standing around and even sitting on people's doorsteps. Maguire quickly abandoned the plan to drink at the Trinity and moved on to the Hope and Anchor.[21]

A further protest in October 1990 saw over 5,000 people gather in Brockwell Park to hear speeches from Tony Benn and Steve Nally, among others. But a breakaway group organised by the Trafalgar Square Defendants Committee headed to Brixton prison, where some of the protesters from the 31 March riot were being held. The usual altercation resulted: hundreds of police blocked the way, their arrogant 'professionalism' riling the angry crowd as they treated people contemptuously. Some people starting throwing cans and bottles. The police reacted aggressively, starting to target people and making arrests. More people joined the fray, with the police pushing the crowd back to Brixton town centre, where people formed barricades in the market place to defend themselves against the riot police. Petrol bombs were thrown and an abandoned police motorbike was set on fire. Over one hundred arrests were made.

In the middle of the Poll Tax campaign, Thatcher resigned. Her exit from Downing Street in November 1990 was always claimed by the left as a result

---

20 On the corner of Effra Road and and Brixton Water Lane. Later renamed The Hobgoblin before being re-branded initially as a Scottish themed pub called Hootanany.
21 Interview with Eamon Maguire, September 2019.

of their efforts to stop the Poll Tax, but the reality was a little more complicated. Of course the Poll Tax movement was exerting a huge pressure on her government. The hated tax had succeeded in uniting the working class alongside many middle class people in angry riots that were shaking the country. Even the non-payment campaign was causing a crisis – a ruling party cannot rule if seventeen-million people refuse to pay the taxes it has imposed. Thatcher had a degree of insolent arrogance about these protests however – she was emboldened by the defeats of the miners, the print workers at Wapping, and the left local government over rate-capping. Perhaps she could have survived the Poll Tax protests, but she couldn't fight on two fronts. The internal divisions in the Conservative Party over Europe threatened to split her party as the number of enemies on her own Parliamentary benches finally mustered their forces to bring her down. Geoffrey Howe's resignation speech as Deputy Prime Minister earlier in the month made clear the level of bad-will among the Tory front bench, as he delivered a twenty minute long excoriating attack on Thatcher's policy towards the European Community. Sensing she was on the ropes, Michael Heseltine challenged her for the leadership, triggering a civil war among Conservative MPs that quickly led to her resignation on 28 November 1990. The Iron Lady was gone, leading to some popular cheers in various inner city parts of Britain that had borne the brunt of her policies. Some glasses were raised in pubs across Lambeth when news came she was gone. It was a kind of bittersweet moment though, her arrogant attitude of invulnerability had led to her downfall so there was a certain pathos, but she had already largely completed her mission. Britain was changed, some believed irrevocably. Deindustrialisation, weaker trade unions, and a local government that could barely tie its own shoe laces without putting it out to competitive tender. Her legacy would leave a searing scar for generations to come.

Clearly, Thatcher leaving Downing Street was a boost for Labour, finally their most formidable opponent was gone. Huge crowds gathered at the Florence Nightingale pub in north Lambeth, just across the bridge from Parliament [today it is The Walrus]. Pubs across the country were crammed with people toasting the demise of the milk snatcher herself, excitedly talking of what was to come next. However, what followed was not a period of peace internally. For Labour, New Realism would outlive Thatcher. The New Realism demanded the heads of the left, the alleged vote losers, those who were accused of unthinkingly and irreparably damaging the image of the party.

In early February 1991 the council narrowly voted to reverse its decision not to allow bailiffs to be deployed against non-payers. Officers had warned them that they faced possible surcharging over the issue. Nevertheless, the vote was close, twenty-five against twenty-six in favour. Steve Nally warned that the councillors that had voted to send in bailiffs should watch out for "the early morning knock".

That came a few days later when three teams of 'Bailiff Busters' left calling cards and "a copy of a threatening letter" with three Tory and two Liberal Democrat Councillors. They claimed to have been woken at 6am by loud bangs on the door with people claiming to be bailiffs threatening to seize their property. Kevin Fernandez helped organise the protest, saying they wanted to highlight that "many people do not know bailiffs have no right of entry, and that they can simply refuse to open the door to them."[22]

But the Labour right also complained of intimidation. Councillor Cathy Ashley, who also worked at Labour HQ and was an LCC member, reported that her car tires had been slashed, implying it was done by left wingers. Ashley was very fond of regaling her stories to any journalist that would listen, and LCC loved to put the claim in any press releases they issued to sympathetic journalists (which was a lot of press releases and a lot of sympathetic journalists). Another Councillor that voted to deploy the bailiffs had the word "scab" graffitied across their door.[23]

Twelves herself was under public scrutiny after she was summoned to appear at Camberwell Magistrates Court. She was processed alongside many other non-payers and a liability order granted against her by the magistrate, the first step towards a potential visit from the bailiffs.

The tax was defeated, in 1992 the Conservative party declared it dead, to be replaced in 1993 with a Council Tax. The entire philosophy behind the Community Charge had been to punish high-spending councils and turn their local population against them, forcing either cuts or possibly electing a low spending Tory Council instead of a Labour one. But the strategy totally backfired; people blamed the Tory government and punished them in a series of devastating by-elections which saw large Tory majorities shredded and overturned. Places like Lambeth were crucial to its defeat. At the time Martin Linton (who went on to be the Labour MP in Battersea) argued in the Guardian that Lambeth's Community Charge was so high that "if the poll tax is going to succeed anywhere in making people march on their town hall and demands cuts in the council's budget, then is would surely be here. But it has not..."[24] The Tory flagship was sunk by torpedoes fired from places like Lambeth.

THE GULF WAR COMES TO SOUTH LONDON

In the middle of the Poll Tax crisis, the first Gulf War broke out when western military forces invaded Iraq to drive Saddam Hussein's forces from Kuwait. The outbreak of war in the Gulf saw protests break out across the country as anti-war activists condemned the military action against Saddam Hussein's Iraq. The bridge across Brixton Road was emblazoned with a large sign saying "We support Brixton" with a number of local business logos

---

22 'Councillors hit by Poll Tax raiders', *South London Press*, Feb 26 1991.
23 Richard Heffernan and Mike Marqusee, *Defeat From the Jaws of Victory* (Verso 1992), p. 284.
24 *The Guardian*, 30 April 1990.

underneath. As the Gulf War got underway, someone had stuck the word 'Iraq' over Brixton in a display of anti-imperialist bravura.

Despite having their hands full with the Poll Tax, the left saw it as important to try and show some kind of act of solidarity with the anti-war movement. Indeed, for Twelves talking about the Gulf War and its impact on the Arab and Muslim community in Lambeth was a welcome relief – possibly even a distraction – from the fact that she was being cajoled into implementing the tax and paying it herself. In his capacity as Peace and Nuclear Affairs Officer, Jon Rogers drafted a motion against the war and presented it to Twelves. It called on the council to hold a special open council meeting to debate the impact of the Gulf War on local residents. The key argument was that any war would push up oil prices, which would have a knock on effect on the economy and no doubt detract from Local Government spending. In that context the motion made a clear anti-war argument, condemned the western attack on Iraq and pointed to the danger of an increase in racism against the local Arab population. One councillor, Josh Arnold-Foster, who worked for the Labour Defence Spokesman, tried to amend the motion but failed. The Labour Group voted overwhelmingly to hold the meeting, with only two votes against and five abstentions.

In a panicked fax, sent on 30 January, Joyce Gould stated that the meeting was "a waste of time and money" and the resolution was a "matter which is not germane to the functioning of the Council in Lambeth",[25] and demanded that it should be withdrawn. Gould also informed the councillors that they were free to break the whip on the resolution if they so wished and that it would not be considered as a breach of party rules. This official sanction from Walworth Road to break the whip was seen as a direct affront to the Labour group, a partisan intervention, given that some of the left themselves would be subsequently suspended by Labour for breaking the whip shortly after the meeting.

Replying to the attack in the *South London Press*, Twelves wrote a letter to the editor in which she defended the remit of the meeting. Her argument focused on the question of community cohesion and the amount being spent on the war in the face of local government cuts. She condemned the "hysterical Jingoism" and cited the need for "racial and religious harmony" in the borough: "if truth is the first casualty of war then in this conflict racial harmony looks like being the second". She also derided the idea that the flying of the Union Jack was anything to do with the meeting, slamming the *South London Press* for "distorting and trivialising the issue by misleading everyone with a silly story about flags."[26] The leader of the Conservative group on the Council, Hugh Jones, opted to use the rhetoric of traitors from within, "There must be Servicemen or Servicemen's families who will feel stabbed in the back by this sort of unpatriotic

---
25 Fax sent to Lambeth Labour group, 30 January 1990.
26 *South London Press*, 8 February 1991.

activity. Council leaders should either support out forces or shut up."[27] This led to *The Sun* chasing Twelves around the Town Hall with a mother of a serving soldier and recorded her berating Twelves for not 'backing the boys' deployed to the Middle East. Twelves retort, that she had a family member in the army too and that was precisely why she opposed the war was studiously ignored by the hack from *The Sun*. The *News of the World* carried the same claim about the Union flag being banned and urged Lambeth Council staff to "Take no notice… patriotism is a noble emotion."[28]

With feelings running so high it was obvious that the council meeting itself would be a volatile and highly charged affair. The room was packed, not just with local residents and anti-war campaigners but with an excitable press corps looking for a story. There was an extended debate, regularly interrupted by shouts from the public gallery. The LCC later accused Steve French of repeatedly shouting "victory to Iraq" and "bomb Israel." These claims were widely circulated in the local press, *The Guardian* and the *Evening Standard*, which not only reported the 'victory to Iraq' claim but also that he had formally apologised for it. In reality, French completely denied the allegations. But rather than establishing any facts, the media perpetuated the story that French had repeatedly shouted 'victory to Iraq' until it becomes a received idea, a fact on the ground.

The LCC also claimed one councillor who opposed the motion was repeatedly heckled and had her microphone tampered with. Eventually the motion was passed, after a gruelling debate, at 1am by twenty-six votes to twenty-four. The press reportage was universally damning; claiming it was everything from unpatriotic or a waste of council resources and time, or both. There were plenty of Labour sources willing to provide quotes to fill newspaper columns. Twelves remained defiant. "We talk about national issues like the environment in the council all the time, but nobody takes them up."[29]

The right were furious at what they saw as the pointless theatrics of the left. Ben Lucas, writing for the Labour Co-ordinating Committee Executive, argued that the Gulf War debate was "an ideal pretext to distract attention from the council's problems and have a go at Neil Kinnock at the same time." Lucas aimed a lot of his fire at *Labour Briefing*, who he labelled the sectarian "hard left".[30]

Sorabji was just as scathing. "Being a local politician in Lambeth is terrible. You don't have any money so all you can ever do is preside over making awful cuts. So, when they have a debate on the Gulf War, for a little while they can forget all that. They can have fun and go back to being working class heroes or ultra-left heroes or whatever."[31] Lucas returned to

---

27 'Patriotism is the last refuge for Lambeth's anti-racists', *Daily Telegraph*, 26 January 1991.
28 'Chin up and fly the Union Jack!', *News of the World*, 27 January 1991.
29 Interview with Joan Twelves, April 2016.
30 'Lambeth and Labour – the Gulf is too great', LCC, February 1990.
31 'Labour Council unable to shake off its culture of incompetence', *The Times*, 7 May 1991.

the central concern of the Labour right, that the antics of the Labour Group were robbing them of a chance of returning a Labour MP in Streatham and of getting a Labour government.

As this crisis played itself out, *Telegraph* journalist, Cassandra Jardine, asked, "why is Joan Twelves committing political suicide?" In the usual manner of the national press, Jardine describes Twelves as conforming exactly to the appearance of a hard left activist: "studiedly unglamorous old cord trousers and thick, woolly, shaggy hair and glasses." Jardine reminded her readers that Twelves was standing in the tradition of "red Ted Knight and the "militant Lesbian" Linda Bellos.[32] Given the heat from the media and the spotlight on them from the national party, it was only a matter of time before Labour's internal disciplinary procedures came knocking on the door of Lambeth Town Hall, gunning for Twelves and her comrades.

---

32 *The Telegraph*, 20 February 1991.

18

Hurtling Towards the Precipice

"Joan Twelves, you are charged with advocating a strategy of confrontation with central government."
"Central government has always had a strategy of confrontation with Lambeth!"[1]

Kinnock had been making noises since mid-February about bringing Lambeth to heel.[2] An inquiry into Lambeth Labour Group was agreed at the NEC on 27 February, and an initial investigatory report was commissioned to report back in a month. Kim Dewdney, the ex-chair of Lambeth Labour Group and ex-chief whip under Bellos and Sorabji, prepared the evidence for the prosecution.

The culture of the witch-hunts in Labour is important to bear in mind here. In their excellent book on the destructive civil war in Labour under Kinnock, Mike Marqusee and Richard Heffernan describe the way the party machine conducted their persecution of the left: "Violations of natural justice were legion. The presumption of innocence was hopelessly subverted. Guilt by association became commonplace. Smears, innuendo and catch all charges proliferated. Hearsay and other forms of uncorroborated evidence were uncritically accepted. Judgements were made on the basis of secret dossiers compiled by anonymous figures whom the accused could never confront. Sentences were based exclusively on subjective political considerations."[3]

When Labour's NEC convened again on 27 March they considered the written submission of evidence from Dewdney and passed a resolution that concluded, "as a result of their continual breaches of the rules of the party, the following named councillors be suspended by the NEC under its powers

---

[1] Paraphrase of Labour NEC documents listing charges against Lambeth Councillors, reply is from interviews with Joan Twelves, August 2017.
[2] Richard Heffernan and Mike Marqusee, *Defeat From the Jaws of Victory* (Verso 1992), p. 283.
[3] Ibid, p. 299.

contained in Clause IX(2)(h)(ii) from holding office, delegation and representation of the party pending further investigation."[4]

The 'named councillors' were Steve French, Lesley Hammond, John Harrison, Alison Higgs, Anne Hollifield, Bill Houghting, George Huish, Julian Lewis, Susanne Roxby, Greg Tucker, John Tuite, Joan Twelves and Rachel Webb. In addition, Steve Nally and Kevin Fernandez, a black Militant activist from Bishops Ward who had riled up the right there once too often, were named as accused. A Labour spokesman told the *Sunday Times* that, "although the inquiry is into the Lambeth Labour group, we will not ignore any evidence of intimidation which involves other party members." He ominously concluded; "We have sorted out Liverpool. We will sort out Lambeth."[5]

In response Herman Ouseley wrote to Joyce Gould in his capacity as Chief Executive: "It is not my business to meddle in the affairs of the Labour Party, but it appears you may not have given due consideration to the utter chaos you are likely to cause by your precipitative action."[6]

The NEC referred the prosecution to the NCC under Clause III(4) of the Constitution Rules and Clause IV(5) of the Constituency Rules. The NEC also recommended that officers from London Region attend Lambeth CLPs and Labour Group meetings, and that Region also draw up the panel for local council elections. All thirteen councillors were charged with engaging "in a sustained course of conduct prejudicial to the Party" and referred to the National Constitutional Committee (NCC).

When he introduced the NCC to the 1986 Party conference, Larry Whitty took pains to explain that it would only be "proportionate" in its disciplinary measures and "efforts at mediation should be tried and exhausted" before any action taken. No mediation was offered to the Lambeth Councillors however, they were issued warnings and then brought up on charges.[7]

The initial allegations which the press focused on included intimidation of fellow councillors at two council meetings relating to the Poll Tax and the Gulf War. These had been repeated in much of the material put out by the LCC, who regularly accused the left of "intimidation," though there was no specifics, and in the file of information handed over to the NEC there were no examples included among the charges. Strange to be so public about supposed threats and then so reticent when it came to investigating them or naming names. When the charges were finally heard, they only consisted of instances where the party whip was broken on the Labour Group. Other charges against several councillors included "voting to invite Sinn Fein councillors" (23 July 1990), voting for a resolution against the Gulf War at a special council meeting (1 February 1991), and voting against using bailiffs to collect Poll Tax arrears (17 February 1991). Other councillors were charged

---

4 Labour NEC minutes, 27 March 1990.
5 'Labour acts on Lambeth poll tax 'threats'', *Sunday Times*, 3 March 1991.
6 Fax from H Ouseley to J Gould, 27 March 1991.
7 Richard Heffernan and Mike Marqusee, *Defeat From the Jaws of Victory*, p. 263.

with publishing articles. Tucker for instance was accused of penning the following articles: "Summer 1989 – Statement in NALGO journal opposing all aspects of the poll tax" and "September 1989 – article in Briefing opposing views of Group".[8] This accusation would seem to indicate that no Labour Councillor could write anything critical of the Labour group policy – a gagging instruction that did not apply to MPs or other party members. It reinforced a view that councillors had no right to criticise policies they considered to be wrong, that the whip extended beyond voting and covered any public views that might be expressed. It looked eerily like thought crimes. But then at this time the NEC was intent on disciplining people for socialist politics, whether Militant or otherwise. Certainly no one from the LCC was criticised for any of their printed materials attacking the positions and resolutions of Lambeth Labour Group, even when it was the majority position.

As leader of the Labour Group, Twelves had additional allegations brought to bear. The NEC heard how, on 1 July, Twelves recommended that no Labour Councillors should pay the Poll Tax, a week earlier she had voted against Poll Tax collection at the council. In her appeal to the NEC, Twelves adopted a more conciliatory tone regarding the Poll Tax, that she saw her role as "resisting implementation by all legal means". Hoey saw it differently, writing to her constituents in Vauxhall complaining about the Council's "regular pastime to push to the very brink of illegality."[9]

Another charge was that five councillors co-signed (along with thirty others) an anti-Poll Tax advert in the *South London Press* calling a demonstration. Again, this was a direct attack by the Labour NEC on the right to express political disagreements with a government policy and to organise opposition to it. Others included several instances of "indicating intention to vote against the whip" and opposing the budget and, in March 1989, moving for an illegal budget against the whip's instructions.

These ran counter to the express remit of the NCC, as stated in the NEC report 1986 Disciplinary Procedures that "no action should be taken relating to the expression of opinion and ideas".[10] By the early '90s, however, the mood in the upper echelons of the Party was to purge and exorcise troublemakers as part of the drive for respectability. As the LCC had opined in one of their local leaflets "Lambeth Council now stands out like a sore thumb. Every other London Labour council has reformed itself, but Lambeth continues on its own part, intent on undermining the Party nationally in order to retain credibility on the hard left."[11]

To try and keep the wolves from the door, Twelves and several allies very publicly paid their poll tax debts. The current councillors and ex-councillors

---

8   NEC pack for disciplinaries against the Lambeth Labour Party members.
9   *The Guardian*, 6 March 1991.
10   Richard Heffernan and Mike Marqusee, *Defeat From the Jaws of Victory*, p. 263.
11   Ben Lucas, 'Lambeth and Labour – the Gulf is too great', LCC, February 1990.

posed with an oversized cheque for £10,000 to the assembled press. From their perspective this wasn't a climbdown. Terry Rich told reporters that "the poll tax is dead" and the reason they were paying is they did not want to contribute to Lambeth's massive deficit.[12] However, this was not enough to prevent the impending disciplinaries.

"PRESSURE"

The attack from the right of the party went beyond the council chamber. The NEC was given a "background" paper that purported to show how some councillors were forced to vote certain ways, due to pressure from Vauxhall and Norwood GCs and the Lambeth LGC. Twelves was clear that the link between the LGC and the councillors was crucial in pushing the demands of rank and file Party members. In her reply to the NEC, Twelves denied that "undue pressure" was brought to bear, arguing that,

> Labour councillors represent the Party and Party members have a right to be consulted and to expect their councillors to be accountable for their decisions and actions.
>
> Many local members are actively involved in the local community (e.g. tenants associations, voluntary organisation management committees, school governors, and need to be able to explain and defend the council's priorities. Others may be involved in organisations and campaigns less affected by what the council does, e.g. health, transport campaigns, but they still see the council as a focus because it is such a dominant force locally. The involvement of local party members in what is happening on the council has been crucial during elections.[13]

The NEC claimed that the factional nature of Lambeth Labour Group was embarrassing the party nationally. Twelves responded that the analysis was too simplistic, that several councillors who had been charged along with her (presumably part of her faction) had voted against her own budgets and that the Bellos group had voted in different ways. If they were factions they were the least disciplined factions you could imagine. What it actually showed was a Labour Group with several different tendencies, but there was a lot of debate, overlap and agreement on various issues. If anything, the most disciplined 'faction' in Lambeth was the LCC, who were usually unanimous in how they voted on policy. But of course the LCC weren't under investigation – this was a witch-hunt of the left, after all.

The left knew that they were heading for a stitch up. They had already been found guilty in the court of media opinion. At the Greater London Conference, Ted Knight spoke from the front against any attack on the

---

12 *Financial Times*, 12 March 1991.
13 Joan Twelves, submission to the NCC hearing.

Lambeth left: "We don't want any purges, do we?"[14] The LCC members in the hall shouted back in pantomime fashion, "oh yes we do!" Worryingly, Phil Cole, senior party manager, who also lived in Lambeth and was in charge of the investigation, was seen applauding the vitriolic attacks on Lambeth.[15] Cole had already had several run-ins with the local left where no one was under any illusions that he held them in great contempt.

The local movement was also clear on the character of the attack. NALGO called a 1,000 strong meeting of its members to pass a motion against the cuts that Twelves was pushing through, but the meeting nevertheless voted to completely oppose the Labour Party's investigation. In his local ward meeting a motion was proposed defending Nally from the witch-hunt. The meeting was being held in Oval House Theatre – John Mann was late and as he approached the door someone jammed a chair under the handle to prevent him getting in for the first half of the meeting.

The accused were summoned to Labour HQ on Walworth Road to account for themselves.

Upon walking into the meeting Nally immediately challenged one of the senior Labour officials in the room. That same official had confronted Nally and Hollifield outside Brixton Town Hall during a Poll Tax Demo and gleefully said that they "couldn't wait to see you two hanging from lamp posts."[16] Hardly an independent adjudicator in an investigatory hearing. Nally was asked to leave the room, and when he returned five minutes later he saw that the official was allowed to stay but sat looking sheepish throughout.

By the time of the NCC meeting the initial charges against Nally were all mysteriously dropped and replaced with one lone accusation: 'being a member of Militant'. Their evidence was a photo of a Militant poster for a public meeting that they claimed had his name on it. Upon looking at it, Nally saw that the poster was blank and only a weather-faded and faint red Militant logo remained. "My name isn't on there. It's blank!", he pointed out. The NCC looked annoyed. "well your name was on there, it just got washed off."[17] Clearly, as was often the case in Labour investigations, any sense of natural justice was suspended. He knew that he was already a condemned man as other Militant comrades had been summarily expelled for being associated with the organisation. Knowing his purge was inevitable, Nally gave the NCC a firm rebuttal on every point. On the way out he passed George Huish. Nally was immediately concerned that his clash with the NCC would rile them up and make them likely to take it out on the next person. True enough, lifelong Labour member George Huish, who had dedicated his adult life to the party and the labour movement, was summarily expelled by the NCC. Nally saw him later, Huish was sobbing at the outcome

---

14 Richard Heffernan and Mike Marqusee, *Defeat From the Jaws of Victory*, p. 286.
15 Ibid.
16 Interview with Steve Nally, August 2017.
17 Ibid.

and wiping his eyes on his jacket sleeve – railroaded out of the party for standing up for his community.

Wielding a file several inches thick, Twelves approached the investigation meeting like a defence lawyer, ready to argue her case. It was particularly galling that Twelves felt she had made compromises and tried to modernise the council and yet she was still facing the gallows. She had been excoriated by the left for selling out, but was still on the chopping block for her left credentials. The main evidence against Twelves was a statement from a UCATT official to the effect that that the council's leadership was inconsistent. Despite having a signed statement from every other trade union in the council and statements of support from Norwood and Vauxhall CLPs in her defence, it was clear that the NEC wanted to proceed purely on the flimsy testimony in front of them.

Gould said that Twelves was charged with being in breach of the decisions of the Labour group, when in fact Twelves was not only leader of that group but the councillors had *backed* her proposals. She was also charged with being part of a regime of intimidation against oppositionists, though there was not a shred of evidence anyone had been involved. In the bizarre world of an NEC investigation, a claim against you with no evidence and no chance of being proven or disproven could still be used to indict you. Furthermore the report concluded "that the council meetings on 1 February and 17 February 1991 were conducted against a background of intimidation, abuse and threats."[18] A peculiar conclusion since no evidence was submitted referring to such actions.

By the end of the miserable affair, the NEC investigation found only one charge with which to report the councillors to the National Constitutional Committee – the famous catch-all accusation loved by bureaucrats of "a sustained course of action prejudicial to the party." This was because "over the last two years there has been a lack of decisive leadership from the senior officers of the Group, in particular the leader, deputy leader and the chief whip." Many on the local left grumbled that the national party had also suffered from a lack of decisive leadership, but none of *them* were being hauled before the NCC. The NCC concluded "That this lack of discipline and order by some Group members coupled with the many contraversial [*sic*] public statements has presented a detrimental view of the party to the electors of Lambeth."[19] This part of the ruling was the most subjective. The only possible gauge for such an attitude would be votes, and Labour had won more council seats and won more votes in Streatham and Vauxhall than before. There were more Labour councillors elected in 1990 than there had been under Knight.

Of course, such an accusation is designed to allow those making the charge to decide the terms of the investigation and the meaning of the

---

18 NCC summary of the investigation.
19 Ibid.

words. What is a sustained course? How many times must you vote against your Group whip for it to become sustained? What conduct is prejudicial? On what grounds is the prejudice to be judged? The left felt that they had stuck to the spirit of the local manifesto and, indeed, the principles of the labour movement as they understood them. But objective decisions and justice was not the purpose of the hearings. The fact of the investigation and the manner in which the NEC felt able to make such judgements demonstrated how far the Labour Party had travelled since the mid-1980s. After all, were Knight and his allies responsible for action "prejudicial to the party" in 1985 despite following party policy agreed at conference? Was it the matter of the whip or something more expansive, a feeling that some of the national leadership had, that Lambeth was a thorn in the side of its so-called modernisation agenda?

The councillors were banned from office, banned from Labour Group meetings, and banned from any Labour party meetings outside their own ward. They were effectively internally exiled – still party members and councillors, but unable to exercise any political power. On the day of the suspensions, the prospective Labour candidate for Streatham, Keith Hill, and Vauxhall MP, Kate Hoey, issued a press release, timed perfectly (they had inside sources to help coordinate it) so that the news would report on how pleased they were that "an unrepresentative minority" had been ousted from the Labour group. "I think the vast majority of people in Lambeth will be pleased Joan has resigned" said Kate Hoey, savouring her victory in the *South London Press*.[20]

Despite everything, the thirteen councillors who had been disciplined maintained their loyalty to the Labour group, voting for their motions to keep the party in power and prevent a Tory/Liberal take over.

Later that day the Lambeth crisis was used by Heseltine to take some of the heat out of the Tory government's own crisis over the Poll Tax. Debating a motion of no confidence in the Conservative Government due to failure of the Community Charge, Heseltine returned one more time to his favourite whipping post of the activities at Lambeth Town Hall. He deployed the well-worn Tory attack line that Labour was unfit to govern because it harboured radicals in its ranks. He goaded Labour MPs with a roll call of the recent suspensions: "The House is entitled to the latest up-to-the-minute information. Today the Labour executive kicked out 13 of Labour's councillors in Lambeth. The Labour leader, Joan Twelves, is out. The mayor, George Huish, is out. The deputy leader, John Harrison, is out. The chief whip, Julian Lewis, is out. Greg Tucker, Mrs. Twelves's partner, is out. I leave it to my right hon. and hon. Friends to interpret that for themselves; whatever he happens to be, he is out on his ear. As all those great luminaries of the Labour establishment get the chop, they have given a new political

---

20 *South London Press*, 27 March 1991.

significance to the meaning of the Lambeth walk."[21] Labour MPs shuffled uncomfortably, for most of them the first they had heard about the NEC's decision was Heseltine's speech.

Tasting blood, Heseltine went further: "Why did the Labour party stop at Lambeth? The truth is that it did not. The national anti-poll tax campaigner, Steve Nally, was heaved out as well. Let us be generous and say with one accord to the leader of the Labour party, "Well done, but why did it take you so long? Now what will you do about all the other councillors and Labour Members of Parliament who will not pay their poll tax?"[22] Heseltine obviously didn't know that Nally was part of the Lambeth investigation as he lived in the borough. But it is worth recognising once again the nature of the Tory attack: to always apply pressure on Labour to go further, to implement more expulsions and suspensions. As ever, the Tories and their allies in the media set the agenda for Labour's internal politics; the party felt huge pressure to respond to the latest outrage from Wapping or Fleet Street, desperate to prove how moderate and reliable they were.

The Labour group on the council became a minority administration. After the suspensions Larry Whitty wrote to the Lambeth Labour Group and instructed the twenty-seven remaining councillors to elect a new leader or they would all face suspension. The NEC were willing to purge the entire Labour group of Lambeth Council if that is what it came to. The Labour group asked to send representatives to meet with the NEC to appeal against Twelves' suspension but they were stonewalled. A few weeks after the disciplinary action, Twelves resigned as leader of the Labour group. Steve Whalley took over as the leader and became head of the council. The era of Radical Lambeth was coming to an end.

---

21 *Hansard*, 27 March 1991.
22 Ibid.

Conclusion
Legacy of Radical Lambeth

> The splendid Victorian town hall, standing proudly in many city centres, increasingly seemed like a dinosaur from a very distant past.
>
> A J Davies[1]

In 1991 Associated Press wrote a largely unsympathetic article about Lambeth titled, 'ultra left presided over stricken borough of Lambeth'. Summarising the situation as "Here the pro-Marxists, gay rights activists, organisers of blacks-only recruitment programs and nuclear-free zones hold out, bankrupt and under attack from both the Conservative government and the Labor Party leadership." Suspended member Joan Twelves is described as "cheerful and chain-smoking".[2] Nearly thirty years later Twelves is still cheerful, though no longer chain smoking. Her hair is shorter but she is still recognisably the embattled woman photographed for the newspaper hatchet jobs all those years ago. She dropped out of politics for a few years after narrowly losing her council seat in Larkhall ward in the 1994 council elections. Her partner, Greg, stayed active in trade union politics, becoming secretary of the powerful Waterloo RMT branch in 1993. Then he got sick with cancer. Joan nursed him until he died in 2008. At his funeral many of the people mentioned in this book turned out to show their respects.

Twelves still lives in the same flat near Oval that she occupied back when she was a councillor. Twelves was sick for several years, meaning that she dropped out of politics. Nevertheless, she kept every piece of paper from her time on the council — her spare room is a treasure trove of leaflets, internal council papers, pamphlets and memorabilia, including a photo of her posing with Jeremy Corbyn in front of the GLC building around 1986 or '87. When I interviewed her, she became very serious, though her wry grin

---

1 A J Davies, *We, The Nation: The Conservative Party and the Pursuit of Power*, (Little, Brown and Company 1995), p. 341.
2 'Ultra Left Presides Over Stricken Borough of Lambeth', April 30, 199

poked through occasionally when she remembered some conflict or exchange from the past. Referring to her legacy and her role in local Labour politics she liked to remark, "Apparently I'm the most dangerous woman in Lambeth!" with a broad smile. "The Councillors are a bit nervous of me because I know how things work!" You have to have a strong ego to survive Lambeth politics.

But the gruelling battles of the 1980s also demonstrated how hard it was for left-wing Labour Party members to affect change from the Council Chambers. Heroic stands were made against Thatcherism but all ultimately went down to defeat. To a large degree the defeats came not from the balance of forces in the borough itself but from the national picture – how different would rate-capping have been if the miners had lasted on strike just two more months and the 'second front' had opened up? Once the key fights had been lost it was a case of rear-guard actions over privatisations and budget cuts, with only the Poll Tax battle proving to be a success, though for the people of Lambeth more so than the Labour Councillors that were sacrificed by the party on the altar of appeasing the right-wing media.

The struggles inside the Labour Party took their toll locally. The 1994 council elections saw a Labour slump, losing sixteen councillors whilst the Liberal Democrats gained twenty, leading to a Liberal Democrat and Tory coalition council for four years. As a consolation, however, Labour finally won the Streatham seat in 1992.

After the events recounted in this book the radical culture in the borough began to noticeably decline. The Council was run by 'moderates', consciously distancing themselves from the politics of the 'bad old days'. The Labour left itself was in historic retreat under the blows of Blairism – not to revive until Jeremy Corbyn became party leader in 2015. But it was not just in Labour, the last of the squats were evicted by the early 2000s, the short-life properties were cleared out a decade later. Carshalton Mansions opposite Brixton Village (on the side of which the *Nuclear Dawn* mural was painted in 1981) was the last of the short-life properties, an almost forgotten relic of a different time. Largely this was due to gentrification – house prices simply became unaffordable for most people and there were no slums left to squat. One example is the fate of the Cooltan social centre on Coldharbour Lane, which was eventually knocked down and the land brought by Barratt Homes to build luxury flats costing £310 a week. The rapacious hunger of developers accelerated under New Labour as local councils like Lambeth saw it as their duty to 'redevelop' the area, but without their own DLOs to do the work, construction was left to companies that demanded a high price – expensive flats and houses with not much for social rent and few of the kind of places that could house an alternative local newspaper. The view in the local community that the local authority is on the side of developers instead of local residents is one that regularly resurfaces. Councillors across the country will point to the strict legislations and plead that they have no choice, that the reforms of the Thatcher era, left largely untouched during Tony Blair's government, mean that their hands are tied. It is notable that successive Labour manifestos since 2010 have contained relatively little on local government until 2019, when Labour stood on a platform to end Right to Buy and routine privatisation of local services. This got nearly 100,000 votes across the three Lambeth constituencies, though Labour was defeated nationally.[3]

There were also huge battles with the council over the austerity regime after 2010. Lambeth Labour had been firmly taken over by Tony Blair's internal pressure group, Progress, who prided themselves on representing a total break from the 'loony left' days. They shared all of the Conservatives criticisms of Ted Knight and his colleagues, they derided gesture politics, and instead set down to the grim task of making cut backs, implementing job losses and calling back services. They had no intention of any community campaigns or working with trade unions to resist cuts – indeed compared to the 1980s no Labour council put up any fight at all. It wasn't until the Corbyn leadership after 2015 that things began to shift in the local Labour Parties, though it is a sign of the times that Labour still categorically, even under Corbyn, committed itself to implementing local government cuts whilst out of power nationally. The much derided dented shield remained Labour policy even when the party was led by individuals who had been so critical of it in the 1980s.

By the late 1980s Lambeth stood as one of the last bastions of municipal socialism – a rich newspaper column filler for stories about the so-called loony left. Clearly there were problems that the left couldn't overcome, and even a sympathetic account has to conclude that there were many problems, often self-inflicted. Dealing with inner-city poverty whilst fighting central government as well as their own party hierarchy meant that the councillors were often isolated, usually embattled against their own officers, and perpetually under siege from the media hate campaign. They largely failed to improve services to the quality that was needed, but then, what council could improve services in the 1980s in a war with central government? As we have seen, the councillors often came up against opposition from their own workforce and the local community, a community which itself was divided with overlapping interests and demands. The decisive showdown with the government over rate-capping failed to mobilise the local community in any great numbers. It seemed like a fight happening somewhere else to other people. It wasn't until the Poll Tax in 1990 that local people rose up, and that was because it impacted directly on their pockets. There are lots of criticisms that could be made, but the richness of the stories of people from the

---

3 The exact figure for Lambeth's voters is unknowable, since Dulwich and West Norwood (DAWN) has three wards in Southwark. It is worth noting that every constituency saw Labour's vote share rise considerably in 2017; Helen Hayes in DAWN got an extra 15.5%, Kate Hoey in Vauxhall 3.5%, Chuka Ummuna 15.5% in Streatham.

borough and the idealism with which they lived and fought should not be forgotten or ignored or laughed at.

As time wore on local radical politics had changed too – the kind of radicalism which produced the Brixton Black Panthers and pioneers like Olive Morris were largely a thing of the past. Rebel Dykes, the 121 Social Centre and the alternative political scene on Railton Road had vanished, though the *Race Today* Collective maintained a building for some time before it was replaced by Brixton Advice Centre. All in all, Lambeth, and Brixton in particular, changed considerably. But there was several institutions from that time that were a direct result of the events of the 1980s. The Brixton Recreation Centre was built for the explicit purpose of mitigating future violent disorder, based on slightly Victorian attitudes that youth who were engaged in sport would be less prone to radicalisation and criminality. The Black Cultural Archives was founded in 1981 by Len Garrison and other educationalists with the intention of providing a place where community memory could be preserved and enriched. There was a very real fear that Thatcherism was trying to physically and politically wipe out the cultural memory of black Britain.

Some of the changes since the battles of the 1980s have been positive. The black and the LGBT community in particular had fought heroic battles during the 1970s and '80s, demanding the right to exist, the right not to live every day under state repression or violence from bigots. Darcus Howe talked about the gradual emergence of "a social ease and confidence now that we have not had before". Not gradual because it was happening peacefully or inevitably, but because people had fought and established that they were here to stay, no matter the National Front, the police baton or the reactionary press. LGBT rights is one example – in the middle of the AIDs epidemic Section 28 was introduced. In 1987 and was viewed by some as 'common sense'. Homophobia was explicit and politically weaponised. Fast-forward ten years to when New Labour was in power and scrapped Section 28 and allowed civil partnerships – the Tories even legalised gay marriage in 2013. Would any of these changes have been possible without the militant Rebel Dykes and Brixton Fairies, or without the fight for survival that gay and lesbian people had put up in the 1970s and '80s?

Cardboard City was eventually dismantled in the late 1990s, part of the redevelopment of the area as the New Labour government put more money into tackling homelessness and rough sleeping. The remaining thirty residents were evicted from the site to make way for an IMAX cinema near Waterloo Station, but were promised accommodation by Lambeth Council. But even that apparent act of generosity was viewed with suspicion, one of the long-term resident, an ex-soldier called Shaun, who had lived at the site for a decade, warned that it just doesn't work. "You offer someone who has been living rough the chance of a permanent home and then give them upwards of £500 to get straight... They have no concept of a normal life and just spend the money on drink or drugs. It might work if the people you are trying to rehabilitate are given some counselling because most of them have no idea what it is like to settle down and live in a flat."[4]

The progress that was made on tackling police institutional racism, on challenging structural racism in employment, would any of that have even been on the agenda without the urban uprisings of the 1980s? By the 1990s significant parts of the establishment were forced to acknowledge the problem that so many knew to exist and make concessions and reforms to meet some of the demands of black communities. Clearly there is still a long way to go but arguably without those acts of resistance, violent and terrifying as they were, things wouldn't change. Would the MacPherson Report into institutional racist in the police have been possible without the bricks thrown in the 1980s? In the late 1970s people still talked about repatriation of all non-whites from the country, today – even with all the Islamophobia and anti-migrant attitudes – no one is countenancing such a reactionary social project. Because colonialism was a violent assertion of power, it was inevitable that post-colonialism and the right to be a black citizen was also something that had to be fought for. As James Baldwin once wrote, "to be black was to confront and to be forced to alter, a condition forged in history."[5] It was on those streets and so many others across Britain that black people fought to make their own history.

It is not all forward steps, however. The initial democratic spirit of the consultative forums for police monitoring established in the 1980s were abandoned and replaced by a Safer Neighbourhood Boards in 2015, an initiative of Boris Johnson when he was Mayor. Instead of volunteer organisations holding regular public meetings with senior police commanders, the SNBs would be made up of 'stake holders' from approved organisations, many of them some way dependent on the council or the police force.

In the popular imagination the notion of Lambeth as a wild, untamed part of central London, rife with corruption, political extremism and eccentric characters, a veritable Dodge City,[6] is occasionally still invoked. This is partially racialised, partially just a suburban prejudice against urban life. But the 'loony left' insult looks very dated today; after all, a number of those policies, gay rights, women's issues, a focus on race relations and equalities more generally, are now standard practices across the public and private sector. Even the nationally recognised Black History Month was devised by a Lambeth Council worker called Ansel Wong and launched in Lambeth by Linda Bellos in 1987, a woman who at the time was under constant attack in the press for *who* she was as much as *what* she did. Even

---

4 BBC, "Cardboard City' meets its Waterloo', 23 February 1998.
5 James Baldwin, *Dark Days* (Penguin 2018), p. 1.
6 Cited in Peter Jones, *From Virtue to Venality: Corruption in the City* (Oxford University Press 2016).

the criticism of the later councillors' supposedly 'confrontational attitude' has to be seen in the context of a mass popular uprising against the Poll Tax by seventeen-million people – it seemed that confrontation was the order of the day. Labour's failure to get with the times and engage with those movements was arguably one of the factors that lost it the 1992 election.

And despite progress in some areas, some of the essential problems still remain. Lambeth continued to struggle. On Saturday, 17 April 1999, a nail bomb in Electric Avenue, right in the heart of the market, exploded injuring forty-eight people. It was planted by David Copeland, a known fascist, who did it specifically to target the local black population in an attempt to ignite a race war. In 2016 a Runnymede Trust report into Lambeth found that it was the worst borough in the country for racial inequality for employment, housing, education and health; its figures markedly worse for black people than in 2001.[7] Was it that the white population had just enjoyed more gains, relative to the black residents, or had the quality of life for many black people gone backwards? In 2014 three gay men were sprayed in the face with ammonia in a homophobic attack outside the Vauxhall Tavern. By 2016 36% of children in Lambeth were still living in poverty. In 2015 it had the highest rate of long term Job Seekers Allowance claimants in London. So much had changed with so many structural problems still remaining.

There are also darker legacies of the past that still linger. It was during the 1980s that the scale of abuse in children's care homes across different local authorities began to come to light. These ranged from lax safeguarding that led to the employment of abusers in some care homes to systematic abuse on a large scale. Council run care homes in Islington, Hackney and Lambeth all ended up in the national media. Five homes were implicated in Lambeth, two of which were homes for children with special needs. At Shirley Oaks (then the largest children's care home in the country) from the 1960s to the early 1980s abuse was carried out on 'an industrial scale' by a network of abusers. In all, 48 children died in Lambeth care homes between 1970 and 1989. A number of Councillors, including Phyllis Dunipace, launched inquiries into individual accusations of abuse from 1986 onwards but these inquiries failed to uncover the systematic nature of the problem. It wasn't until the 1989 Children's Act and then a follow-up law in 1999 that concepts like 'safe guarding' and 'child protection' were even seriously considered.

There is still a cultural and political memory of the 1980s, and even the 1970s, locally. The fight against gentrification, with Lambeth Council regularly criticised as being in the pockets of developers, produced Reclaim Lambeth in 2016, a protest that started off in Windrush Square, headed to the Town Hall, past an estate agents on the high street (which had its window smashed), before heading to the police station, which was

---

7   Farah Elahi and Omar Khan, *Ethnic Inequalities in London Capital For All* (Runnymede Trust 2016).

temporarily besieged before twenty police stormed out with batons and pepper spray and cleared protesters away. Some of those radical habits die hard.

But in difficult and dangerous times it is often the small ray of lights that shine brightest. Perhaps the most remarkable story I came across during research involved a Lambeth resident's trip to China in 1989, where she ended up in Tiananmen Square with the pro-democracy protesters. She went to visit the assembled students and activists gathered in their encampment in the middle of the city, singing the *Internationale* and seeing themselves, alongside the movements in Eastern Europe and Russia, as the dawn of a new era of radical democracy. On her jacket and bag they saw all the badges she had collected from the various campaigns that were being run in Lambeth. When they excitedly asked if they could have them to put on next to their own stickers and badges, she gladly handed them over. That afternoon a *Financial Times* journalist spotted groups of young Chinese people, hopeful for a better future, walking around Tiananmen Square adorned with badges saying, 'Lambeth NALGO says no to cuts!' and 'Lambeth Council against water privatisation'.[8] It seems the spirit of radical Lambeth could even even be found on the other side of the world.

---

8   *Financial Times*, 9 June 1989.

Bibliography

BALDWIN, J., *Dark Days*, Penguin, London, 2018
BUNCE, ROBIN, FIELD, PAUL, *Darcus, Howe, A Political Biography*
BUTCHER, H. AND LAW, I. ET AL, *Local Government and Thatcherism*, Routledge, London, 1990
COCKBURN, C., *The Local State: The Management of Cities and People*, Pluto Press, 1977
DAVIES, A. J., *We, The Nation: The Conservative Party and the Pursuit of Power*, Little, Brown and Company, London, 1995
FIRELDHOUSE, R., *Anti-Apartheid: A history of the movement in Britain*, 2005
GOSS, S., *Local Labour and Local Government: A Study of Changing Interests, Politics, and Policy in Southwark from 1919 to 1982*, Edinburgh University Press: Edinburgh, 1982
HARMER, H., *The Longman Companion to the Labour Party; 1900-1998*, Routledge, 2014
HEFFERNAN, R AND MARQUSEE, M., *Defeat From the Jaws of Victory: Inside Kinnock's Labour Party*, Verso, 1992
JACOBS, B., 'Labour Against the Centre: the Clay Cross Syndrome', *Local Government Studies*, Vol. 10, 1984
_____, *Black Politics and Urban Crisis in Britain*, Cambridge University Press, 1986
JEFFERS, S., AND HOGGETT, P., 'Like Counting Deckchairs on the Titanic: A Study of Institutional Racism and Housing Allocations in Haringey and Lambeth', *Housing Studies*, Vol 10 Issue 3, 1995
JONES, E., *Neil Kinnock*, Robert Hale Ltd, London, 1994
JONES, P., *From Virtue to Venality: Corruption in the City*, Oxford University Press, Oxford, 2016
LANSLEY S., GOSS S., AND WOLMAR C., *Councils in Conflict: The Rise and Fall of the Municipal Left*, Macmillan, London, 1989
LIVINGSTONE, K., *If Voting Changed Anything, They'd Abolish It*, Collins, London, 1987
_____, *You Can't Say That!*, Faber and Faber, London, 2011

LOUGHLIN, MARTIN, *Legality and Locality: The Role of Law in Central-local Government Relations*, Clarendon Press, Oxford, 1996
MANDELSON, P., *The Third Man*, Harper Collins, London, 2010
MCKENZIE, S., *The Twentieth Century Lambeth*, Sutton Publishing, 1999
SAINT, A. (ED.), *Politics and the People of London: The London County. Council, 1889-1965*, The Hambledon Press, London, 1989
SHAW, E., *The Labour Party Since 1979: Crisis and Transformation*, Routledge, 2002
SHIPLEY, P., *The Riots and the Far Left, Journal of Ethnic and Migration Studies*, Taylor & Francis, 1981
WAINWRIGHT H., *Labour: A Tale of Two Parties*, The Hogarth Press Ltd, London, 1987
WHITE, J., *London in the Twentieth Century: A City and Its People*, Random House, 2008
WILSON, E., *A Very British Miracle: The Failure of Thatcherism*, Pluto Press, London, 1992
WILSON, D. AND GAME, C., *Local Government in the United Kingdom*, Palgrave MacMillan, Basingstoke, 1998

Index

Amalgamated Engineering Union (AEU) 158,
Alternative Economic Strategy (AES) 17, 18, 29, 120, 155
Anarchists 1, 2, 25-6, 63, 71, 114, 146, 179
Anti-Nazi League (ANL) 55, 59, 60
Apartheid (South Africa) 137-139, 141-3
Atkin, Sharon 102, 103, 105, 123, 164, 173
Amalgamated Union of Engineering Workers (AUEW) 99, 106

Broadcasting, Entertainment, Communications and Theatre Union (BECTU) 136
Bellos, Linda 109, 115, 121, 125, 141, 145, 155, 158, 168, 180, 194, 203
   Becomes leader of the Council 122-4
   Homophobia towards, 125, 189
   Resigns as leader 163-6
Benn, Tony 17, 119, 156, 184
Bercow, John 124-5, 126, 161
Blake, Jonathan 136
Blake, William 5
Black community 6, 92, 99, 129, 137
   encountering racism 54-5, 58, 59, 62-4, 67, 70, 72
Black People Against State Harassment (BASH) 60
Blunkett, David 94, 100n, 101, 154, 180n
Boatemah, Dora (Housing Activist) 147-50
Boateng, Janet 96
Boston, Janet 101, 104, 109, 121
Bowering, Bill 15, 61
Bright, Mike 61, 103
British Black Panthers 25, 55,
Brixton 6, 18, 53, 84, 96, 112-13, 118, 136, 138, 146, 161, 178, 181, 187
   Uprising (1981) 62-72
   Uprising (1985) 111-16
Brixton Academy 53
Brixton Black Women's Group 25, 53
Brixton Defence Committee 67-8, 91
Brixton Fairies 131, 202

Broadwater Farm 115

Cakebread, Stuart 100, 101, 104
Callaghan, James 17
Cardboard City (Waterloo) 202-3
Civil & Public Servants Association (CPSA) 20
Clapham 7, 84, 118
Clay Cross Council 30, 41, 85
Cockburn, Cynthia 11, 19
Communist Party of Great Britain (CPGB) 27
Corbyn, Jeremy 181, 199, 200, 201
Crighton, Sean 111
Crisis in Local Government Conference 36-40

Direct Labour Organisation 22-4, 124

Fraser, John (Norwood MP) 44, 70, 114
French, Steve 122, 124, 125, 169, 188, 192

Gay Liberation Front 129
General Election,
   1979 33, 34
   1983 85-6, 119, 153
   1987 153, 178
   1992 204
General and Municipal Workers Union 38, 120n
Grant, Bernie (MP) 100, 109, 122, 172-3, 174
Greater London Council (GLC) 18, 46, 78, 85, 88, 94, 96-8, 104, 105, 136, 199
Groce, Dorothy 'Cherry' 112-13, 115, 116
Gulf War 186-9, 192
Gutzmore, Cecil 60, 67

Hall, Ed 109, 126
Hammond, Len 64
Hammond, Leslie 64, 121, 192
Hannon, Noel 90
Hatton, Derek 95
Healy, Gerry 12
Heath, Ted 30
Heseltine, Michael 35, 65-6, 73, 87, 99, 185, 197-8
Hodge, Margaret 109

Hoey, Kate 172, 173, 174, 175, 193, 197, 201n
Holland, Stuart 17, 91, 111-12, 155
Hollamby, Edward 27-8
Homelessness 5, 151-2, 202-3
Housing
   Co-operatives 145, 146
   Housing Action Trust 147 -150
   NALGO opposition to Right to Buy 47-9
   Racial discrimination 14, 18
   Right to Buy 39, 45-9, 201
   St Agnes Place 14, 57
   Squatting 13,14, 24-7, 66
   Villa Road 21, 26
Howe, Darcus 56, 62

Inner London Education Authority (ILEA) 59, 97, 99, 105, 167, 169
International Marxist Group (IMG) 37, 122, 173
Irish Republicanism 32, 33, 69, 71, 86, 139, 168

James, CLR 56, 141
Johnson, Lynton Kwesi 56, 62, 64

Kean, Hilda 100, 101
Kinnock, Neil 79, 94, 95, 97, 120, 153, 171-2, 191
Knight, Ted 12, 23, 36, 40, 46, 51, 62, 65, 73, 94, 105, 109, 119, 121, 123, 125, 126, 163, 167, 196, 201
   Becomes leader of Lambeth Labour, 15
   Criticism of the police 63, 66
   Left, criticism of 40-1, 43
   Rate-capping campaign 86-8, 92-109
   Union opposition 49-51

Labour Campaign for the Defence of Brixton 68
Labour Coordinating Committee (LCC) 120, 156, 158, 159, 166, 167, 178, 186, 188, 192, 193, 194, 195
Labour Herald 104, 105
Labour Party 8, 36, 40, 135, 180
   Black Sections 122, 154, 173
   Investigates Lambeth Left 191-8
   Young Socialists 12, 19, 89
Labour Briefing 19, 88, 159, 162, 166, 193

Lambeth Central By-Election 59
Lambeth Council
   Anti-Apartheid solidarity 39, 85n, 141-2
   Budgets 35, 36, 39-40, 42-4, 49, 73-4, 87, 155-9
   Mortgaging the Future 153, 156
   Nicaragua Solidarity 79-83
   Nuclear Free Zone 83-4
   Police 139-40
Lambeth TUC 59, 92, 141
Leigh, Mary (Lambeth Conservative council group leader) 48, 75, 109, 121, 130-1
LGBTQ 7,18, 26, 71, 119, 122-3, 129-36, 174-5, 202
   AIDS crisis 92, 129-31, 133, 135, 175, 202
   Miners' solidarity 91-2
   Section 28 134-5, 202
Lesbians and Gays Support the Miners (LGSM) 90, 91, 92
Liverpool 19, 33, 69, 70, 93, 107
Livingstone, Ken 42, 43, 181
   rate-capping 96, 97-8, 99, 104, 123
Local government
   Competitive tendering 31, 167, 178
   Finance Act (1982) 86
   Local Government Act (1972) 106
   Rate capping; 86-109
   Section 114 183
Local Government Committee (LGC) 14, 74, 123, 125, 156, 158, 163n, 165, 167, 168, 194
Local Elections,
   1978 14-17
   1982 75-6, 85
   1986 121
   1994 199, 200

Mandelson, Peter 16, 66, 119, 172
Mann, John 11-12, 195
Marley, Bob 14, 57, 89
Marxism 12, 15, 19, 26, 39, 43, 71, 73, 74, 76, 119, 129, 140, 199
Marxism Today 97, 119, 163
McDonnell, John 88, 96, 97, 98, 104
Media 2, 13n, 23, 57, 62, 66, 81-8, 117, 132-3, 187, 201
   Loony left 1, 132-3

Militant Tendency 18, 67, 68, 93, 123, 179, 181, 192, 193, 195
Miners' Strike (1984-85) 88-92, 95, 98,
Morris, Olive 25, 202
Municipal Socialism 17-20, 35, 36

NALGO 20, 34, 37, 38, 39, 43, 76, 80, 83, 84, 99, 103, 106, 154, 157, 160, 161-3, 164, 182, 193, 195, 205
    Black Workers Group 50
Nally, Steve 90, 172, 184, 192, 195, 198
Narayan, Rudi 67, 68, 174
National Front 7, 54, 58, 202
National Union of Miners (NUM) 32, 88-90, 99
National Union of Public Employee (NUPE) 20, 38, 39, 94, 106
National Union of Teacher (NUT) 20, 39, 42, 59, 68
New Cross Fire 61, 112
Nicaragua 79-83, 115
Norwood 13, 15-16, 43, 78, 80, 154, 158, 167-8, 194, 196
Nuclear Free Zone 83-4, 162, 199

O'Malley, John 99, 104n, 171n

Osamor, Martha 60, 171-2, 174
Ouseley, Herman 11, 192

Payne, Cynthia 8
Peach, Blair 60
Policing 32, 111-112
    Racism 14, 33, 55, 58, 62, 111-13, 116-17
    SPG 60
    Sus Laws 60-1, 62, 63, 64, 68
Poll Tax 166, 167, 177-86, 192, 193, 198, 201
Porter, Shirley (Westminster Council) 21-2
Powell, Enoch 54

Race Today 56, 67
Racism 7, 11, 12, 203
    Government 58
    Mugging 58-60, 63, 116-17
Railton Road (AKA The Front Line) 25, 54, 56, 64, 65, 70, 71, 72, 131, 202

121 Centre 25-6
Rastafarianism 14, 57-8, 70, 137
    Marcus Garvey 137
Rates 99, 104
    Clapham Rates Action Group 73
    Lambeth Supplementary rate increase (1980-81) 39-40
    Left opposes increases 19, 37
    Debate over rate capping strategy 93-96
    End of rate capping campaign 103-104
    Rate capping court case 105-8
    Rate Payers Alliance 74, 75, 76
Red Wedge 153
Revolutionary Communist Party 174
Right to Buy, *see* Housing
Rock Against Racism (RAR) 34, 55
Rogers, Jon (NALGO) 162, 181, 187
Royal Vauxhall Tavern 92, 132, 204

Scarman, Lord Leslie George 67-70, 111, 116
Sheffield 93
Shelton, William (Streatham MP) 48, 142
Sheridan, Tommy 127
Smith, T., Dan (Newcastle Council) 21
Social Democratic Party (SDP) 16, 120
Socialist Campaign for a Labour Victory 19
Socialist Organiser 39
Socialist Workers Party 67, 76, 99
Sorabji, Dick 122, 156
    become Council leader 166-9, 180, 188
Smith, Hazel 80
Spare Rib 90, 122
Squatting, *see* Housing
Stimpson, David 13, 14, 15, 16
Strauss, George (Vauxhall MP) 33-4
Streatham 6, 40, 118, 197

Tapsell, Anna 50, 107, 154-155
Transport and General Workers Union (TGWU) 38, 39, 41, 118
Thatcher, Margaret 37, 58, 62, 86, 87, 93, 125
    Resigns 185

Thatcherism 29-32, 37, 51, 120, 152, 154
Tribune 94, 95n
TUC (Trade Union Congress) 36, 39, 40, 42, 68, 97, 141-2
Tucker, Greg 122, 124, 163, 164, 168, 181, 192, 197, 199
Turner, Neil 40
Twelves, Joan 121, 122, 124, 169, 175, 180, 187, 188, 189, 192, 197, 199-200

UCATT (Unite Construction, Allied Trades and Technicians) 13, 20, 38, 80, 106
Unemployment 18, 35, 45, 57, 64, 68, 71, 73, 87, 89, 113, 115, 118, 127, 136, 142, 153

Vauxhall 7, 8, 17, 33-4, 82, 104, 154, 155, 163, 171-5, 193
Vauxhall By-election 171-5

Wadsworth, Marc 14In, 171, 173, 174
Waller, Michael (Lambeth NALGO) 20, 37, 38, 43, 49
Wandsworth Council 22, 23, 45, 55, 73, 74, 130, 145
  comparisons to Lambeth 77, 102, 140, 179, 181
Wapping dispute 160, 185, 198
Warburton, Matthew 14, 15, 24, 25, 39, 45, 46, 65
Webb, Rachel 123, 125, 168, 180, 192
Whalley, Joan 84
Whitelaw, Willie 64, 111
Wilson, Harold 17
Windrush 53
Winter of discontent 31
Women 26, 49, 50, 83, 88
  Brixton Black Women's Group 25, 53, 60
  GLC 18
  Lambeth Women's Support Group 89
  policing 117, 118
  Women Against Pit Closures 89
Workers Revolutionary Party (WRP) 12, 15, 67, 108

Also from
BREVIARY STUFF PUBLICATIONS

Victor Bailey, CHARLES BOOTH'S POLICEMEN, *Crime, Police and Community in Jack-the-Ripper's London*
£17.00 • 162pp *paperback* • *2 colour and 8 b/w images* • 140x216mm • ISBN 978-0-9564827-6-1

Victor Bailey, ORDER AND DISORDER IN MODERN BRITAIN, *Essays on Riot, Crime, Policing and Punishment*
£15.00 • 214pp *paperback* • 5 *b/w images* • 191x235mm • ISBN 978-0-9570005-5-1

Roger Ball, Dave Beckwith, Steve Hunt, Mike Richardson, STRIKERS, HOBBLERS, CONCHIES & REDS, *A Radical History of Bristol, 1880-1939*
£18.50 • 366pp *paperback* • *101 b/w images* • 156x234mm • ISBN 978-0-9929466-0-9

John Belchem, 'ORATOR' HUNT, *Henry Hunt and English Working Class Radicalism*
£17.50 • 248pp *paperback* • 191x235mm • ISBN 978-0-9564827-8-5

Alastair Bonnett & Keith Armstrong (eds.), THOMAS SPENCE: THE POOR MAN'S REVOLUTIONARY
£15.00 • 214pp *paperback* • 156x234mm • ISBN 978-0-9570005-9-9

Norah Carlin, REGICIDE OR REVOLUTION?, *What Petitioners Wanted, September 1648 - February 1649*
£18.50 • 358pp *paperback* • 156x234mm • ISBN 978-1-9161586-0-3

Nigel Costley, WEST COUNTRY REBELS
£20.00 • 220pp *full colour illustrated paperback* • 216x216mm • ISBN 978-0-9570005-4-4

Ariel Hessayon (ed.), THE REFINER'S FIRE, *The Collected Works of TheaurauJohn Tany*
£25.00 • 552pp *paperback* • 156x234mm • ISBN 978-0-9570005-7-5

Catherine Howe, HALIFAX 1842, *A Year of Crisis*
£14.50 • 202pp *paperback* • 156x234mm • ISBN 978-0-9570005-8-2

Philip Ruff, A TOWERING FLAME, *The Life & Times of the Elusive Latvian Anarchist Peter the Painter*
£17.00 • 284pp *paperback* • 156x234mm • ISBN 978-0-9929466-5-4
£25.00 • 284pp *hardback* • 156x234mm • ISBN 978-0-9929466-8-5

David Walsh, MAKING ANGELS IN MARBLE, *The Conservatives, the Early Industrial Working Class and Attempts at Political Incorporation*
£15.00 • 268pp *paperback* • 191x235mm • ISBN 978-0-9570005-0-6

David Walsh, THE SONS OF BELIAL, *Protest and Community Change in the North-West, 1740-1770*
£16.00 • 272pp *paperback* • 156x234mm • ISBN 978-0-9929466-9-2

Ralph Anstis, WARREN JAMES AND THE DEAN FOREST RIOTS, *The Disturbances of 1831*
£17.00 • 242pp *paperback* • 191x235mm • ISBN 978-0-9564827-7-8

For further information visit
www.breviarystuff.org.uk

Also from
BREVIARY STUFF PUBLICATIONS

John E. Archer, BY A FLASH AND A SCARE, *Arson, Animal Maiming, and Poaching in East Anglia 1815-1870*
£17.00 • 282pp *paperback* • 156x234mm • ISBN 978-1-9161586-2-7

Bob Bushaway, BY RITE, *Custom, Ceremony and Community in England 1700-1880*
£16.00 • 206pp *paperback* • 191x235mm • ISBN 978-0-9564827-6-1

Malcolm Chase, THE PEOPLE'S FARM, *English Radical Agrarianism 1775-1840*
£12.00 • 212pp *paperback* • 152x229mm • ISBN 978-0-9564827-5-4

Malcolm Chase, EARLY TRADE UNIONISM, Fraternity, *Skill and the Politics of Labour*
£17.00 • 248pp *paperback* • 191x235mm • ISBN 978-0-9570005-2-0

James Epstein, THE LION OF FREEDOM, *Feargus O'Connor and the Chartist Movement, 1832-1842*
£17.00 • 296pp *paperback* • 156x234mm • ISBN 978-0-9929466-1-6

James Epstein, RADICAL EXPRESSION, *Political Language, Ritual, and Symbol in England, 1790-1850*
£15.00 • 220pp *paperback* • 156x234mm • ISBN 978-0-9929466-2-3

Chris Fisher, CUSTOM, WORK & MARKET CAPITALISM, *The Forest of Dean Colliers, 1788-1888*
£14.00 • 198pp *paperback* • 156x234mm • ISBN 978-0-9929466-7-8

Barry Reay, THE LAST RISING OF THE AGRICULTURAL LABOURERS, *Rural Life and Protest in Nineteenth-Century England*
£15.00 • 192pp *paperback* • 191x235mm • ISBN 978-0-9564827-2-3

Buchanan Sharp, IN CONTEMPT OF ALL AUTHORITY, *Rural Artisans and Riot in the West of England, 1586-1660*
£15.00 • 204pp *paperback* • 191x235mm • ISBN 978-0-9564827-0-9

Dorothy Thompson, THE CHARTISTS, *Popular Politics in the Industrial Revolution*
£17.00 • 280pp *paperback* • 191x235mm • ISBN 978-0-9570005-3-7

E. P. Thompson, WHIGS AND HUNTERS, *The Origin of the Black Act*
£16.00 • 278pp *paperback* • 156x234mm • ISBN 978-0-9570005-2-0
£30.00 • 278pp *hardback* • 156x234mm • ISBN 978-0-9929466-6-1

Roger Wells, INSURRECTION, *The British Experience 1795-1803*
£22.00 • 372pp *paperback* • 191x235mm • ISBN 978-0-9564827-3-0

Roger Wells, WRETCHED FACES, *Famine in Wartime England 1793-1801*
£23.00 • 412pp *paperback* • 191x235mm • ISBN 978-0-9564827-4-7

David Worrall, RADICAL CULTURE, *Discourse, Resistance and Surveillance, 1790-1820*
£15.00 • 186pp *paperback* • 156x234mm • ISBN 978-0-9929466-4-7

For further information visit
www.breviarystuff.org.uk

www.ingramcontent.com/pod-product-compliance
Lightning Source LLC
Chambersburg PA
CBHW030817190426
43197CB00036B/552